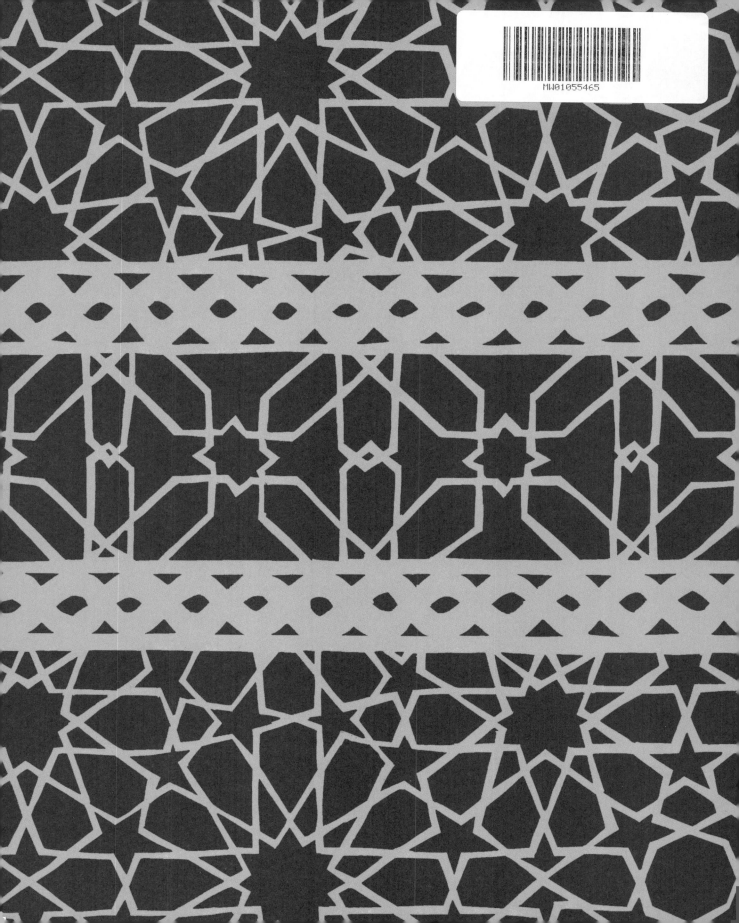

QOHELET
SEARCHING FOR A LIFE WORTH LIVING

PHILOSOPHICAL
COMMENTARY

ILLUMINATIONS
AND COMMENTARY

MENACHEM FISCH

DEBRA BAND

FOREWORD ELLEN F. DAVIS

PREFACE MOSHE HALBERTAL

B

BAYLOR UNIVERSITY PRESS
2023

Unless otherwise stated, biblical quotations are from *The Koren Jerusalem Bible*, Koren Publishers Jerusalem, copyright 2008. Used by permission. All rights reserved.

Cover design by Debra Band
Cover images adapted from the Frontispiece, *Qohelet: Searching for a Life Worth Living,* by Debra Band and Menachem Fisch.
Book design by Debra Band

Typeset English text set in Williams Caslon and Trajan Pro. Typeset Hebrew text set in Adobe Hebrew, with text from the DavkaWriter text library.

Printed and bound in China through Porter Print Group, Bethesda, Maryland
First printing, 2023.

12 13 14 15 16 17   10 9 8 7 6 5 4 3 2 1

ISBN: 978-1-4813-1873-0
Library of Congress Control Number: 2022945634

The publication of this book was made possible by a generous gift from
Sharon and Steven Lieberman

in honor of their children
Rachel Shoshana and Jaryn Louis,
Jessica Michal,
and Benjamin Shai and Hannah Dorit,
and their granddaughter, Mackenzie Rebecca.

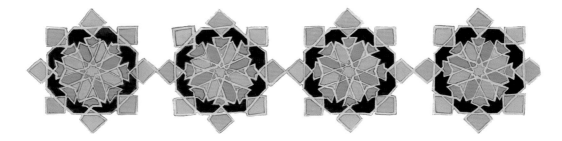

In loving memory of our parents and cousins,
Josephine Swift Roskies and Harold Fisch

Their memories are our blessings.

PRAISE FOR
QOHELET: SEARCHING FOR A LIFE WORTH LIVING

If our life seems to go nowhere, our enjoyment of things seems shallow, our understanding of things seems thin, our attempt to pursue justice seems to get nowhere, where do we go? We could always read Ecclesiastes, with this illuminating commentary. Among the many studies of the book, it is like no other in offering two Jewish perspectives, a philosopher's and an artist's, and incorporating a wondrous profile of artwork with which one could sit for a long time.
—*John Goldingay, Senior Professor, Fuller Theological Seminary*

Band and Fisch's Qohelet commentary is a feast for both eyes and mind. Qohelet, roughly a contemporary of Aristotle, jumps off the page into the interstices of our own struggle to make sense of how God wants us to understand ourselves and how we had best conduct our lives. These two religious Jews let Qohelet speak from the Jewish canon, not about, or on behalf of, Judaism but about the human condition. The calligraphy is clear yet absorbing in both Hebrew and English, with the Hebrew fully vocalized and with Masoretic cantillation marks. Qohelet urges us to enjoy life's pleasures fully, being ever mindful of their evanescence in the face of inevitable death.
—*Ellen T. Charry, Margaret W. Harmon Professor of Systematic Theology Emerita, Princeton Theological Seminary*

Qohelet: Searching for a Life Worth Living is an important contribution to philosophical theology, which rereads Qohelet through a philosophical lens. This book corrects scholarly misperceptions of Qohelet as a strange outlier in the Bible and in ancient Judaism and instead retells the story of its relevance in Western thought. The contribution of Qohelet as an important voice for reflective and philosophical thinking in ancient Judaism was not lost on the rabbis. Moreover, this book demonstrates that the voice of Qohelet can now be heard in conversation with the history of Western philosophical reflections. Fisch and Band weave philosophical commentary, rabbinic reflection, and artistic illumination together into a new inheritance of Qohelet.
—*Hindy Najman, Oriel and Laing Professor of the Interpretation of Holy Scripture, University of Oxford*

This wonderful book offers a biblical, philosophical, artistic, and (ultimately) theological account of one of the deep treasures of wisdom in Scripture, Ecclesiastes. Seeing the tension between the absolute timeless norms of divine expectation and the inherent transience of all human reckoning and understanding in Qohelet's account, Fisch offers us a deeply reflective account of the book, which takes both the urgent divine call and the limits of human knowing just as seriously. Only a philosopher and text scholar of Fisch's extraordinary calibre could offer so rich a commentary and, moreover, do so beautifully in partnership with Debra Band's art and calligraphy.
—*Tom Greggs, Marischal Chair of Divinity, University of Aberdeen*

Qohelet is the one book in the Hebrew Bible that is essentially a philosophic meditation, written, like all genuine philosophy, in the first person. Only a genuine philosopher like Menachem Fisch could enter the mind of this unique biblical author by making the author's questions his own. Debra Band's illuminations and commentary beautifully complement Fisch's meditation on Qohelet.
—*David Novak, J. Richard and Dorothy Shiff Professor of Jewish Studies and Philosophy, University of Toronto*

This inventive, probing, and thought-provoking volume argues that the biblical book of Qohelet (Ecclesiastes) is a singly authored composition propounding a coherent philosophy of life, one that is highly pertinent today. The accompanying artwork, drawing imaginatively and learnedly upon Jewish and non-Jewish traditions alike, enriches the reader's appreciation of this enigmatic ancient text.
—*Jon D. Levenson, Albert A. List Professor of Jewish Studies, Harvard Divinity School*

Illuminated manuscripts have a rich tradition, to which this gem adds creatively. Not only do Debra Band's exquisite micrography, calligraphy, and artwork invite us to marinate in and meditate on Qohelet's suggestive composition; Menachem Fisch adds a unique and penetrating philosophical analysis. This work takes us from the ancient world of the Bible through medieval traditions of illumination and into a reading of Qohelet as a harbinger of postmodern thinking. What a ride!
—*The Rev. Peter A. Pettit, Teaching Pastor, St. Paul Lutheran Church, Davenport, Iowa*

Debra Band's illuminations in *Qohelet: Searching for a Life Worth Living* illustrate her outstanding ability to marry art with text. Her intriguing paintings balance the rich commentary in an elegant embrace. Her vision rests upon Menachem Fisch's accompanying analysis of the biblical text. Band's artistic view illuminates the book and sets forth in a compelling visual narrative the words of both biblical text and the other sources upon which the paintings draw. We are fortunate to have such a wonderful display of art interpreting the written word.
—*Laura Kruger, Curator Emerita, Dr. Bernard Heller Museum, Hebrew Union College, New York*

"Vanity of vanities, all is vanity," wrote the mysterious author of the biblical Qohelet—Ecclesiastes, in English, from the Greek. "There is nothing new under the sun." For generations, the meaning of this haunting outlier text seemed clear and even merciless: in its endless cycling, nothing in the cosmos lasts, so nothing matters. Even if God is real, human life is, in the end, unreal and can have no real purpose. Resignation is the only valid response: at best, "living for the moment"; at worst, existential despair. But what if there *were* something new under the sun? In this fresh approach to Qohelet, philosopher Menachem Fisch and scholar-artist Debra Band radically re-vision a text whose interpretation was "settled." Through exciting exposition that ranges from the history of rabbinical thought to analytical philosophy to the pain of personal loss, and illumined by Band's glowing paintings, the authors return us to the original Hebrew word on which Qohelet pivots: *hevel*. When *hevel* is not read figuratively but is restored to its literal meaning as "vapor" or "mist," an unexpected theology is revealed. What if the text were never a meditation on absurdity, after all, but instead "a vivid portrayal of the limits of human knowledge"? These

limits can inspire us to return to our deepest human challenge: How should we live? Fisch and Band show how we can take up the question again in fascination—and even more, in hope. An unforgettable book.
—*Kimberley C. Patton, Professor of the Comparative and Historical Study of Religion, Harvard Divinity School*

Of the making of books on Ecclesiastes-Qohelet, there is seemingly no end, and yet this one truly stands out. Debra Band, a renowned visual artist, and Menachem Fisch, a distinguished philosopher, together explore one of Judaism's—and indeed, the Western world's—most provocative and elusive books and offer us new ways of reading the text and imagining the experiences and struggles it evokes. Whether Ecclesiastes is relatively new territory for you or whether you've spent decades studying and puzzling over it, you will undoubtedly find new insight and inspiration in this remarkable book. Band and Fisch offer us a feast for the eyes, the mind, and the heart.
—*Rabbi Shai Held, President and Dean, the Hadar Institute*

What a rereading of this fascinating scripture! Menachem Fisch's decades of study, in which he has worked to combine rigorous and self-critical philosophy, immersion in rabbinic Judaism, and perceptive attention to life, have been distilled into this profound interpretation of the book of Ecclesiastes. The portrayal of types of foolishness rings uncomfortably true, and Qohelet's positive wisdom is something each of us needs to learn—for the sake of our personal, political, economic, intellectual, and religious lives. Not only that: because of Debra Band's accompanying visual illuminations, this is a new seeing as well as a new reading.
—*David F. Ford, Regius Professor of Divinity Emeritus, University of Cambridge*

This is an exquisite combination of pictorial imagination with abstract reflections of the most philosophical book of the Hebrew Bible, penned by two experts in their respective domains. Menachem Fisch's fresh interpretation of the ultimate message of Ecclesiastes as a portrayal of a transient—in lieu of a futile—world is a permanent contribution that will guide any serious reader of the book in the future. A more balanced attitude toward the magnificent worldview that pretends to reflect a king's experience of life decodes an original type of ancient Jewish religiosity, which has more optimistic valences than previously assumed.
—*Moshe Idel, Max Cooper Professor in Jewish Thought at the Hebrew University, Jerusalem*

TABLE OF CONTENTS

FOREWORD
Ellen F. Davis

magine what a wise philosopher-king of mature years—let's call him "Solomon"—might write as a legacy statement. That is the task that the ancient Jewish sage known to us as Qohelet set for himself, and the result is the book known to many as Ecclesiastes, the Greek rendering of Qohelet's peculiar name ("convener of an assembly"). "Of making many books there is no end," Qohelet wrote (Qoh 12:12), and his own book has generated countless more through the ages. Likely he himself would find this superabundance of commentary "a weariness of the flesh" (Qoh 12:12). Yet in this volume, contrary to Qohelet's famous dictum, there is something genuinely "new under the sun." Menachem Fisch is a contemporary philosopher living near Qohelet's home city of Jerusalem, and Debra Band is a visual artist fluent in the cultural iconography of the Mediterranean world through the centuries; both are deeply steeped in traditional Jewish learning and a critical appreciation of modern science. Here they combine two lifetimes of expertise in an imaginative yet rigorous analysis of Qohelet's intellectual and existential journey. Their literary, philological, philosophical, and visual responses expand and gradually overturn established understandings of Qohelet's line of thought.

The exegetical power of their reading rests on two critical perceptions that counter the views of most readers, professional as well as lay. First they trace a single complex philosophical argument as it unfolds through the book, from the first verse to the last. In contrast to Fisch and Band's perception of a comprehensive literary and philosophical integrity, it is a commonplace among Bible scholars to treat "the words of Qohelet" (Qoh 1:1) not primarily as a narrative account but rather as an anthology of collected sayings. The whole might be seen as a bundle of contradictions, and the point of gathering them is precisely to demonstrate the "absurdity" of the human condition.[1] Equally common is the view that the plain sense and force of his words is deliberately blunted, most markedly in the final coda (12:13–14), by the heavy hand of an editor who inclines to a piety more traditional than the sage's own.

The second critical perception on which Fisch and Band's treatment rests is a crucial point of Hebrew semantics, namely, with respect to Qohelet's signature exclamation, "All is *hevel*!" (Qoh 1:2, *et passim*. They assert that Qohelet does not say or mean, "Vanity of vanities, all is vanity"—though countless English speakers quote him to that effect, often with no notion of source or context. Rather, taking their cue from the most literal sense of the Hebrew word, "vapor," they interpret the whole work in accordance with "the *hevel* premise": any knowledge or judgment of a person or a thing, a state of affairs or a projected course of action, is inescapably "uncertain, time-bound, questionable, context-dependent, and transient."

Menachem Fisch's detailed philosophical and exegetical commentary has its perfect complement in Debra Band's 58 full-page illuminations and the commentaries that explicate them. This is an illuminated text in the strongest sense: each development in Qohelet's emerging worldview is reflected in multidimensional, sometimes astonishing, images. While Fisch discovers a coherent philosophical perspective taking shape chapter by chapter and tracks the subtle literary means by which the movements in the argument are marked, Band's illuminations underscore its coherence by providing an unexpected kind of narrative setting. Taking seriously, though not literally, the ostensible claim to Solomonic authorship, Band creates an extended visual parable. Imaginatively traveling across time, space, and cultures, she relocates Qohelet-Solomon in the thirteenth-century Alhambra palace in Granada, the jewel of Moorish rule in Andalusia; its elegant rooms, gardens, and vineyards provide much detail for the illuminations. Much like the narrative superscriptions that stand at the head of various psalms, linking prayers of lament and thanksgiving with events in the life of King David (e.g., Pss 3:1, 18:1, 51:1–2), these visual depictions give specificity to Qohelet's rumination on the meaning of life. By connecting the sage's words to one concrete historical setting, Band helps readers imagine how they might also speak into and illumine other circumstances, including our own.

The Alhambra stimulates Debra Band's visual imagination but does not contain it. The images themselves constitute a multilingual and intercultural conversation across the centuries about "searching for a life worth living," and readers can use their own imaginations to follow strands within the visual conversation and discover new insights. Here it must suffice to witness one potential interaction. In the third chapter, which Fisch identifies as "Qohelet's great turning point," from questioning the value of human achievement in itself "to deliberating its possible value in the eyes of God" (page 108), Qohelet concludes with his *hevel* premise: "all is vapour … and all return to dust" (Qoh 3:16–20; see commentary on page 115). Band's image shows a once-elegant palace wall crumbling to dust, and the pattern of its mosaic is adapted from the twelfth-century synagogue in Toledo, "appropriated and converted to a church … following the expulsion of the Jews from Spain in 1492" (page 116). The Hebrew and English passages from the book of Qohelet are framed (respectively) by lines from Psalm 49 and the eighteenth-century Christian poet Thomas Gray: "The paths of glory lead but to the grave."

Compare that image of dereliction and defeat with the final palace image in the final illumination (page 84). Night falls over the beautiful silhouette of the Alhambra, framed by the golden bowl, which is one of Band's recurrent images for the fragility of what is precious (see Qoh 12:6). Now the bowl is cracked, though still beautiful. Surrounding the bowl is a micrographic border composed of forty-four(!) poems composed by Shmuel haNagid (d. 1056), the famous Jewish grand vizier who ruled in Granada. The minutely inscribed poems, laid out in a design from a tiling pattern found within the palace complex, sum up the medieval poet's insistence—and likewise, that of Qohelet himself—on pursuing and cherishing what is lovely, despite its impermanence and the reality of our own death.

This volume is a work of art and a work of religious philosophy, like Qohelet's own book. And like the ancient sage, Debra Band and Menachem Fisch have given us a work not intended to settle a question but rather to stimulate searching and conversation, both in the context of community. May that hope be fulfilled through its readers.

NOTE

[1] See Michael V. Fox, *Qohelet and His Contradictions* (Decatur, Ga.: Almond Press, 1989); and *A Time to Tear Down and a Time to Build Up: A Rereading of Ecclesiastes* (Grand Rapids: Eerdmans, 1999). "Absurdity" is his rendering of Qohelet's term *hevel*.

PREFACE
Moshe Halbertal

The book of Qohelet is a genuinely intriguing and perplexing composition, and careful readers of the book have struggled with the question of its meaning and coherence. Does the book present a dark and nihilistic vision of life? Does it recommend a joyful embrace of the here and now? Does it posture an ironic indifference to all human efforts, including the effort of making sense of it all? Does it aim altogether to provide a stable position besides exploring this array of shifting attitudes and moods? And there is yet a further perplexity, raised to the level of a religious and spiritual scandal: How did Qohelet find its place as part of sacred scripture? Every canonical compilation, including the Bible, presents a multiplicity of voices, and such a plurality is part of the attractiveness and strength of canonical authority and standing. But Qohelet is not another voice within a sacred symphony; its message seems to be directly antithetical to the essence of biblical religion. History in Qohelet is not grasped as a sphere of God's presence but rather as a repetitive cycle of events lacking direction and aim. Humanity's tortuous search for guidance throughout the book is not aided by divine revelation and command. Qohelet is totally devoid of covenantal promise and obligation that presumes to bond humans to God and God to humans. It is no wonder that the canonicity of Qohelet has been a contested matter from its inception, and the fact that within the tradition its sacred standing was finally secured is indeed astonishing. The achievement and brilliance of Debra Band and Menachem Fisch's book is that it attempts to provide a compelling answer to the twofold perplexity. It presents us with a coherent and fascinating reading of Qohelet, and it beautifully explores its deep religious meaning.

At the heart of Band and Fisch's approach is the following methodological insight: an answer can be understood only when the question it has aimed to address is fully grasped. A journey that has felt directionless can make sense once its motivating starting point is clarified. The first and most important insight of Band and Fisch's book is in the argument that the starting point of Qohelet's journey—the declaration—*hevel havalim*, has been misunderstood by many of its readers. *Hevel* in the traditional reading of Qohelet has been translated as vanity, or meaninglessness. Thus, in this reading the author begins his quest by declaring the assumed meaninglessness of life. If this is indeed the starting point of Qohelet's search, then many readers who have accepted it have been perplexed as to whether the rest of the book serves as an affirmation of its title or is an attempt to provide a rebuttal to it. Band and Fisch read the term *hevel* as designating what is transient, passing and temporal, rather than what is meaningless and vain. Qohelet's search thus focuses on the question of the human condition of temporality, and, in light of this starting point, Qohelet's further exploration is brilliantly illuminated. Following Qohelet's quest with the guidance of Band and Fisch becomes a revelatory experience, not only in its interpretative depth but also as a book that—though inspired by Qohelet—stands on its own in addressing an unsettling feature of life.

Temporality has been viewed as an existential quality that undermines weight and meaning. If our efforts don't leave a stable, persistent mark, if they evaporate with no cumulative force, then we seem to work in vain. Moreover, our achievements suffer from an even greater fragility, since future generations may retroactively determine the meaning of our efforts in directions that stand against what we have labored to achieve. Our efforts might not only evaporate leaving no mark; they might be abused and misdirected by our heirs. Family fortunes that have been laboriously accumulated and that were once targeted toward philanthropic purposes might turn out to have corrupting effects in the hands of decadent heirs and might even degenerate to become monstrous tools of exploitation. Founding generations of nations and states that once labored to secure their inhabitants' freedom and to produce a flourishing system of social cooperation entrust the fate of their efforts to future leaders that might turn state power into a vehicle of tyranny and aggression. The past, in that respect, is not sealed and secured; it is at the mercy of the future. These sets of existential human concerns might be addressed by readjusting our expectations for everlasting impact, by letting go of our omnipotent fantasies of shaping the future. Internalizing our finitude would thus allow us to have joy in what is not complete, in the temporality of our lives. But Band and Fisch's book reads Qohelet as struggling with another dimension of temporality, a struggle that would not be answered by such humble acceptance. The temporal, in their reading, affects not only the weight of our efforts but the reliability of our judgments and beliefs and the validity of our norms. Our epistemic fallibility is thus not exclusively an existential predicament but rather a daunting religious and moral concern. How can we adhere to the just and the right knowing that our judgments and beliefs are transient, that what was accepted in the past has been discovered to be repugnant in the present, and that we don't have any assurances that in the future the same critical light will not be shed on our essential convictions and norms? Given that we finite creatures are accountable to God's judgment, this uncertainty attains a painful religious edge. Qohelet, in the reading offered by Band and Fisch, articulates the way in which humans ought to confront this moral and religious predicament. *Qohelet: Searching for a Life Worth Living* presents to us an outstanding combination of meticulous and exquisite interpretive and artistic work and an inspiring philosophical and human exploration of the way to recognize and live before God under the shadow of epistemic and moral temporality and fallibility.

Acknowledgments

As Qohelet anticipated the completion of his book, he famously mused, "Of making many books there is no end," as though exhausted with the effort. In contrast, as we conclude our work of interpreting his book, we are exhilarated—not only by our fascination with his thoughts but by the pleasures of working with the many fine people who helped us bring our interpretation of Qohelet to light.

Debra writes:

For many years, I had wanted to take on the book of Qohelet, even prior to a Shabbat dinner at the home of my cousin Menachem and his wife, Hanna, during a meet-the-family trip to Israel with my then-new husband, Michael Diamond. When, during the delicious meal, Menachem casually asked me about my plans for my next project (I was then working on my Kabbalat Shabbat book), I replied that I really wanted to work on Qohelet and had made a couple of false starts over the years; vapor still clouded the book's meaning. "I've written on Qohelet—let me send you the article," he offered. The following week, I downloaded and devoured the article—lo, the fog began to dissipate. Menachem graciously agreed to discuss a joint project (What? An illuminated manuscript of so abstract a text?), and light began to penetrate Qohelet's mists.

Edward Gamson helped me identify sources of medieval Muslim geometric patterns that became essential in re-creating details of the décor of the Alhambra and other Andalusian buildings more completely and reliably than my own library, photographs, and drawings. Kathy Bloch, of the Asher Library of the Spertus Institute, and Ann Brener, of the Library of Congress, generously helped me track down sources that appear in my artwork and commentary. Janice Meyerson has edited this volume—as she has several of my recent books— improving its precision and clarity. My friendship with Janice and her husband, Raymond Scheindlin, has long inspired my work; indeed, Ray's studies and translations of medieval Sephardic poetry have been an essential part of this project. Judry Subar, my neighbor, friend, and cherished *hevrutah* (study partner) for many years, spent years of Monday evenings studying the rabbinics on Qohelet with me and my husband, Michael. Jud also meticulously proofread the entire body of Hebrew calligraphy within the illuminations. My father-in-law, Arnold J. Band, has held me to a model of critical clarity and integrity throughout my career, and I have been grateful for his comments on this work as well.

The period of our labors on this book were the last years of my beloved mother, Josephine Swift Roskies, to whom this book is dedicated, along with her beloved cousin Harold Fisch. My mother's unceasing passion for my painting, since my earliest childhood "illustrated stories," encouraged me throughout my career, and her model of practical Jewish life has been my guide. More recently, when she could express little else, she brought all her old ebullience to her excitement about my partnership with Menachem—whom she loved so well—as we worked together to shed light on her favorite book of the Bible. Her memory will always inhabit these paintings for me, and her memory will always be a blessing.

Above all, I am grateful to my husband, Michael Diamond, MD, for the infinite devotion and support that he has offered in this project, whether his eagerness to trek across Andalusia together, his patient waiting during my sudden stops in order to sketch and photograph (especially in the Alhambra), his passion for studying the related rabbinic literature with Jud and me, or his eternal eagerness to discuss every aspect of this project. Truly, my cup runneth over.

Menachem writes:

As I explain in my introduction, the reading of Qohelet presented in the following pages originated over three decades ago in a conference marking my father's retirement from Bar-Ilan University. I am immensely grateful for the many long and hard discussions of the text that we managed to enjoy, until his death in 2001. I dedicate my share of this project—which, if not for his splendid essay of Qohelet, would never had been written—to his loving memory.

The initial ideas presented at that conference survive intact in the present work. But in order to read Qohelet by means of them, as the profound, sustained, and systematic work of pre-revelatory religious philosophy presented here, my own philosophy and understanding of the rabbinic literature required years of thorough rethinking. These were made possible by the two remarkably vibrant institutions that I have had the privilege to call my intellectual homes: the Cohn Institute for the History and Philosophy of Science and Ideas at Tel Aviv University; and the Shalom Hartman Institute, Jerusalem. My deepest gratitude goes to their two visionary founders: the late professors Yehuda Elkana and Amos Funkenstein of the former; and the late Rabbi David Hartman of the latter.

Of my many philosophical partners in dialogue, I would like to single out Yitzhak Benbaji, Yemima Ben-Menahem, Lorraine Daston, Noah Efron, Moritz Epple, Paul Franks, Eli Friedlander, Michael Friedman, Snait Gissis, Simon Goldhill, Niccolò Guicciardini, Don Howard, Matthias Lutz-Bachmann, Elijah Millgram, Adi Ophir, Hilary Putnam, Heiko Schulz, Yossef Schwartz, Orly R. Shenkar, Alfred I. Tauber, Zvi Tauber, Till van Rahden, Jeremy Wanderer, and Christian Wiese, for unwittingly proving my main contention: that the normative constraints on self-criticism can be breached only by exposure to the keen normative critique of trusted others, which they have generously supplied in abundance.

As my philosophy of self and rationality gradually took form, so did my understanding of the rabbinic literature as a wide-reaching, and profoundly dialogical, exegetical, and legal undertaking, centrally informed by that very contention. Here, too, I have been blessed by partners in dialogue and study, of whom I would like to single out Shlomo Biderman, Daniel Boyarin, Ellen F. Davis, Yael Fisch, Moshe Halbertal, Israel Knohl, Yedidah Koren, Laura Lieber, Menachem Lorberbaum, Shlomo Naeh, Peter Ochs, Kimberley C. Patton, Peter Pettit, Ishay Rosen-Zvi, Avi Sagi, Adiel Schremer, Haim Shapira, Suzanne Last Stone, Claudia Welz, Noam Zion, and Noam Zohar.

My talk at my father's conference yielded three short essays on Qohelet, the last of which was published in 1995. I returned to the book in various talks, study groups, lecture courses, and seminars—(chief among them at a riveting Hartman Institute seminar on Qohelet organized by Ilana Pardes and Adi Ophir) but did not feel ready to commit anything more to writing—until Debra raised the subject at our Shabbat table, and jolted me into realizing that perhaps I was ready. I am profoundly grateful to Debra, not only for proposing the tempting prospect of engaging Qohelet together, but for my much-needed wake-up call to return to the book, finally better equipped to render its philosophical potential explicit.

My deepest gratitude goes to Hanna, my beloved wife and keenest critic, who has steadily stood beside me during the twists, splits, and turns of my scholarly pursuits. Hanna warmed immediately to the idea of collaborating with Debra on Qohelet, and has cheered us on enthusiastically ever since. "Who can find a woman of worth" (Proverbs 31).

DEBRA AND MENACHEM WRITE:

Sometime after that fateful Shabbat dinner—we had both been busy with other projects—we met for a weekend at the home of Ellen Davis and her husband, Dwayne Huebner, to plan the project, when Menachem was at Duke for a series of lectures. Since then, Ellen, who was already acquainted with Menachem's approach and has known and supported Debra's work for years, has played godmother to this book. Ellen has often discussed this project with both of us as it has grown, sharing her deep knowledge of the text, her excitement, and her aesthetic sensitivity and then introduced us to Baylor University Press. We are deeply honored by her contribution of the elegant foreword to this volume.

Noah Efron, Oren Harman, Deborah Harris, Kimberley C. Patton, Alvin H. Rosenfeld, and Brent A. Strawn read parts of the book and generously shared advice of many kinds.

We are grateful to Dave Nelson, Cade Jarrell, David Aycock, Jenny Hunt, Kasey McBeath, and Michelle McCaig of Baylor University Press for their enthusiasm and care at bringing this book to light. Matthew Miller of Koren Publishers Jerusalem graciously granted us the rights to use the translation of Qohelet by Harold Fisch from the Koren Jerusalem Bible. Rene Porter and her staff at Porter Print Group, in particular, Jared Stevens, as ever with Debra's work, took on the task of producing this beautiful book with extraordinary energy and skill.

We are grateful beyond words to Sharon and Steven Lieberman, whose passion and generosity, which have been poured into Debra's work over many years, have enabled the publication of this book. We are proud that our work figures among their good works in Jewish life and learning.

Much of the work of this book took place against the background of the first years of the Covid-19 pandemic. Indeed, Debra's studio is located in the Washington, D.C. area, only a few miles from the foci of American public policy. This surreal period, during which so many millions across the world needlessly lost their lives and loved ones, has been a modern realization of Qohelet's warnings about the hazards of reckless government (see chapters 9 and 10). We acknowledge the ghastly cost of this tragedy, and we only hope that this work, in some small measure, can help leaders appreciate the need for human prudence in this world, even while they pray for divine providence. Finally, we hope that this work will help all of us, whatever our status, navigate a fulfilling path through this challenging world.

Introduction
Making Sense of Qohelet

Menachem Fisch

A Labor of Love

Many great love affairs are sparked by a chance encounter, and in their early stages a third party is often involved. In that respect, my love affair with the book of Qohelet is no exception. I know no other text quite like it. It is certainly the one with which I have grappled most fervently for the last thirty years. Over the years, Qohelet proved to be far more than a book I felt obliged to reckon with. It is a text that beckoned me, drew me in, and ended up engaging me like no other. As I hope to explain in the following pages, I read Qohelet not as a detached philosopher pondering the prospects of living a meaningful life under conditions of perpetual doubtfulness but as an anxious and engaged deeply religious philosopher grappling with the profound problem of how to live a meaningful religious life under such conditions. Thus I read it as intimately addressing my own deepest concerns as a religiously engaged contemporary philosopher of science and religion.

I did not come across Qohelet by chance. I was as aware of the book as any synagogue-goer would be, long before I fell in love with it. But my love affair with this remarkable book owed its beginning both to chance and to the towering presence of a third party.

The third party involved was my father, Harold Fisch, whose essay "Qohelet: A Hebrew Ironist," was published in 1988.[1] As chance had it, Ellen Spolsky invited me to deliver a paper at a conference honoring my father's retirement that she was organizing at Bar-Ilan University later that year. I could not refuse but did not have a clue as to what I might talk about at such a gathering. I was a young analytical philosopher of science at the time, much taken by Karl Popper's thinking,[2] who had also done some work on early Victorian science and philosophy—nothing remotely relevant to my father's work. I was relatively well acquainted with it but felt ill-equipped to engage it in a meaningful way—until I happened upon his essay on Qohelet. He read Qohelet like no one before him, bringing his profound knowledge of late Renaissance humanism to bear on the text. His brief mention of Popper toward the end offered me a much needed entry point.[3] Coming to terms with my father's ingenious reading of Qohelet left me love-struck by the book, not because I thought that he had gotten it right but because I believed that he had not. The paper that I presented at the conference marked a first and crucial step toward articulating an alternative reading that I could live with: an undertaking that reaches its current state of fruition, dear reader, in the present volume. It also signaled a significant turning point in my philosophical career. As I shall explain, the two are closely connected. But let us start at the beginning.

The Mystery of Qohelet

The book of Qohelet is an extraordinarily difficult text to make sense of, especially religious sense—and not because its language is especially challenging; compared with much of the prophets and many of the Psalms, let alone Job, Qohelet seems to speak loud and clear. The problem with Qohelet is that it is notoriously difficult to place in the relevant contexts capable of lending it religious significance. Bible scholars speculate about when and where the book might have been composed, and by whom. Similar efforts are invested in speculating about the historical circumstances of its canonization. Convincing as they may be, such speculations have little relevance to people of faith such as myself. For most such people, to explain Qohelet's biblical status requires squaring its apparent concerns and message with those of the Bible's other books in a manner that makes religious sense to them, rather than to its original canonizers. This would not explain why the book was canonized, but it would certainly render the fact that it was canonized less mysterious. Convincing oneself that Qohelet does not jar too harshly with the rest of our religious canon carries little historical conviction, yet even this more existential approach to Qohelet proves to be exceedingly problematic.

R. B. Y. Scott, translator and interpreter of Qohelet for the Anchor Bible, speaks for many in claiming that Ecclesiastes "is the strangest book in the Bible, or at any rate the book whose presence in the sacred canons of Judaism and of Christianity is most inexplicable.... It diverges too radically [from the Law and the prophets]. In fact, it denies some of the things on which the other writers lay the greatest stress—notably that God revealed himself and his will to man, through his chosen people Israel."[4] For Scott, Qohelet does not present an exegetical problem. He believes that he understands the book's argument and message. His only problem is to explain how such a book could be considered part of the Bible.

The rabbinic literature, by contrast, debated the meaning of the text, along with its biblical status. Those who opposed its canonization are said to have registered a double worry, deeming it inappropriate because, in their opinion, its words sometimes contradict one another[5] and sometimes lend themselves to heresy.[6] Those who favored canonizing Qohelet obviously read it differently, as neither inconsistent nor heretical. But much more is needed to justify granting a text biblical status than its being consistent and religiously inoffensive.

Scott does not raise the question of Qohelet's consistency but does lay great stress on its apparent incongruity with the teachings of the rest of the Hebrew canon. It is a question for which he ultimately has no answer and, being Christian perhaps, can afford not to address by implying that it is up to Qohelet's "religious fellow Jews" to do so:

> In Ecclesiastes, God is not only unknown to man through revelation; he is unknowable through reason, the only means by which the author believes knowledge is attainable. Such a God is not ... the covenant God of Israel. He is rather the mysterious, inscrutable Being whose existence must be presupposed as that which determines life and the fate of man, in a world man cannot change, and where all his effort and values are rendered meaningless.... Thus, in place of a religion of hope and obedience, this writer expresses a mood of disillusionment and proffers a philosophy of resignation. His ethic has no relationship to divine commandments, for there are none.... The author is a rationalist, an agnostic, a skeptic, a pessimist, and a fatalist.... In most respects his views run counter to those of his religious fellow Jews.[7]

I have quoted Scott at length because his seems to be the accepted view. Most readers deem the bulk of the text to be fundamentally at odds with the rest of the biblical canon and take comfort in its closing statement that, after all is said and done, man's duty is to fear God and obey his commandments. But if the sole purpose of Qohelet's twelve dense chapters was merely to affirm the submissive religiosity of that one verse, it presents, as Scott wryly observes, "a remarkable example of the indirect method."[8]

My father's subtle reading of Qohelet reaches the same conclusion, but unlike any other, it reads the twelve chapters leading up to it as a powerful theo-philosophical argument. Hosea and Qohelet, he suggests, should be read as jointly exploring the nightmarish consequences of withdrawal from the covenantal relationship that binds God and Israel. "If the darker passages of Hosea show us God threatening to withdraw himself from man," he writes, "then Ecclesiastes shows us what happens when man withdraws himself into the inwardness of his own consciousness and distances himself from God."[9] He reads Qohelet accordingly as an essentially ironic text that amounts in its philosophical claim to a sophisticated reductio ad absurdum of the very possibility of self-sufficient anthropocentric knowledge of the true and the good. Hence the inevitable conclusion: "The end of the matter, when all is said and done: Fear God and keep his commandments, for that is the whole[10] … of Man" (12:13). "From this point of view," he writes, Qohelet presents "the nearest thing to humanism that the Bible has to offer, even a radical humanism"[11]—a humanism that is meticulously explored, he argues, and wholly exploded. Despite its ingenuity, many modern readers would be inclined to reject such a reading of Qohelet as religiously inappropriate, if only for its dismissal, by implication, of Renaissance humanism and its undeniable scientific, literary, artistic, philosophical, and political yieldings, as "utter futility."[12]

Discomfort with such a reading is further intensified by the second mystery surrounding Qohelet. Unlike that of its canonization, this second puzzling aspect of the book represents an exclusively Jewish concern. I am referring to Qohelet's liturgical placement in the Jewish festival cycle. How might the rabbis have read the text to deem it appropriate for public ritual reading during the festival of Tabernacles? What could have rendered Qohelet's gloomy meditations and, according to my father, its disturbing denunciation of all human accomplishment fitting for the festival singled out by the Torah as a time of special rejoicing (Deut 16:14–15)?

A Reading Takes Form

Qohelet's frequent use of the first person is unique. He draws you in by allowing you to be privy to his talking to himself. He muses and deliberates aloud, exploring possible alternatives and rejoinders, rebutting counterarguments, and weighing things in various ways, with the fierce intensity of personal engagement. From its first employment in 1:12, Qohelet's use of the first person succeeds in communicating an intimacy, urgency, and credibility like no other biblical text. He does not purport to preach God's Word, as do the prophets, to represent a well-formed position, as do the characters of Job, or to articulate common truths, as in Proverbs. It is a philosophical text that conveys credibility by its utterly frank personal idiom, much like that of Montaigne's *Essays*, as opposed to the detached, objectifying third-person idiom of most philosophical works—the dialogue form of Job and the Platonic dialogues being the most extreme.

Qohelet's journey is as emotional as it is philosophical. He despairs and rejoices, fumes and jokes. The cruel candidness of his musing aloud is as captivating as it is contagious. The questions referred to in the previous section pose a serious challenge to anyone seeking to make sense of the book's biblical and liturgical placing.

Some thirty years ago, it was with these concerns in mind that I assessed and contended with my father's essay, which I deemed then, and still deem, to be the best piece written on it, from a contemporary point of view. But I also found it deeply disturbing—and not only for the reason mentioned above. If Popper had taught me anything, it was that science thrived, not through its ability to prove its findings, which is impossible, but through its ability to criticize them relentlessly. Rationality, at its best, treats the fruits of reason as likely to be wrong, rather than tries vainly to prove them right. Popper deemed science the epitome of rationality in this regard. Reason could be applied to great effect to destabilize and disprove what we take to be true but could not prove itself to be baseless or futile. That is a contradiction in terms.

The very idea that God's commandments could be understood, feared, and obeyed without the benefit of rational comprehension struck me as overly fundamentalist, especially against the backdrop of the rabbinic texts that undertook to discern them. In attempting to determine our religious obligations, the talmudic literature—described by Moshe Halbertal as Judaism's "formative canon"[13]—subjects virtually every one of God's revealed words to the critical scrutiny of an extraordinarily broad array of disputing human perspectives that seem never able to reach agreement, except on practical matters of law, and even then, only by provisional majority vote.

Thus the idea of viewing talmudic deliberation through a Popperian philosophical lens began to take form, and with it—because of my father's brief mention of Popper in his paper—that of fashioning a reading of Qohelet different from his, one that was equally capable of making sense of the text but in a way that reinforced my emerging understanding of talmudic epistemology in Popperian terms.

It was a worthwhile effort, to which much of what I do to this day owes its origin, though I could not know that at the time. What was immediately evident, even before I had finished reading the paper at the conference, was the effect that it had on my father. Mine was the only paper at the conference that constructively challenged an aspect of his work, and he was delighted. He sat beaming in the front row, and was on his feet with the first question the minute I sat down. We continued to discuss Qohelet in earnest long after the event. It was a text we read very differently by allowing our very different academic, intellectual, and even religious worlds to bear upon it. Arguing about Qohelet enabled us to enrich our own positions by enjoying the lively challenge of someone equally serious but committed very differently. Qohelet thus facilitated a wonderfully meaningful meeting ground with my father's thinking and world of values, as well as a dialogical engagement with him that lasted long after he died—which was all the more significant, given our profound and unbridgeable political differences.

The first fruits of that initial effort were outlined in my contribution to the volume commemorating the conference, edited by Spolsky in 1993.[14] A four-lecture series delivered shorty after at the Van Leer Institute, Jerusalem, and published in Hebrew in 1994[15] enabled me to further develop the tripartite structure of my initial offering at the conference, with chapters devoted to the philosophy of science, still much in Popperian spirit, to the talmudic literature's musings on its undertaking, and to a reading of Qohelet along lines anticipating those of the present study.

What none of this early writing took note of was that it was set in motion by a work I considered superb yet profoundly wrong. My budding new reading of Qohelet owed its origin and existence to the critical challenge of a reading very different from my own, a critical challenge I could never have self-mounted. Popper stressed the importance of criticism for setting a creative effort in motion, but his philosophy, like mine at the time, failed to register the crucial difference between applying criticism and being challenged by someone whose perspective differed from one's own. Through my Popperian eyes, I viewed myself at the time as offering a friendly critique of my father's reading by proposing a different one of my own. What I only later realized was that I was naively reversing the arrow of causation. My reading took form in an effort not to criticize my father but to rise to the challenge of the critical effect that his reading had had on me, a challenge I could never have set myself.

This later realization eventually marked my philosophical parting of ways with Popper and set the agenda for virtually everything I have since done, which, as I now realize, was sparked unknowingly thirty years ago in preparing for that fateful conference. The realization that one could get a proper critical hold on one's own convictions only by being exposed to criticism leveled by people with whom one disagreed also turned out to be a key element in Qohelet's thinking, as I gradually came to understand.

Qohelet may have started out for me as yet another intriguing text, of which, due to the chance circumstances of my father's conference, I felt religiously and philosophically obliged to make better sense. But what I have come to realize is that grappling with Qohelet for years, in an attempt to better understand it, was just as much a self-grappling in an attempt to better understand myself. All engaged philosophical readings of past thinkers are, to some extent, tendentious. We cannot help seeing with our own eyes and understanding in terms of what we understand. In the past thinkers we appreciate, we most often see ourselves reflected. But in the case of Qohelet, it was less a process of *finding* myself *in* the text, than of forming my thinking in attempting to read it. Attempting to understand Qohelet yielded a process of philosophical self-discovery or self-formation that I did not think possible. It was not a process of reading in or of reading out but a dialectic combination of both.

The philosophical excitement and exhilaration that I feel each time I return to Qohelet has not abated over the years. I owe to the impact on my thinking of my father's reading of Qohelet my appreciation of the indispensable role of external critique. To Qohelet itself I owe the more elusive realization that one's own thinking is better served by attempting to come to terms with that of another thinker, than by merely talking to oneself.

Reason's Problematic Limits

My philosophical work on rationality and scholarly engagement with the talmudic literature remain the key for how I read Qohelet, but they have both changed and deepened over the ensuing years, lending a crucial added dimension to my initial reading of the book. A brief preliminary word about each will help explain why I regard Qohelet as such a religiously significant philosophical work.

I remain committed to Popper's famous identification of rationality and criticism. To act rationally (as opposed to acting impulsively or instinctively) is to act for a reason. And we have reason to act when we consider something in our world to be sufficiently amiss as to merit repair or replacement. Rationality thus consists in a willingness to keenly seek problems out, look them in the eye, and act to put them right.

What goes sorely missing in Popper's account is rationality's essentially normative component. To judge something to be sufficiently amiss to consider putting it right, and to consider those we criticize—whether ourselves or others—to be wrong not to attend to it is to issue a complex normative judgment. Wrongs and failings are breaches of norms and will furnish reasons to act only for those whose norms they are. What might seem wholly satisfactory to a secular liberal might well strike a devout orthodox Jew, for instance, as reason to take urgent and decisive action.

Our normative commitments also serve in holding ourselves in normative check. We chide ourselves, as we chide others, for being inattentive, careless, or neglectful of what we know is right. We take ourselves to be accountable to the norms and standards to which we are committed and blame ourselves for failing to live up to them. But the demands of rationality extend further, to our commitments themselves. We expect others, as they expect us, to be responsible not only for living up to our commitments but for living up to commitments that are worthy of living up to. The secular mostly criticize the religious for being religious, not for not being religious enough, just as liberals are mostly criticized by conservatives for being liberal, not for failing to fully live up to their liberal aspirations.

The great diversity of human commitment across cultural boundaries in place and time renders the task of holding our own standards of propriety in normative check all the more urgent. On the one hand, mere awareness of the fact that radically different forms of life exist and flourish, and realizing that the one to which we happen to be committed owes to the wholly accidental circumstances of our birth and *Bildung*, does not weaken its hold on us, or subvert our devotion and willingness for self-sacrifice for our God, king, and country, our family and friends, our chosen life projects, our ideas and ideals, what and whom we wholeheartedly care for, and those we hotly detest.

On the other hand, the fact that so many people are committed differently demands that we take responsibility for our own form of life by creating rational critical distance between ourselves and who we are. If that sounds like a contradiction in terms, it was meant to; for how is it possible to step outside ourselves in such a way? How can we effectively subject our norms and standards to our own normative appraisal if it is by means of those very norms and standards that we normatively appraise? But then, how can it *not* be possible? It is unthinkable that the ethical, political, religious, and scientific standards to which we are presently committed would be immune to our own normative scrutiny. Yet no philosopher of science, mind, or agency has been able to show how, as philosopher of mind John McDowell puts it, our standards can be impeached by being subjected to their own reflective scrutiny.[16] The problem of rationally breaching rationality's normative constraints has stumped the entire philosophical community and has animated my work for the last several years.

Rationality, at its best, requires an internalized normative framework in order to perform its critical work. Such frameworks are the time-bound children of historical place and time. They are embedded and embodied in the languages we speak and the environments of thick relations constitutive of the lives we live. As rational as we might aspire to be, we cannot break the glass ceiling of our heartfelt commitments by mere self-reflection. And yet, as I have tried to show with respect to rational agency in general[17] and to scientific framework transitions,[18] as well as to talmudic dialogism,[19] normative criticism leveled at us by others, though unable to persuade us to replace our norms, can still have a destabilizing effect on their hold on us. External criticism is capable of ambivalating us sufficiently toward the norms in challenges, to create the self-critical distance necessary for changing our minds. A discursive environment of differently committed trusted critics is hence a necessary condition for holding our own commitments in rational check—a feat that we are incapable of achieving alone.

The four main elements of this brief excursion into my philosophical work of late—the identification, à la Popper, of rationality and criticism; the normative basis of all criticism; the contingent time- and culture-boundness of all human commitment; and the necessary role of external, different-minded critics in holding our commitments in critical check—combine to explain the rationality of scientific revolutions (which Thomas Kuhn deemed to be no more rational than religious conversions or gestalt switches),[20] as well as the talmudic canon's self-understanding. As the following pages purport to show in picture and prose, they also hold the key for a new and exciting reading of Qohelet.

Rhythms and Moods

Apart from undertaking to make better sense of the text, our proposed reading of Qohelet addresses the book's biblical status, as well as its liturgical place, differently from other readings. It diverts sharply from the interpretive strategy adopted by Scott, Harold Fisch, and countless other readers of the book, in refusing to view Qohelet as promoting a negation of human wisdom, even if, as Fisch argues, it is a negation achieved by a supreme act of reflexive rational self-critique. In the course of the book, certain rival viewpoints are indeed dismissed by reducing them to absurdity. But not all is ultimately reduced by Qohelet to "nothingness and futility," as Fisch and many others insist, by translating the text's keyword *hevel*.[21] In fact, the meaning of *hevel* for Qohelet is plausibly far less harsh.

An initial motivation for the reading presented here will be shown to originate in the Mishna's mythical account of the controversy surrounding the canonization of the book of Qohelet and its eventual resolution, but my reasons for adopting that particular route owe to the very texture of the book, or rather, to its distinct change of tone and rhythm mid-argument—a feature of the text that systematically goes unnoted.

Qohelet sets forth from a premise that he nowhere takes back: that all, but all, is *hevel*—whatever the word means; and he proceeds to ask: if so, what profit or achievement can people boast in all of (or, in any of) their labor under the sun? Note that if Qohelet's claim that everything a person can ever think or do amounts to "nothingness and futility," the question of its possible advantage or value is rendered rhetorical. Under conditions of utter futility, all human endeavor is worthless.

Qohelet's initial response to the challenge that he set himself in the opening verses seems to bear out such a reading. Undertaking to "seek and search out by wisdom concerning all things that are done under the heaven" leads him to conclude that "it is a sore task" (the Hebrew phrase *inyan ra*—"an evil matter"—is markedly harsher) and to fall a little over a chapter later into what has to be the darkest depth of despair in the Hebrew Bible:

> Then I saw that wisdom excels folly, as far as light excels darkness.… As it happens to the fool, so it happens even to me; and why was I then more wise?… For of the wise mn as of the fool there is no enduring remembrance… And how does the wise man die? Just like the fool. Therefore I hated life … for all is *hevel* and a striving after the wind. And I hated all my labor in which I have laboured under the sun.… Therefore I went about to cause my heart to despair of all the labour which I took under the sun. (2:13–20)

Up to this point, one could well read the text, as most do, as describing Qohelet's disconcerting realization that all human wisdom can ever boast is irrefutable proof of its own worthlessness, painfully leveling the wise and the fool and rendering the prospects of a meaningful human life "*hevel* and a great evil" (2:21). What all such readings fail to note is that the end of chapter 2 does not mark the culmination of Qohelet's argument but only its point of departure. For the well-known opening of chapter 3 registers a major change of rhythm and mood—nicely captured by the rhythmic, upbeat music of Pete Seeger's well-known 1959 rendition of "Turn, Turn, Turn." In realizing that "for everything there is a season and a time for every purpose under the heaven," that there is "a time to plant and a time to uproot the planted; … a time to weep and a time to laugh; … a time to keep and a time to cast away," Qohelet clearly appears to undergo a dramatic change of heart that allows him to reembrace life and, more important, to revisit the question from which he set forth—now, however, without a trace of despair: "What profit has the worker for his toil? I have seen the task which God has given the sons of men to be exercised in it" (3:9–10). The possible worth of human toil is no longer stated rhetorically. Qohelet has come to see (to "see" in Qohelet is to understand) the task that God has set us, which he no longer deems to be a "sore" task, no longer an *inyan ra*.

One does not have to understand Qohelet's precise reasons for despairing of life at the end of chapter 2, or those responsible for his change of heart at the beginning of chapter 3, to appreciate that the famous "Song of Seasons" marks a transformative moment in his reasoning. Yet no reading of the book as a negation and dismissal of human reason takes note of it.

The same is true for the book's closing chapter and a half, where one need not understand Qohelet's overall argument to appreciate the glaring contrast between his horror and despair at the end of chapter 2 and the joyous affirmation of human life and calm acceptance of its inevitable and natural conclusion in death of chapters 11 and 12: "Truly the light is sweet and a pleasant thing it is to behold the sun. For if a man live many years, let him rejoice in them all; yet let him remember the days of darkness, for they shall be many. All that comes is *hevel*.... Rejoice, O young man, in thy youth, and let thy heart cheer thee in the days of thy youth" (11:7–9).

Human toil and reason might have seemed to Qohelet, in the closing verses of chapter 2, alarmingly and unsurmountably worthless; but by the end of his discourse—beginning in the opening verses of chapter 3 and culminating in the last two chapters—Qohelet seems to have made his peace with whatever gave rise to his initial despair. Long before declaring that the fear of God and observing his commandments is the "whole of man" in the book's penultimate verse, the deep and initially heart-wrenching problem concerning the very worth of human reason and conduct seems to have been resolved to Qohelet's satisfaction. The reading proposed in the following pages seeks to make detailed sense of the text along these lines: to discern the precise nature of the problem that exercises Qohelet and the complex and perceptive way in which he tackles, and eventually solves, the problem. As noted, it is a reading that turns on a plausible yet decidedly different understanding of *hevel* from most—and one that takes its cue from the rabbis' myth-history of Qohelet's canonization.

THE TALMUDIC PRISM

According to the Mishna, Qohelet's canonization was long disputed by the so-called Houses of Shammai and Hillel and was decided in favor of the Hillelites "on the very day R. Elazar b. Azaria was appointed head of the yeshiva."[22] The yeshiva in question is the Jabne center, and the day in question is, according to the Babylonian Talmud's legendary account of its establishment and demise, "that very day" of the Hillelite takeover led by R. Joshua b. Ḥanania and R. Elazar b. Azaria.[23] The association of Qohelet's religious viability with talmudic Hillelism is insignificant for the historical question of the book's actual canonization but is highly relevant to that of how the rabbis might have read it. It is here that I find my cue for the reading of Qohelet as I propose. For readers less familiar with what the two Houses stand for in rabbinic literature (and the formative role played in it by that of Hillel), a brief background and word of explanation are in order.

The rabbinic literature of late antiquity differs from other religious canons in the radical and wholly unadjudicated diversity of exegetical and halakhic opinion that it harbors and its keen argumentative style, but it has precious little to say about either. However, in one brief, well-known legend concerning the Hillelite-Shammaite dispute and its heavenly resolution, the Babylonian Talmud, the crowning achievement of that literature, offers a rare glimpse of how it understands its own undertaking.[24]

The legend introduces the deeply divided Houses of Hillel and Shammai as the paradigm of real halakhic and meta-halakhic dispute, each claiming that the law be decided according to them—until a heavenly voice is said to have issued forth, ruling enigmatically that while both positions are to be equally considered "the words of the living God," halakhic decision-making is to follow the House of Hillel.

The first part of the heavenly ruling is understandable. If the law is best developed in conditions of real disagreement, a plurality of differently committed voices must be valued and ensured—hence, the need to deem all disputing parties to the debate to be religiously viable. Yet for the law to benefit from debate, energetic disagreement is not enough. For dispute to have an impact, at least one party must be willing to change its mind in the face of criticism. This, the Talmud explains, is why the Hillelite approach merited heavenly endorsement.

But its precise wording is what renders this passage truly exceptional. The Hillelite position was endorsed, it explains, because, unlike the Shammaites, the Hillelites were *noḥin va'aluvin*. In talmudic Hebrew, the term *noḥin* means "flexible," as opposed to "dogmatic"—wary of being wrong and willing to change one's mind.[25] But that is not enough. The Hillelites knowingly coupled their flexibility with a willingness to be proved wrong by others; not only *noḥin* "flexible" but *aluvin*, "open to criticism" (literally, "willing to be insulted by being proved wrong"). It is one thing to be willing to admit being wrong, but quite another to realize that it is impossible to gain a critical grip on one's own heartfelt commitments. The Hillelites, the Talmud goes on the explain, would not only hear their rivals' arguments but granted them precedence over their own—to which the Palestinian Talmud perceptively adds: "and they would [often] take the Shammaite position to heart, and retract their own." To side with the Hillelites is hence to realize the severe limitations of self-criticism and to recognize the need, therefore, for the kind of potentially transformative challenge that only a real and equally dedicated opponent can provide, as well as to actively seek such engagement. For the Hillelites, exposure to external critique was a norm of halakhic rationality.

It is easy to see why I find the position attributed by both Talmudim to the endorsed House of Hillel profoundly significant. I have read and reread this well-known legend in almost everything I have written on talmudic discourse since turning to the rabbinic literature in the wake of my father's conference. But although it was looking me in the face, I failed to grasp its full philosophical significance before completing *The View from Within*, over twenty years later, which opened the door for a re-appreciation of Qohelet.

But there is more to talmudic Hillelism. The Houses of Hillel and Shammai are not described in rabbinic literature as schools of halakhic thinking but as bearers and transmitters of Hillelite and Shammaite halakha. When attributed an initial halakhic position, it is not one that they had arrived at by reason but one of their received traditions. And received halakhic tradition is not an interlocutor in the Talmud's horizontal halakhic debate but a vertical source of halakhic authority. It is here that another important and fundamental difference emerges between the two Houses. The Shammaites, neither *noḥin* nor *aluvin*, view themselves as charged with the solemn obligation to transmit God's one true revealed Word, which they believed was passed down to them. The Hillelites view themselves as charged with very different responsibilities. They humbly believe that humankind's inherent fallibility, our tendency to misunderstand and err, extends to the traditions transmitted to us by our forebears. They see themselves, therefore, as religiously obligated to adopt a critical, reformative stance toward their legacies and understandings. They do not deny that God revealed his will to man by word and prophet; what they do deny is the conceit that our understanding of God's word and will, forever cast in human idiom and image, can ever be deemed to be *the* one God-given truth—a position that thoroughly problematizes any simplistic fundamentalist reading of Qohelet's ending verses.

Like the Shammaites, the Hillelites take their religious understandings and halakhic legacies with utmost seriousness and conviction. However, aware of their own and their forebears' likelihood to err, they are equally committed to holding them in critical check. To do so effectively, they realize, requires exposing them to the critique of those committed differently. Therefore, they welcome diversity of opinion and conviction, even regarding religious fundamentals. They are the true pluralists and the truly rational.

Talmudic Hillelism not only resonated closely with my newfound philosophy but profoundly informs the radical diversity of opinion and keen dialogism characteristic of both branches of the rabbinic literature's extensive undertaking: its midrashic enterprise of interpreting Scripture and its halakhic enterprise of deliberating and erecting a system of law. It subsequently informs the bifocal lens of my recent thinking, on the one hand, and the Mishna's mythic identification of the Hillelites as being ultimately responsible for Qohelet's canonization, through which I propose to read the book. Read from such a Hillelite perspective, Qohelet emerges not as the strangest book in the Hebrew Bible, as Scott submits, but as perhaps the most important one—not merely for me but for talmudic Judaism.

HEVEL'S THE WORD

As I have remarked, any reading of Qohelet must first contend with the book's central term: *hevel*. For it is under the contention, nowhere retracted, that all, but all is *hevel*, that Qohelet's entire argument unfolds. In biblical Hebrew, *hevel* means "vapor" or "mist" and is frequently employed to denote "nothingness," "futility," "emptiness," "insignificance," "nonsense," or "inconsequentiality," especially when applied to idolatry, as in Isa 30:7; 49:4; Jer 2:5; 10:3, 15; 16:19; and many more. But *hevel* is also taken more literally to denote mist-like impermanence, transience, and temporality, something inherently time-bound, here today but gone tomorrow, especially when human existence is compared to divine absolute permanence, as in Isa 57:13; Ps 39:6; 78:33; and, especially, 144:4: "Man is like a breath [*hevel*]; his days are like a shadow that passes away."[26]

I propose to read Qohelet's notion of *hevel* in the latter, rather than the former, sense of the term, careful not to instinctively equate the time-bound and temporal with the empty, futile, and the senseless.[27] Being a discourse on possible human achievement and the limits of human wisdom, rather than on the value or viability of other gods, it makes much better sense to attribute to Qohelet the notion of *hevel* consistently reserved by the Hebrew Bible to human transience than to attribute to it what is reserved consistently for the senselessness and vacuity of idol worship.[28]

To claim that the human condition is inherently time-bound; that what we are now absolutely sure of, is likely to be refuted tomorrow; that our legal systems, technologies, social institutions, sciences, and deepest normative convictions are the inherently contingent, perspectival, historical products of the particular circumstances of our time and place; that even if absolute truth was staring us in the face, we would have no way of recognizing it as such; or that all, but all is *hevel* in the second sense of the term, is a very different claim from deeming them all to be but "nothingness and futility." To inquire about the worth of human endeavor if human endeavor is deemed to be inherently "empty of meaning and worth" is to pose a rhetorical question. To inquire about the worth of human endeavor under conditions of time-bound temporality is not only a different question entirely—and by no means rhetorical—but is precisely the predicament in which talmudic Hillelites constantly found themselves—and which philosophers like myself find themselves today. From such a Hillelite perspective, the idea of avoiding the forever precarious uptake of human reason in favor of submissive reliance on blind obedience to divine dictate begs all the questions without solving any. For to obey God's command requires us to understand it, and such understanding will always be as inherently precarious as any other feat of human reasoning.

Thus, I read Qohelet as a concerned and deeply troubled religious philosopher wrestling with the profound problem of how to live a worthy life in the eyes of God under such conditions. How can we ever boast to live up to the absolute standards by which God will judge us, lacking the very ability to recognize them as such? It is a problem that, I believe, Qohelet solved to his satisfaction with great, surprisingly modern, and highly relevant philosophical acuity.

It is hence an interpretation that diverges considerably from the vast majority of common, religiously motivated, and scholarly readings of the book. Enough has been said in these introductory pages about our reasons for reading it as we do to justify embarking on our interpretive project. But its ultimate viability can be vouched for only by the extent to which it succeeds in making detailed sense of the entire text, of which, dear reader, only you can be the judge. To allow the text to speak for itself and unfold naturally in the light of our proposed reading, we shall refrain in what follows from arguing for it. Our introductions, notes, and commentaries to each of its chapters will not be polemical, and we shall not be making our case by criticizing other readings.[29] We assume that the vast majority of our readership will have read Qohelet at least in part—and even if not, they will have some preconception of what the book is about, against which the reading we propose will have to prove its mettle.

For the same reason, we shall not be offering a verse-by-verse running commentary. My introductions to each chapter will explain how I understand the shape of Qohelet's deliberations, the lessons that he endorses and those that he rejects, and how it relates to the book's broader undertaking and evolving argument. The chapter will then be presented in Hebrew and in English, accompanied by Debra Band's rich and intricate artwork and commentary. In my concluding essay, I shall explain how the mystery of the book's liturgical placing is also addressed. But it is now time to allow Qohelet to speak for himself.

NOTES

[1] Harold Fisch, "Qohelet: A Hebrew Ironist," in idem, *Poetry with a Purpose: Biblical Poetics and Interpretation* (Bloomington: Indiana University Press, 1988), 158–78.

[2] Popper believed that scientific theories could never be proved but could be falsified; and that science advances by trial and error, by keenly testing its hypotheses and modifying or replacing them when they are refuted.

[3] H. Fisch, "Qohelet: A Hebrew Ironist," 174–75.

[4] R. B. Y. Scott, *The Anchor Bible*, vol. 18: *Proverbs, Ecclesiastes* (Garden City, N.Y.: Doubleday, 1965), 191.

[5] Babylonian Talmud (hereafter, b.), Kidushin 30b.

[6] Qohelet Rabbah, 1:4.

[7] Scott, *The Anchor Bible*, 192.

[8] Scott, *The Anchor Bible*, 192.

[9] H. Fisch, "Qohelet: A Hebrew Ironist," 158.

[10] Following KJV, the Hebrew phrase *ki ze kol ha'adam* is invariably rendered by Christian translators as "this is the whole *duty* of man" or "of humankind," while, with the exception of the Jerusalem Bible, Jewish translators tend to steer closer to the Hebrew, with "this is the whole man" (JPS), or "the entire man." Interestingly, while Harold Fisch reads Qohelet as the Bible's equivalent or "answer" to Pope's "Essay on Man" ("Qohelet: A Hebrew Ironist," 172f.), in the Jerusalem

Bible version, he opts for KJV's rendition of 12:13, rather than remaining truer to the more general Hebrew phrasing.

[11] H. Fisch, "Qohelet: A Hebrew Ironist," 158–60.

[12] H. Fisch, "Qohelet: A Hebrew Ironist," 160.

[13] Moshe Halbertal, *People of the Book: Canon, Meaning, and Authority* (Cambridge, Mass.: Harvard University Press, 1997), 3–6.

[14] Menachem Fisch, "The Perpetual Covenant of Jewish Learning," in *Summoning: Ideas of the Covenant and Interpretive Theory*, ed. E. Spolsky (Albany: SUNY Press, 1993), 91–114.

[15] Menachem Fisch, *"To Know Wisdom": Science, Rationality and Torah Study* [Hebrew] (Tel Aviv: Hakibbutz Hameuchad, 1994).

[16] John McDowell, *Mind and World* (Cambridge, Mass.: Harvard University Press, 1996), 81–82.

[17] See, esp., Menachem Fisch and Yitzhak Benbaji, *The View from Within: Normativity and the Limits of Self-Criticism* (South Bend, Ind.: University of Notre Dame Press, 2011).

[18] Menachem Fisch, *Creatively Undecided: Toward a History and Philosophy of Scientific Agency* (Chicago: University of Chicago Press, 2017).

[19] First in Menachem Fisch, "Deciding by Argument versus Proving by Miracle: The Myth-History of Talmudic Judaism's Coming of Age," *Toronto Journal of Theology* 33, no. 1 (2017): 103–27, and more fully in idem, *Covenant of Confrontation: A Study of Non-Submissive Religiosity in Rabbinic Literature* [Hebrew] (Ramat Gan: Bar-Ilan University Press, 2019).

[20] I am referring to the paragraphs of Kuhn's *The Structure of Scientific Revolutions*, 2d ed. (Chicago: University of Chicago Press, 1970) that John Earman dubs "purple." See Earman, "Carnap, Kuhn, and the Philosophy of Scientific Methodology," in *World Changes: Thomas Kuhn and the Nature of Science*, ed. P. Horwich (Cambridge, Mass.: MIT Press, 1993), 9–36, with reference to *The Structure*, 94, 111–14, 150, 151. The view is forcefully restated in Kuhn's Postscript-1969 appended to the 1970 ed., where he declares: "The conversion experience that I likened to a gestalt switch remains therefore at the heart of the revolutionary process" (Kuhn, 204).

[21] See, e.g., Michael V. Fox, "The Meaning of *Hebel* for Qohelet," *Journal of Biblical Literature* 105, no. 3 (1986): 409–27, who surveys the relevant literature concluding, not unlike Fisch, that for Qohelet, "the reliability of the causal nexus fails, leaving only fragmented sequences of events which, though divinely determined, must be judged random from the human perspective.… The belief in a reliable causal order fails, and with it human reason and self-confidence. But this failure is what God intends, for after it comes fear. And fear is the only emotion that Qohelet explicitly wants God to arouse" (427). For a comprehensive survey of renderings past and contemporary of *hevel* for Qohelet, see Russell L. Meek, "Twentieth- and Twenty-First-Century Readings of *Hebel* (הֶבֶל) in Ecclesiastes," *Currents in Biblical Research* 14, no. 3 (2016): 279–97.

[22] Mishna, Yadaim, 3:5.

[23] See, esp., b. Berakhot 27b–28a and Bava Metzia 59b. Menachem Fisch, *Rational Rabbis: Science and Talmudic Culture* (Bloomington: Indiana University Press, 1997), pt. 2, chap. 3, offers a detailed account of the Jabne legends, which is challenged by Daniel Boyarin, *Border Lines: The Partition of Judaeo-Christianity* (Philadelphia: University of Pennsylvania Press, 2004), chap. 5.

[24] B. Eruvin 13b. The remainder of this section briefly summarizes the analysis of the legend presented in M. Fisch, "Deciding by Argument versus Proving by Miracle," and in greater detail in idem, *Covenant of Confrontation*, chap. 1.

[25] See, e.g., b. Sanhedrin 3a, where *noḥin* is explicitly contrasted with *mehudadin* ("dogmatic").

[26] A usage also employed by the rabbis. See, e.g., b. Shabbat 34a–b; 39b; 51a; Yevamot 80b; Bava Metzia 107b; Bava Batra 75a. See also Yerushalmi, Terumot 45d; Pesaḥim 34a.

[27] As does Scott, who translates Qohelet's premise as "A vapor of vapors (says Qohelet). Thinnest of vapors. All is vapor," but adds in a footnote: "[H]evel denotes a breath empty of substance and also transient. The writer's thesis is that everything in a man's experience in this world … is empty of meaning or worth.… Hence … his efforts to achieve something are ultimately futile." In similar fashion, Harold Fisch also identifies the *hevel* mist with emptiness: "The wisdom that turns in upon itself and finds its aim as well as its origin in man himself is a wisdom without remembrance.… That is why it is *hevel*, a mist, an emptiness" ("Qohelet: A Hebrew Ironist," 160).

[28] In his survey of past and present readings of *hevel* in Qohelet, Meek claims that while "early Jewish interpretations" tended to interpret *hevel* metaphorically as connoting mist-like "ephemerality and transience" ("Twentieth- and Twenty-First-Century Readings," 280–82), "early Christian interpretation … tended toward a more negative understanding" connoting futility, pointlessness, and falsity. However, readings of the former, "Jewish" variety, though metaphorical, end up with a similar claim—that because it is radically transient, our mist-like existence is worthless. The same goes for the vast majority of twentieth- and twenty-first-century readings that he surveys (with the exception of Martin Shuster; see following footnote).

[29] Martin Shuster's insightful "Being as Breath, Vapor as Joy: Using Martin Heidegger to Re-Read the Book of Ecclesiastes," *Journal for the Study of the Old Testament* 33, no. 2 (2008): 219–44, comes closest to the interpretation of *hevel* presented here. Shuster understands *hevel* as connoting mist-like "contingency," i.e., "an acknowledgement of the fundamental historical nature of human existence" (231), captured in Heidegger's famous coupling of Being and Time. Shuster, however, fails to develop this thought further. He makes no mention of the epistemological problem to which Qohelet's *hevel* premise gives rise, the additional anxiety due to the religious dimension of the book, to Qohelet's proposed solution, or to his dealings with the opposition.

13

INTRODUCTION
APPROACHING THE BOOK OF QOHELET
Debra Band

My first conversation with Qohelet followed a family tragedy, during the week of Sukkot when I was thirty-one. Upon returning home from synagogue late in the evening after Kol Nidre (the evening service that begins Yom Kippur) a few days earlier, the telephone rang. Alarmed—for, as an observant Jew, my mother would not ordinarily touch electronics on a festival—I heard her voice through the answering machine. I grabbed the phone, and heard her cry that my stepbrother, Jonathan, only a few months older than I, lay in the hospital, dying from brain trauma suffered in a traffic accident that afternoon. I left my young children at home in Berkeley with my husband, David, and managed to arrive in Montreal in time for the funeral, and entered a maelstrom of shock and grief that I had never yet experienced, although the near-death of my second child soon after birth the previous year had been a near-miss. The shiva was cut short by the festival of Sukkot,[1] but the family still continued to gather at Jonathan's home with his wife and toddler children after synagogue services. One evening, having returned to my parents' house before others, I picked the book of Qohelet off their library bookshelf. I cannot remember what drew me to it—perhaps this was the evening after it was chanted in synagogue. I spent the rest of the evening circling their foyer gripping the book, my eyes glued to Qohelet's words.

Before that night, I had dutifully followed the annual chanting of the book of Qohelet each year in synagogue each Sukkot, but had never paid much attention to it. Why did Qohelet's words resonate in me that night? All I can remember about my reaction is feeling, "Oh, *he* understands how random death can be." Many years have passed since that night, crowded, as for many of us, with both intense joy and terrible grief; throughout, Qohelet has stayed with me. I suspect that that evening, I absorbed some sense of his understanding that we *all* live subject to an inscrutable divine will, and the best we can do is to live every moment as well, as deeply, and as intentionally as we can, while we can … for life drifts away.

Life drifts away. *Hakol hevel*. Menachem Fisch's literal understanding of Qohelet's key word, *hevel*, as "vapor," or "mist," instead of the common English interpretations of "vanity," or "futility," immediately hints at the dispassionate—to many, calming—common sense that Qohelet achieves through his appreciation of the transience of human life and accomplishments. Life is short, and we can never fully predict or understand our fortunes or the heritage we leave behind us—hence, the best we can do is to live life lovingly, kindly, and fully. As Menachem has described in his introduction to Qohelet's philosophy, and as I will expand on below, reading *hevel* as "vapor," instead of "vanity," or "futility," radically changes our understanding of the text.

Yet, as Menachem writes, Qohelet struggles with an even more painful problem than mortality. How can any individual find true wisdom, when even the most powerful person knows that, limited by both the human vantage point "under heaven" and the unpredictable limits of human life, he or she can never perceive the full scope of God's expectations of each of us? He knows that God exists—this is hardly the work of an atheist. But from a human perspective, God is remote and, to humankind, unpredictable. So how best to live in God's eyes, how to learn wisdom, how even to understand what God demands from each of us?

¹²I Qohelet was King over Yisra'el in Yerushalayim. ¹³And I gave my heart to seek and search out by wisdom concerning all things that are done under the heaven: it is a sore task that God has given to the son of man to be exercised with. ¹⁴I have seen all the works that are done under the sun; and, behold, all is vapor and a striving after wind. ¹⁵That which is crooked cannot be made straight: and that which is wanting cannot be numbered. (Qoh 1:12–15)

Below, you will find our attempt to come to terms with both the torment and serenity that Qohelet offers by probing his writings through philosophy and painting. Menachem has shared the philosophical approach to understanding this biblical book. Let me explain the value of fusing a visual interpretation to a scholarly understanding of the book of Qohelet, and then introduce you to the artwork ahead.

Why Illuminate the Book of Qohelet?

In Song of Songs Rabbah, the main compendium of midrash on that biblical love poetry, rabbis praise Qohelet for teaching wisdom—they mostly understood his name as a kind of pen name for the wise King Solomon. Solomon, the midrash passes down, elucidated the meaning of Torah through parables that illustrated the concepts of Torah, and thus made God's intent comprehensible to the human mind. Solomon "pondered the words of the Torah and investigated [the meaning of] the words of the Torah. He made handles to the Torah. You find that till Solomon came there was no parable."[2] The rabbis elaborate on the great value of parable, which might, on the surface, seem like a superficial distraction:

> Let not the parable be lightly esteemed in your eyes, since by means of the parable a man arrives at the true meaning of the words of the Torah. If a king loses gold from his house or a precious pearl, does he not find it by means of a wick worth a farthing? So the parable should not be lightly esteemed in your eyes, since by means of the parable a man arrives at the true meaning of the words of the Torah.[3]

The illuminated book you have before you is founded on parable. When I began this project, many people—even those who knew and appreciated my previous works—asked, incredulous, how I could possibly attach visual imagery to this highly abstract text. However, just as in my earlier work—indeed, exactly as the rabbis observed that Solomon used *verbal* parables to draw out the implications of this enigmatic book—I use *visual* metaphor to draw out the subtle meanings that we find in Qohelet.

Readers of my earlier books may already be acquainted with my approach to crafting visual interpretations of traditional Jewish texts. As I have written in those works, my compositions begin with a representation of reality that usually makes sense in the world of our own experience—or even the mystical world that some of these texts describe. Following Erwin Panofsky's[4] analysis of "disguised symbolism" in the work of the masters of medieval northern Europe—particularly, van Eyck, a reproduction of whose *Arnolfini Wedding Portrait* has hung over my worktable since college—I introduce values and ideas related to the text at hand through symbolic images in ways that usually make logical sense. While the overall painting usually creates a coherent, easily understood, material reality, examining the symbolism of individual items within it reveals a more complex world of ideas. In our increasingly visual age, when the word "icon" has sprung far from its roots in religion and art history into everyday conversation, a vibrant Jewish visual vocabulary—able to convey complex abstract philosophical, ethical, and spiritual ideas in a glance, using imagery rooted in millennia of diverse Jewish sources—acquires a new relevance in Jewish society. I use and expand this Jewish symbolic vocabulary that I have developed in my work over three decades to explore the meanings of Qohelet's often abstract thoughts. So this Jewish illuminated book does far more than simply decorate text pages with pretty gold and color. Rather, the imagery and emotion of the paintings heighten the drama of the text and add to our meditation our spontaneous reflections on the text by raising relevant ideas drawn from our cultural surround. Within this book, as in my previous works, the full meaning of the symbolism—the full message of each painting—is laid out in the commentary that corresponds to each illuminated page. Menachem Fisch offers commentaries on each chapter that explore Qohelet's concerns within. Readers of my earlier books may recognize the small honeybee hidden in each of these paintings of Qohelet's gardens and palace. My Hebrew name, Devorah, is the Hebrew word for "honeybee" and plays with the medieval manuscript tradition of the scribal colophon, the brief paragraph in which the scribe identified himself that ended many medieval Christian and Jewish manuscripts. Just as the honeybees that now fly in and out of my hives pollinate the blossoms in the area and provide my family and friends with honey, we hope that these paintings and essays will nourish your understanding and pleasure in your own life.

The Central Metaphor: Human Life as a Palace

Just as our struggle to realize true wisdom—how God wants us to live—is limited by the human life span and the inherent time-boundedness of all human knowledge and endeavor, as Qohelet so poignantly reminds us, so do even the grandest, most exquisitely decorated, of our architectural monuments suffer the effects of time. Indeed, like many human artifacts, their very styles may be time-bound; for instance, after fire destroyed the roof and spire of Paris's treasured Notre Dame Cathedral, a brief discussion took place about whether the thirteenth-century structure should be duplicated in every detail, or whether the new roof might take a more modern form.[5] In the paintings in this volume, I compare human life and deeds ("labors," as Qohelet would say) to a grand palace, gorgeously decorated, full of lives bursting with energy and conversation, beauty and tragedy. Yet despite all its riches and grandeur, even this palace will crumble in time. This palace metaphor draws upon a tradition prominent across centuries of midrash, comparing the heavens to a palace, the human world to an orchard or garden. As I seek to lend light and dimension to Qohelet's ideas in these illuminations, I extend the palace metaphor to human life and deeds—and what grander palace than the Alhambra, the wondrously beautiful medieval palace and gardens of the Muslim Nasrid rulers of Granada. Despite all its magnificence, all the almost audible ghosts of the glittering and powerful people who strode its expanses, even the Alhambra crumbles slowly into the red dust from which it arose.

This most glorious of palaces—not only the seat of Muslim rulers but also a home of the vivid Jewish court life of medieval Andalusia—becomes the central symbol for human life and deeds as I interpret and envisage Qohelet's struggle to understand a path to a wise and deeply fulfilling life. Archaeological remains of First and Second Temple–period Jerusalem, as well as trees in all their seasonal phases and particular symbolic values within midrashic literature, flesh out the sense of the essentially time-bound beauty, fragility, and limitations of human experience. Poetry and prose from across not only the Hebrew Bible but across Western civilization—much of which reflects Qohelet's influence—as well as imagery from some of the most ecstatic and also horrific aspects of human experience of our own day enter the paintings to help reveal the enduring reality of Qohelet's thought in our own daily lives. Together I employ these human creations to conjure a parable, a visual midrash, of Qohelet's struggle to understand the workings of the universe, wisdom—at its root, what God demands of us—in the face of the limitations of the human vantage point "under the sun" and the evanescence of human life and deeds.

16

Qohelet is obsessed by the limitations of the human view of the entirety of Creation, of God's intent for the individual, humanity, the world, and the consequent transience and insubstantiality of all human standards of truth and goodness. Even nowadays—perhaps twenty-four centuries since Qohelet's lifetime, when we can send probes to test the environments of planets throughout our home galaxy—we cannot probe the fullness of divine will, he would say. God is in heaven, figuratively "above the sun." Humanity's view is restricted to the material sphere. Indeed, the phrase "under the sun" appears twenty-nine times, and "under heaven," appears three times. Although Abraham walked with God and Moses took dictation of the Torah directly from God and today we manipulate materials at the atomic level and create primitive life from amino acids, human existence is irrevocably separate from the Creator of all time and matter. So how might I visually convey the vastness of God, our inability to assuredly determine God's expectations of each of us?

Modern cosmology offers a metaphor for God's remote vastness. For many years—most notably, in my 2016 book, *Kabbalat Shabbat: The Grand Unification*—I have used imagery of the deep sky—far beyond our sun—as a metaphor for the all-surrounding, all-suffusing divine presence. The plastic of my computer keys, the garden that surrounds me as I sit writing on my deck, the sunlight and air and, indeed, the energy of the gentle breeze blowing the air around me are all matter that has been processed through the stars countless times since the moment of Creation. My late first husband, David Band, an astrophysicist, was fond of quoting a phrase popularized by both astronomer Carl Sagan and folksinger Joni Mitchell: "We are all stardust." Jewish mysticism holds that all space, time, and matter—all phenomena, whether material or spiritual—are sparks of the divine. Indeed, the kabbalistic tradition describes the moment of Creation in terms strikingly congruent with the modern cosmological theory of the Big Bang.[6] Thus, throughout these paintings, another key metaphor for God's all-suffusing presence is a particular astronomical image. Throughout the book, you will find adaptations of the Hubble Space Telescope's famous image of the "Ultra Deep Field" of space, which combines astronomical observations in all energy frequencies, from ultraviolet through near-infrared, to reveal an image of the heavens from the early universe era (a few hundred million years after the Big Bang!) through the image's compilation in 2014.[7] We are truly far beneath the sun.

Yet, as omnipresent as he knows God is, Qohelet asserts that God and God's intent for us and all the world are hidden from us. Like the firmament that God's words called up on the second day of Creation, an impenetrable barrier and difference in kind divides the human and divine spheres. Just as the stars of the cosmos have reprocessed all matter continually since the moment of the universe's creation, human comprehension of God's intent for us changes across time. In my visual midrash, the deep sky symbolizes the way in which the human vantage point "under the sun" limits our view of the depths and height of God, as well as God's intentions for us and expectations of us.

And all our deeds—our very selves—are finally ephemeral, like vapor, as Qohelet muses. Mist drifts across the paintings of Qohelet's words, expressing the evanescence of even our most concrete labors. Yet Qohelet achieves a kind of understanding that, although it cannot really answer his question, at least offers him, as well as us, a measure of serenity, and even joy, as we live our lives.

Before entering Qohelet's palace, let us explore who he might have been and when he might have lived and then attempt to acquire a sense of his surroundings.

Jewish tradition ascribes the book of Qohelet to King Solomon (tenth century B.C.E.), renowned for his wisdom and the luxurious wealth and power of his reign from Jerusalem. Yet while the book's author dons the cloak of the great king, he likely lived more than half a millennium later.

When did Qohelet live and write? Scholarly debates on the book of Qohelet's dating continue, but linguistic analyses of the text lead many scholars to place it in Israel in the third or fourth century B.C.E., that is, roughly two centuries following the 538 B.C.E. restoration of the Judaean leadership to Jerusalem by the Persian king Cyrus, following his conquest of the Babylonian Empire. The book of Qohelet includes no Greek words; thus much modern scholarship holds that it was composed before Hellenistic influence took root in Judaea, in the wake of Alexander the Great's conquest of the Persian Empire, in 332 B.C.E.;[8] the second-century B.C.E. book of Ben Sirach appears to have been acquainted with the book of Qohelet,[9] so it certainly predates that. We cannot divine the concerns that prodded this man to write this book, but a brief examination of Jerusalem society during the Persian period will help us understand the conditions that influenced his community and may have influenced his search for wisdom. Were we walking through Persian-period Jerusalem to meet this wisdom teacher, how might Qohelet's world look? What might we hear and see on the streets of Persian-period Jerusalem?

To begin with, the Hebrew language we would hear would no longer be quite the same as the language spoken before the Babylonian exile. The book of Qohelet's Hebrew shows the influence of the Aramaic language learned in Babylonia during the generations that grew up during the exile, as well as Persian words introduced into Hebrew texts under Israel's Persian rulers. Again, given the lack of the Greek loanwords that began to enter Hebrew following Alexander's conquest, we would deduce that we were walking through Jerusalem while it was governed by the Persian Empire.[10]

We would find ourselves making our way through the streets of a small but currently secure and prosperous city. Our view would be dominated by the Second Temple, standing now for a century or two, a more modest structure than the glorious white-and-gold edifice (as Herod would later redecorate it), but unquestionably the heart of the city. Roughly a century after the Persian king Cyrus permitted the Jewish exiles to return to their capital city (539 B.C.E.), the Second Temple had been constructed (515 B.C.E.),[11] and the city had become the administrative capital of the Persian province of Yehud Medinata, part of the larger satrapy known in the Persian Empire as "Across the River," meaning west of the great Euphrates.[12] Nowadays, we are familiar with the early twenty-first-century outlines of the Old City of Jerusalem as the city was redrawn by successive conquests. The Jerusalem of Qohelet's day, however, was smaller, perhaps thirty acres, with a likely population of four to five thousand people.[13] Jerusalem was the core of Yehud, which spread across what is now southern Israel. The Northern Kingdom of Israel had been conquered by Assyria, its population killed or exiled centuries earlier, in 722 B.C.E.

The Persian kings, like many other conquering powers of the day, generally offered both legal and financial support to the indigenous religious and political authorities of subject nations, in return for loyalty and military support. Under the Persian rule, however, Jerusalem's safety, socioeconomic conditions, and morale had already risen and fallen repeatedly. Early in the Persian period, Cyrus, Darius, and, later, Artaxerxes sent generous support to rebuild the city and the Temple after conquering Babylonia and assuming control of Israel, and the consequent public optimism even raised messianic expectations.

Ezra described the optimism of the first Passover celebration at the newly reconstructed Temple. He described how the returned exiles "kept the feast of unleavened bread seven days with joy: for the Lord had made them joyful and turned the heart of the king of Ashshur to them, to strengthen their hands in the work of the house of God, the God of Yisra'el" (Ezra 6:22). Later, the city suffered as the flow of funds from the Persian crown ceased because of fiscal constraints during the rule of Xerxes I (486–465 B.C.E.). Royal taxes on the populace remained burdensome; construction and maintenance of city walls were cut back, all disrupting life in the city. Ezra and Nehemiah tell of how, in the mid-fifth century B.C.E., the city's walls were breached, Temple practices were interrupted, and social division and intermarriage increased, all endangering the welfare of the Jewish capital.[14] By the fourth century, however, Jerusalem was comparatively calm, and the merchant and Temple administrative class within which he lived and taught prospered.

If we had we walked through Persian-period Jerusalem streets to meet with Qohelet, we would have encountered both wealth and poverty. Qohelet's frequent castigation of the wealthy for their oppression of the poor implies not only prosperity but also significant social stratification across the city's population:

> I … considered all the oppressions that are done under the sun, and behold the tears of such as were oppressed, and have had no comforter; and on the side of their oppressors there was power; but they had no comforter. (4:1)

Economy and Society

The Babylonian exile disrupted the traditional agrarian lifestyle and economy of Judaea. In Judaea, the bulk of the population worked farms and practiced local trade and barter, while the monarchy dominated larger-scale trade; but following the Persian conquest of Babylonia, the Persian crown imposed its own state control of Yehud's agricultural lands. Nehemiah, like other populist leaders across the Persian Empire, attempted to minimize the dislocation by returning fields and vineyards to their original owners.[15] Local agricultural barter and trade among Judaean farmers similarly diminished under Persian control of the land, and Jews who returned from exile entered into pursuits other than farming, such as shopkeeping, banking, and long-distance trade around the wider eastern Mediterranean basin. Coinage of silver and other metals, including coins from as far away as Greece, had come into common use in Jerusalem by the mid-fifth century.

Social stratification widened in the wake of the shift from agrarian life to money-based commercial life. Tax burdens rose and fell at the whim of the Persian state, and although the Persian monarchy awarded grants, it also suddenly retracted them. Private commercial ventures prospered or failed, and while even a slave might grow fortunes from initially small investments in land or commerce, vast fortunes might vanish following commercial failure or changes in taxation. Reversals of fortune such as Qohelet mentions became commonplace across the society. The social changes that sprang up in the wake of the new money-based economy ripple throughout Qohelet's characterizations of the human relationship with God and among people down here "under the sun." We will see how frequently Qohelet mentions silver, meaning coinage;[16] (worldly) labor and profit; a continual, arbitrary, and unpredictable risk of losing fortunes; and greed and social injustice. Consider one criticism of the wealthy: "He who loves silver shall not be satisfied with silver; nor he that loves abundance with increase: this is also vapor" (5:9).

Jerusalem became thoroughly integrated into the larger Mediterranean urban culture. The archaeological record reveals constant trade among Yehud, Persia, Egypt, Greece, and Cilicia (modern southern Turkey).

"The kitchen pots, as well as heavy bronze anklets worn by girls, or weapons of men were now the same in the whole Levant, united under Persian sway. Greek painted pottery, Phoenician amulets and Egyptian idols are equally typical of Palestine in the fourth century."[17]

The Temple

Before even a year had elapsed after his conquest of Babylonia in 539 B.C.E., the Persian king Cyrus permitted the exiled Jews to return to Jerusalem and rebuild the Temple, as he did with other conquered peoples. Ezra (6:2–5) records:

> Memorandum: In the first year of King Cyrus, King Cyrus issued an order concerning the House of God in Jerusalem: "Let the house be rebuilt, a place for offering sacrifices, with a base built high…. The expenses shall be paid by the palace. And the gold and silver vessels of the House of God which Nebuchadnezzar had taken away from the Temple in Jerusalem and transported to Babylon shall be returned, and let each go back to the Temple in Jerusalem where it belongs; you shall deposit it in the House of God."[18]

The nature of Temple ritual itself highlights the unique, even revolutionary, quality of Qohelet's inquiry. First and foremost, the Temple was the site for Israel's chief public worship of God, the sacrifices of animals, and agricultural produce. Priests assisted by Levites accomplished these rites following exact protocols and procedures considered to have been dictated by God to Moses. That these sacrifices pleased God was beyond doubt—after all, the priests followed his direct instructions; that much of the divine world the priests knew that they understood.[19] Tentativeness was not part of the Temple ethos. Qohelet's frustration with the tentativeness of human knowledge in the face of its need for immutable wisdom stretched far beyond the worldly details of Temple ritual.

The Persian government recognized Jerusalem as a temple-city, the religious and governmental center of Yehud. Persia granted significant local autonomy to its subject peoples; within Yehud, such self-rule laid the groundwork for the development of rabbinic law. The Second Temple was completed in 515 B.C.E. by Persia's Jewish governor, the Judaean prince Zerubbabel, whose lineage as the grandson of the penultimate king of Judaea, Jeconiah, lent him authority within the Jewish province. The Second Temple—again, still a simple structure, not yet the renowned glowing marble edifice remodeled by Herod in the late first century C.E.—stood at the center not only of Jerusalem's religious life but also its political and economic landscape.

The Temple itself, headed by the High Priest, enjoyed rights to supplies of sacrificial animals and tax exemptions for personnel, including priests and Levites—encouraging, as Lee Levine points out, its leadership's loyalty to the Persian crown.[20] Reforms instituted by Ezra and Nehemiah increased the centrality of the Temple's role in lay life beyond its sacrificial role. Ezra's institution of regular public Torah readings bound the people closer to the sacred texts and with the concept of the *brit*, the covenant between God and Israel. Scholars—scribes and sages—began to develop the earliest halakhic midrash as a way of rooting out the legal intent within biblical texts. "Over the course of time," Levine writes, "the learned argument began to hold sway over apodictic rulings, and the Scribe or sage assumed a role in some ways equal to and even surpassing that of the priest and prophet."[21] The scribes' analyses of biblical text became the root of all subsequent classical Jewish legal and homiletic exegetical writings. Elias Bickerman points out that consequent to this democratization of Jewish legal authority, the First Psalm "presents as the model of happiness not the officiating priest in the Temple, but rather the Sage who meditates on the Torah day and night."[22] It is here that Qohelet's insistent inquiry into the uncertainty of human understanding and subsequent diversity of human opinion, as we read him, might have found its origin.

THE BOOK OF QOHELET IN THE CONTEXT OF ANCIENT NEAR EASTERN WISDOM LITERATURE

The book of Qohelet is part of a contemporaneous Wisdom tradition that spread across the southeastern Mediterranean basin from at least the third millennium B.C.E. Wisdom literature may be described as texts studying the moral and ethical dimensions of human relationships and the pursuit of happiness in the context of worldly behavior, rather than primarily exploring the relationship between humankind and the world of divinity. Oliver Rankin described Israel's Wisdom literature as the "documents of Israel's humanism … because its general characteristic is the recognition of man's moral responsibility, his religious individuality and of God's interest in the individual life."[23]

Within the Jewish context, Wisdom literature leaves room for human choice, for causes other than divine underlying human events; yet unmistakably, God has a role in human affairs, whether from near or apparently from afar. Psalm 37, one of a number of Wisdom psalms sung at the Temple, recognizes freedom of choice and suggests that those who practice generosity will be rewarded directly for their choices:

> I have been young, and now I am old;
> yet I have not seen a just man forsaken, and his seed begging bread.
> He lends generously and all times; and his seed is blessed.
> Depart from evil and do good; and dwell forevermore. (Ps 37:25–27)

As we will find, Qohelet takes a different approach to the immediacy of divine reward. Other Wisdom literature canonized in the Hebrew Bible, in addition to the book of Qohelet and the Wisdom psalms (many of which were likely composed during the Second Temple period), include the book of Proverbs, the book of Job, and the Song of Songs. The third-century B.C.E. Wisdom of Sirach (book of Ecclesiasticus), preserved only in Greek but originally written in Hebrew, and the first-century B.C.E. Wisdom of Solomon, composed in Greek, figure among non-canonized Jewish Wisdom texts.

Jewish Wisdom books had many counterparts across Egypt, Mesopotamia, and ancient Ugarit (now northern Syria); scholars debate the relative influence of Egyptian and Mesopotamian influence on the book of Qohelet.[24] Egyptian Wisdom literature, of which one of the earliest texts, *The Instruction of Ptahhotep*, dates from the fourth millennium B.C.E., tended to phrase ideas as instructions of a parent to a child, similar to passages in both Proverbs and Qohelet. Compare, for instance, Ptahhotep's advice to a young person with the eleventh chapter of Qohelet:

> Follow your heart as long as you live,
> Do no more than is required,
> Do not shorten the time of "follow-the-heart,"
> Trimming its moment offends the *ka*.
> Don't waste your time on daily cares
> Beyond providing for your household;
> When wealth has come, follow your heart,
> Wealth does no good if one is glum.[25]

Qohelet advises:

> [9]Rejoice, O young man in thy youth; and let thy heart cheer thee in the days of thy youth, and walk in the ways of thy heart, and in the sight of thy eyes: but know thou, that for all these things. God will bring thee into judgment. [10]Therefore remove vexation from thy heart, and put away evil from thy flesh: on account of childhood and youth being vapour.

Like Ptahhotep, Qohelet urges young people to follow their hearts before youth vanishes; but unlike the Egyptian writer, he reminds his readers that divine judgment—which he has already repeatedly declared inscrutable—will most certainly follow.

Babylonian Wisdom literature similarly extends to the third millennium B.C.E., and many commentators have remarked upon the shared concerns about life's brevity in the *Epic of Gilgamesh* and the book of Qohelet. Consider these works' advice to enjoy life while possible. As the grieving Gilgamesh journeys to find the secret of eternal life, following the death of his friend Enkidu, a tavern-keeper warns him:

> You will never find the eternal life
> that you see. When the gods created mankind,
> they also created death, and they held back
> eternal life for themselves alone.
> Humans are born, they live, then they die,
> this is the order that the gods have decreed.
> But until the end comes, enjoy your life,
> spend it in happiness, not despair.
> Savor your food, make each of your days
> a delight, bathe and anoint yourself,
> wear bright clothes that are sparkling clean,
> let music and dancing fill your house,
> love the child who holds you by the hand,
> and give your wife pleasure in your embrace
> That is the best way for a man to live.[26]

Qohelet echoes this thought, but with a difference (9:7–11):

> [7]Go thy way, eat thy bread with joy, and drink thy wine with a merry heart; for God has already accepted thy works. [8]Let thy garments be always white; and let thy head lack no oil. [9]Live joyfully with the wife whom thou lovest all the days of the life of thy vapor, which he has given thee under the sun, all the days of thy vapor: for that is thy portion in life, and in thy labor in which thou dost labor under the sun. [10]Whatever thy hand finds to do, do it with thy strength, for there is no work, nor device, nor knowledge, nor wisdom, in She'ol, whither thou goest. [11]I returned, and saw under the sun, that the race is not to the swift, nor the battle to the strong, nor yet bread to the wise, nor yet riches to men of understanding, nor yet favor to men of skill; but time and chance happens to them all.

Qohelet, however, is tortured not only by life's brevity but by the impossible problem of understanding precisely how God wants him (and all of us) to live in the face of our brief lives down "under the sun." As he writes in the beginning (1:13):

¹³And I gave my heart to seek and search out by wisdom concerning all things that are done under the heaven: it is a sore task that God has given to the son of man to be exercised with.

MEETING QOHELET

The identity of the man who donned the cloak of wise King Solomon is, of course, lost. His book offers little in the way of an obvious "narrative world," the daily circumstances against which he analyzes the human condition. Nonetheless, we may make some informed, if tentative, guesses about the society to which he reacted. Robert Gordis suggested that Qohelet might have been a retired teacher from one of Jerusalem's Wisdom academies that educated the wealthy youth destined for careers within Yehud's leadership.[27] The book of Proverbs mentions the master-disciple relationship within these schools,[28] and Gordis imagined his former students visiting him late in his life. He was almost certainly aged, probably living alone, bereft of his wife and children. He seemed to care urgently about guiding his former students, now likely adults engaged in influential careers in government or the Temple, no longer naive students but experienced officials disillusioned by the daily realities of power. Gordis imagined this aged teacher feeling the pressure to record his insight into the wisest life that he has been able to find.[29]

Just as we cannot know Qohelet's identity, we cannot know his familial or social background. Although it is possible that he might have risen from poverty, his writing implies that he was accustomed to being close to wealth, influence, and power. While this philosopher criticizes the wealthy and arrogant who misuse their power, Gordis suggests that he might have criticized social injustice and oppression with more heat had he himself grown up in want;[30] indeed, when he describes poor laborers, he seems to express a sense of aloof, if genuinely concerned, noblesse oblige rather than painful personal experience.

If Qohelet lived in Persian-period Jerusalem, his education and intellectual outlook would have been greatly influenced by the growing Tanakh—in particular, the Torah, whose laws shaped Temple practice and whose texts, as we observed above, were studied for their practical legal implications and taught by the scribes. The age of prophecy had ended long before, and the books of the prophets, with their emphasis on social justice, were now considered integral to Jewish culture. Qohelet echoes prophetic concern with social justice throughout his writings.[31] Apart from his own "eponymous" book, the composition of the writings continued throughout Qohelet's day. For instance, the depiction of the Persian court presented in the book of Esther suggests that its author had intimate familiarity with the Persian court at Susa, and modern scholarship dates the redaction of Job, the Song of Songs, and Psalms to the Second Temple period.

Although we cannot plumb the concerns that motivated Qohelet to write this book, the social attitudes that he passed on to his readers seem to point to at least some of his personal interests and passions. The first chapter immediately expresses Qohelet's (or his imagining of Solomon's) delights in a luxurious life in a grand palace, handsome servants, orchards, food, wine, and music—his whole life as master of all he surveyed.

As we will see throughout the book, his urging to enjoy life's gifts while possible, particularly in the "Allegory of Old Age" in chapter 12, indicates advanced age and perhaps even infirmity; he reflects on the joys of youth and urges his readers to enjoy all of life before age eliminates the possibility.

Readers of my earlier works are accustomed to finding extensive imagery drawn from midrashic collections interpreting those works (such as Song of Songs Rabbah, on the Song of Songs; or Ruth Rabbah, interpreting the book of Ruth) and their targumim, or vernacular Aramaic paraphrases, which developed to probe the biblical books' hidden meanings, associations, and legal and moral implications. Although the paintings include much midrashic imagery relating to many biblical books in the paintings in this volume, you might notice a surprising paucity of midrashic imagery drawn from Qohelet Rabbah and Targum Qohelet. Its near-absence reflects the early rabbis' complicated attitudes toward this unusual book. For instance, Song of Songs Rabbah and its corresponding targum interpret the biblical love poetry in a coherent allegory of the love between God and Israel; Ruth Rabbah and Targum Ruth see in the story of the young Moabite woman who will become King David's great-grandmother a coherent model of acceptance of Jewish law; Psalms Rabbah offers largely homiletic support for the Psalms' assurance that God protects individuals and the people of Israel. Qohelet Rabbah, in contrast, seems puzzling for *avoiding* a coherent interpretation of the text but instead mostly comprising a collection of comments relating Qohelet to other biblical texts, by way of interpreting those. By the end of this book, you will understand the lack of a coherent interpretation in Qohelet Rabbah.[32] At the same time, Targum Qohelet expresses discomfort with the literal words of Qohelet, consistently interpolating additional text that changes the book's meaning to certainty about how *olam haba*, a blessed life after death, can be achieved by following Jewish law—turning the biblical text on its head. Here, we offer you a philosophical understanding and interpretive illuminations that face Qohelet head-on.

THE TRANSLATION USED HERE

The English translation of Qohelet and other biblical verses that you will find in this work are adapted from the translation prepared by the Israel Prize–winning scholar of English and Hebrew literature Harold Fisch, published by Koren Publishers in 2008. The *Koren Jerusalem Bible* adapted and modernized (including replacing English versions of Hebrew names with transliterations of their original Hebrew) the translation revised by M. Friedlander in the British 1881 *Jewish Family Bible*, developed for use in the United Synagogue of Great Britain. The Friedlander translation, in turn, is based on the King James "Authorized Version" of 1611. We made slight revisions in the Fisch translation—primarily, as you might have guessed by now, by changing the translation of the word *hevel* from "vanity" to "vapor."[33]

We share with you here the literary elegance and linguistic accuracy of this translation, ultimately founded, as it is, on the beautiful King James Version, still acclaimed more than four hundred years since its appearance. We believe that this translation best conveys the grandeur of Qohelet. For the sake of fidelity to the Hebrew text, we have maintained the male pronouns that the book of Qohelet usually associates with people; Hebrew is a gendered language, and, as has traditionally been the case in English and many other languages, the male pronoun generally enfolds all people, regardless of gender. In the illuminations, wherever it makes sense, I include women in my representation of humankind—I, the artist, am, after all, a woman, and see myself fully included in Qohelet's moral and ethical world. We hope that you will enjoy the eloquence and accuracy of the English text as well as the Hebrew.

Come, my friend, let us meet Qohelet.

NOTES

[1] In Jewish tradition, while the shiva grieving period is only interrupted by Shabbat and resumes afterward, it is ritually, if not emotionally, *ended* by biblically appointed festivals.

[2] H. Freedman and Maurice Simon, eds., *Midrash Rabbah*, vol. 9: *Song of Songs*, trans. Maurice Simon (London: Soncino, 1939), 9.

[3] Freedman and Simon, *Song of Songs*, 10.

[4] See the discussion of "disguised symbolism" in Erwin Panofsky, *Early Netherlandish Painting: Its Origins and Character* (New York: Harper and Row, 1971), 201.

[5] French premier Emmanuel Macron favored a more modern design using modern materials "avec beaucoup d'humilité, mais la bonne dose d'audace." See https://www.elysee.fr/emmanuel-macron/2019/05/24/prix-pritzker-darchitecture-2019.

[6] Howard A. Smith, *Let There Be Light: Modern Cosmology and Kabbalah—A New Conversation Between Science and Religion* (Novato, Calif.: New World Library, 2006).

[7] H. Teplitz et al., "Hubble Ultra Deep Field 2014," NASA photograph found at *Astronomy Picture of the Day*, June 5, 2014, https://apod.nasa.gov/apod/ap140605.html. In July 2022 the James Webb Space Telescope released its first images, among them a new and even sharper version of this image. See https://apod.nasa.gov/apod/ap220713.html.

[8] Yet, as Bible scholar Nili Samet has recently shown, Qohelet displays interesting Greek influence—not in his language, but in the content of argument. See Nili Samet, "Qoheleth's Idiolect and Its Cultural Context," *Harvard Theological Review* 114, no. 4 (2021): 451–68.

[9] Michael V. Fox, *The JPS Bible Commentary: Ecclesiastes* (Philadelphia, Jewish Publication Society, 2004), xiv. See also: Robert Gordis, *Koheleth: The Man and His World* (New York: Schocken, 1968), 67.

[10] Choon-Leong Seow, *The Anchor Bible*, vol. 18C: *Proverbs, Ecclesiastes* (New York, Doubleday, 1997), 12–15.

[11] Lee I. Levine, *Jerusalem: Portrait of the City in the Second Temple Period (538 B.C.E.–70 C.E.)* (Philadelphia: Jewish Publication Society, 2002), 18.

[12] Elias Bickerman, "The Historical Foundations of Postbiblical Judaism," in *Emerging Judaism: Studies on the Fourth & Third Centuries B.C.E.*, ed. Michael E. Stone and David Satran, 9–43 (Minneapolis: Fortress, 1989).

[13] Levine, *Jerusalem*, 33.

[14] Levine, *Jerusalem*, 19.

[15] Levine, *Jerusalem*, 27.

[16] Philip J. King and Lawrence E. Stager, *Life in Biblical Israel* (Louisville, Ky.: Westminster John Knox, 2001), 193–99.

[17] Bickerman, "The Historical Foundations of Postbiblical Judaism," 16.

[18] Levine, *Jerusalem*, 9.

[19] We should note that early Jewish mysticism, full of inquiry and speculation, also began among the Temple priesthood, but that is a separate matter from the quotidian rites of sacrifice. See Rachel Elior, *The Three Temples: On the Emergence of Jewish Mysticism* (Oxford: Littman Library of Jewish Civilization, 2005).

[20] Levine, *Jerusalem*, 18.

[21] Levine, *Jerusalem*, 31.

[22] Bickerman, "The Historical Foundations of Postbiblical Judaism," 18.

[23] O. S. Rankin, *Israel's Wisdom Literature: Its Bearing on Theology and the History of Religion* (New York: Schocken, 1969), 3.

[24] Seow, *The Anchor Bible*, 60.

[25] Seow, *The Anchor Bible*, 61.

[26] Stephen Mitchell, *Gilgamesh: A New English Version* (New York: Free Press, 2004), 168.

[27] Gordis, *Koheleth*, 77. Contrary to the prevailing scholarly understanding today, Gordis places the composition of Qohelet at around 250 B.C.E., nearly a century after the Greek conquest of Yehud. However, this difference in dating does not conflict with other aspects of his speculative portrait of the man.

[28] Lawrence H. Schiffman, *From Text to Tradition: A History of Second Temple & Rabbinic Judaism* (Hoboken, N.J.: Ktav, 1991), 32.

[29] Gordis, *Koheleth*, 85. Although Gordis offers an interesting portrait of Qohelet as a man, we do not concur with his conclusions about the meaning of Qohelet's writing.

[30] Gordis, *Koheleth*, 77.

[31] Gordis, *Koheleth*, 79.

[32] Early in this project, I was convinced that the Jewish mystical literature must have explored the book of Qohelet, which, after all, is a search for Wisdom. In kabbalah, Wisdom is the first emanation of divine energy from *keter* (crown), the innermost core of divinity. Arthur Green generously helped me locate the very few commentaries on the book written by kabbalistic writers; each turned out to be a fairly standard commentary on the *p'shat*, the simple meaning of the text, rather than a mystical interpretation.

[33] Another notable modern translation of *hevel*, rejecting "vanity" or "futility," is Robert Alter's use of "merest breath." However, "breath" ties the concept to the human (or animal) life, whereas Qohelet relates the term to more than animal life; all endeavor, all the material world, is *hevel*. See Robert Alter, *The Wisdom Books: Job, Proverbs and Ecclesiastes* (New York: W. W. Norton, 2010), 339.

THE ILLUMINATIONS

FRONTISPIECE

The words of

Qohelet

the son of David, king in Yerushalayim.
² Vapour of vapours, says Qohelet,
    vapour of vapours, all is vapour.
³ What profit has a man of all his labour,
    wherein he labours under the sun?

דִּבְרֵי קֹהֶלֶת בֶּן־דָּוִד מֶלֶךְ בִּירוּשָׁלָ‍ִם: הֲבֵל הֲבָלִים אָמַר קֹהֶלֶת הֲבֵל הֲבָלִים הַכֹּל הָבֶל: מַה־יִּתְרוֹן לָאָדָם בְּכָל־עֲמָלוֹ שֶׁיַּעֲמֹל תַּחַת הַשָּׁמֶשׁ:

⁴One generation passes away, and another generation comes.
but the earth abides for ever.
⁵ The sun also rises, and the sun goes down,
and hastens to its place where it rises again.
⁶The wind goes towards the south, and veers to the north;
round and round goes the wind and on its circuits the wind returns.
⁷All the rivers run into the sea; yet the sea is not full;
to the place where the rivers flow, thither they return.
⁸All things are full of weariness: man cannot utter it;
the eye is not satisfied with seeing, nor the ear filled with hearing.
⁹That which has been, it is that which shall be—:
and that which has been done is that which shall be done;
and there is nothing new under the sun.
¹⁰ Is there a thing whereof it may be said, See, this is new:
but it has already been in the ages before us.
¹¹There is no remembrance of former things;
nor will there be any remembrance of things that are to come
among those who shall come after.

דּוֹר הֹלֵךְ וְדוֹר בָּא וְהָאָרֶץ לְעוֹלָם עֹמָדֶת: ^ד

וְזָרַח הַשֶּׁמֶשׁ וּבָא הַשָּׁמֶשׁ ^ה

וְאֶל־מְקוֹמוֹ שׁוֹאֵף זוֹרֵחַ הוּא שָׁם:

יהוֹלֵךְ אֶל־דָּרוֹם וְסוֹבֵב אֶל־צָפוֹן ^ו

סוֹבֵב׀סֹבֵב הוֹלֵךְ הָרוּחַ וְעַל־סְבִיבֹתָיו שָׁב הָרוּחַ:

כָּל־הַנְּחָלִים הֹלְכִים אֶל־הַיָּם וְהַיָּם אֵינֶנּוּ מָלֵא ^ז

אֶל־מְקוֹם שֶׁהַנְּחָלִים הֹלְכִים שָׁם הֵם שָׁבִים לָלָכֶת:

כָּל־הַדְּבָרִים יְגֵעִים לֹא־יוּכַל אִישׁ לְדַבֵּר ^ח

לֹא־תִשְׂבַּע עַיִן לִרְאוֹת וְלֹא־תִמָּלֵא אֹזֶן מִשְּׁמֹעַ:

מַה־שֶּׁהָיָה הוּא שֶׁיִּהְיֶה וּמַה־שֶּׁנַּעֲשָׂה הוּא שֶׁיֵּעָשֶׂה ^ט

וְאֵין כָּל־חָדָשׁ תַּחַת הַשָּׁמֶשׁ:

יֵשׁ דָּבָר שֶׁיֹּאמַר רְאֵה־זֶה חָדָשׁ הוּא ^י

כְּבָר הָיָה לְעֹלָמִים אֲשֶׁר הָיָה מִלְּפָנֵנוּ:

אֵין זִכְרוֹן לָרִאשֹׁנִים ^{יא}

וְגַם לָאַחֲרֹנִים שֶׁיִּהְיוּ

לֹא־יִהְיֶה לָהֶם זִכָּרוֹן עִם שֶׁיִּהְיוּ לָאַחֲרֹנָה:

Qohelet was King over Yisrael in Yerushalayim. [13] And I gave my heart to seek and search out by wisdom concerning all things that are done under the heaven: it is a sore task that God has given to the son of man to be exercised with. [14] I have seen all the works that are done under the sun: and, behold, all is vapour and a striving after wind. [15] That which is crooked cannot be made straight: and that which is wanting cannot be numbered. [16] I spoke to my own heart saying: See, I have acquired great wisdom, surpassing all those who were before me in Jerusalem: for my heart has seen much of wisdom and knowledge. [17] And I gave my heart to know wisdom, and to know madness and folly: I perceived that this also was a striving after wind. [18] For in much wisdom is much grief, and he that increases knowledge increases sorrow.

I said in my heart

Come now, I will try thee with joy,
therefore enjoy pleasure;
and, behold, this also was vapour.
² I said of laughter, it is mad,
and of joy, What does it achieve?
³ I sought in my heart to stimulate my body with wine
(yet guiding my heart with wisdom) and to lay hold of folly
till it might see what see what was good for humankind,
which they should do under the heaven all the days of their life.

אָמַרְתִּי אֲנִי בְּלִבִּי

לְכָה־נָּא אֲנַסְּכָה בְשִׂמְחָה וּרְאֵה בְטוֹב

וְהִנֵּה גַם־הוּא הָבֶל:

לִשְׂחוֹק אָמַרְתִּי מְהוֹלָל

וּלְשִׂמְחָה מַה־זֹּה עֹשָׂה:

תַּרְתִּי בְלִבִּי לִמְשׁוֹךְ בַּיַּיִן אֶת־בְּשָׂרִי

וְלִבִּי נֹהֵג בַּחָכְמָה וְלֶאֱחֹז בְּסִכְלוּת

עַד אֲשֶׁר־אֶרְאֶה אֵי־זֶה טוֹב לִבְנֵי הָאָדָם

אֲשֶׁר יַעֲשׂוּ תַּחַת הַשָּׁמַיִם מִסְפַּר יְמֵי חַיֵּיהֶם:

⁴I made great works for myself; I built houses;

I planted vineyards; ⁵I made gardens and orchards,

and I planted trees in them of all kinds of fruits;

⁶I made pools of water, from which to water

a forest of growing trees:

הִגְדַּלְתִּי מַעֲשָׂי בָּנִיתִי לִי בָּתִּים נָטַעְתִּי לִי כְּרָמִים:

עָשִׂיתִי לִי גַּנּוֹת וּפַרְדֵּסִים וְנָטַעְתִּי בָהֶם עֵץ כָּל־פֶּרִי:

עָשִׂיתִי לִי בְּרֵכוֹת מָיִם לְהַשְׁקוֹת מֵהֶם יַעַר צוֹמֵחַ עֵצִים:

⁷I ACQUIRED male and female servants, and had servants born in my house also I had great possessions of herds and flocks, more than all who were in Yerushalayim before me: ⁸I gathered also silver and gold and the treasure of kings and of the provinces: I acquired men singers and women singers, and the delights of the sons of men, women very many. ⁹So I was great, and increased more than all that were before me in Yerushalayim: also my wisdom remained with me. ¹⁰And whatever my eyes desired, I did not withhold from them; I did not restrain my heart from any joy for my heart rejoiced in all my labour and this was my portion of all my labour.

¹¹THEN I LOOKED UP AT ALL THE WORKS THAT MY HAND HAD WROUGHT AND AT THE LABOUR THAT I HAD LABOURED TO DO AND BEHOLD ALL WAS VAPOUR AND A STRIVING AFTER WIND AND THERE WAS NO PROFIT UNDER THE SUN.

¹²And I turned myself to behold wisdom, and madness, and folly: for what can the man do who comes after the king? Even that which has been already done. ¹³Then I saw that wisdom excels folly, as far as light excels darkness. ¹⁴The wise man's eyes are in his head; but the fool walks in darkness; and I myself perceived also that one event happens to them all. ¹⁵Then I said in my heart, As it happens to the fool, so it happens even to me; and why was I then more wise? Then I said in my heart, that also is vapour. ¹⁶For of the wise man as of the fool there is no enduring remembrance seeing that which now is shall, in the days to come, be entirely forgotten. And how does the wise man die? Just like the fool. ¹⁷Therefore I hated life because the work that is done under the sun was grievous to me for all is vapour and a striving after wind. ¹⁸And I hated all my labour in which I had laboured under the sun because I must leave it to the man who shall come after me. ¹⁹And who knows whether he will be a wise man or a fool? Yet shall he have rule over all my labour in which I have laboured, and in which I have shown myself wise under the sun. THIS ALSO IS VAPOUR.

קָנִיתִי עֲבָדִים וּשְׁפָחוֹת וּבְנֵי-בַיִת הָיָה לִי גַּם מִקְנֶה בָקָר וָצֹאן הַרְבֵּה הָיָה לִי מִכֹּל שֶׁהָיוּ

לְפָנַי בִּירוּשָׁלָ‍ִם: כָּנַסְתִּי לִי גַּם-כֶּסֶף וְזָהָב וּסְגֻלַּת מְלָכִים וְהַמְּדִינוֹת עָשִׂיתִי לִי שָׁרִים

וְשָׁרוֹת וְתַעֲנוּגֹת בְּנֵי הָאָדָם שִׁדָּה וְשִׁדּוֹת: וְגָדַלְתִּי וְהוֹסַפְתִּי מִכֹּל שֶׁהָיָה לְפָנַי בִּירוּשָׁלָ‍ִם

אַף חָכְמָתִי עָמְדָה לִּי: וְכֹל אֲשֶׁר שָׁאֲלוּ עֵינַי לֹא אָצַלְתִּי מֵהֶם לֹא-מָנַעְתִּי אֶת-לִבִּי

מִכָּל-שִׂמְחָה כִּי-לִבִּי שָׂמֵחַ מִכָּל-עֲמָלִי וְזֶה הָיָה חֶלְקִי מִכָּל-עֲמָלִי:

וּפָנִיתִי אֲנִי בְּכָל-מַעֲשַׂי שֶׁעָשׂוּ יָדַי
וּבֶעָמָל שֶׁעָמַלְתִּי לַעֲשׂוֹת וְהִנֵּה הַכֹּל
הֶבֶל וּרְעוּת רוּחַ וְאֵין יִתְרוֹן תַּחַת הַשָּׁמֶשׁ:

וּפָנִיתִי אֲנִי לִרְאוֹת חָכְמָה וְהוֹלֵלוֹת וְסִכְלוּת כִּי מֶה הָאָדָם שֶׁיָּבוֹא אַחֲרֵי הַמֶּלֶךְ אֵת

אֲשֶׁר-כְּבָר עָשׂוּהוּ: וְרָאִיתִי אָנִי שֶׁיֵּשׁ יִתְרוֹן לַחָכְמָה מִן-הַסִּכְלוּת כִּיתְרוֹן הָאוֹר

מִן-הַחֹשֶׁךְ: הֶחָכָם עֵינָיו בְּרֹאשׁוֹ וְהַכְּסִיל בַּחֹשֶׁךְ הוֹלֵךְ וְיָדַעְתִּי גַם-אָנִי שֶׁמִּקְרֶה אֶחָד

יִקְרֶה אֶת-כֻּלָּם: וְאָמַרְתִּי אֲנִי בְּלִבִּי כְּמִקְרֵה הַכְּסִיל גַּם-אֲנִי יִקְרֵנִי וְלָמָּה חָכַמְתִּי אֲנִי

אָז יוֹתֵר וְדִבַּרְתִּי בְלִבִּי שֶׁגַּם-זֶה הָבֶל: כִּי אֵין זִכְרוֹן לֶחָכָם עִם-הַכְּסִיל לְעוֹלָם בְּשֶׁכְּבָר

הַיָּמִים הַבָּאִים הַכֹּל נִשְׁכָּח וְאֵיךְ יָמוּת הֶחָכָם עִם-הַכְּסִיל: וְשָׂנֵאתִי אֶת-הַחַיִּים כִּי רַע עָלַי

הַמַּעֲשֶׂה שֶׁנַּעֲשָׂה תַּחַת הַשָּׁמֶשׁ כִּי-הַכֹּל הֶבֶל וּרְעוּת רוּחַ: וְשָׂנֵאתִי אֲנִי אֶת-כָּל-עֲמָלִי

שֶׁאֲנִי עָמֵל תַּחַת הַשָּׁמֶשׁ שֶׁאַנִּיחֶנּוּ לָאָדָם שֶׁיִּהְיֶה אַחֲרָי: וּמִי יוֹדֵעַ הֶחָכָם יִהְיֶה אוֹ סָכָל

וְיִשְׁלַט בְּכָל-עֲמָלִי שֶׁעָמַלְתִּי וְשֶׁחָכַמְתִּי תַּחַת הַשָּׁמֶשׁ גַּם-זֶה הָבֶל:

20 Therefore I went about to cause my heart to despair of all the labour which I took under the sun. 21 For there is a man whose labour is with wisdom, and with knowledge, and with skill; yet he must leave it for a portion to a man who has not laboured in it. This also is vapour and a great evil. 22 For what has a man of all his labour, and of the striving of his heart in which he labours under the sun? 23 For all his days are pains, and his work a vexation: even in the night his heart takes no rest. This also is vapour. 24 There is nothing better for a man, than that he should eat and drink, and that he should make his soul enjoy good in his labour; but this also I saw, that it was from the hand of God. 25 For who can eat, or who can enjoy pleasure, more than I? 26 Surely He gives to a man that is good in His sight, wisdom, and knowledge, and joy: but to the sinner He gives the task of gathering and heaping up, that He may give it to one who is good before God.

THIS ALSO VAPOUR AND A STRIVING AFTER WIND

כ וְסַבּוֹתִי אֲנִי לְיַאֵשׁ אֶת-לִבִּי עַל כָּל-הֶעָמָל שֶׁעָמַלְתִּי תַּחַת הַשָּׁמֶשׁ:

כא כִּי-יֵשׁ אָדָם שֶׁעֲמָלוֹ בְּחָכְמָה וּבְדַעַת וּבְכִשְׁרוֹן וּלְאָדָם שֶׁלֹּא עָמַל-בּוֹ יִתְּנֶנּוּ חֶלְקוֹ גַּם-זֶה הֶבֶל וְרָעָה רַבָּה:

כב כִּי מֶה-הֹוֶה לָאָדָם בְּכָל-עֲמָלוֹ וּבְרַעְיוֹן לִבּוֹ שְׁהוּא עָמֵל תַּחַת הַשָּׁמֶשׁ:

כג כִּי כָל-יָמָיו מַכְאֹבִים וָכַעַס עִנְיָנוֹ גַּם-בַּלַּיְלָה לֹא-שָׁכַב לִבּוֹ גַּם-זֶה הֶבֶל הוּא:

כד אֵין-טוֹב בָּאָדָם שֶׁיֹּאכַל וְשָׁתָה וְהֶרְאָה אֶת-נַפְשׁוֹ טוֹב בַּעֲמָלוֹ גַּם-זֹה רָאִיתִי אָנִי כִּי מִיַּד הָאֱלֹהִים הִיא:

כה כִּי מִי יֹאכַל וּמִי יָחוּשׁ חוּץ מִמֶּנִּי: כִּי לְאָדָם שֶׁטּוֹב לְפָנָיו נָתַן

חָכְמָה וְדַעַת וְשִׂמְחָה וְלַחוֹטֶא נָתַן עִנְיָן לֶאֱסוֹף וְלִכְנוֹס לָתֵת

לְטוֹב לִפְנֵי הָאֱלֹהִים

גַּם-זֶה הֶבֶל וּרְעוּת רוּחַ:

A time to be born, and a time to die;   עֵת לָלֶדֶת וְעֵת לָמוּת

a time to plant,   עֵת לָטַעַת

and a time to pluck up that which is planted;   וְעֵת לַעֲקוֹר נָטוּעַ:

A time to kill, and a time to heal;   עֵת לַהֲרוֹג וְעֵת לִרְפּוֹא

a time to break down, and a time to build up;   עֵת לִפְרוֹץ וְעֵת לִבְנוֹת:

A time to weep, and a time to laugh;   עֵת לִבְכּוֹת וְעֵת לִשְׂחוֹק

a time to mourn, and a time to dance;   עֵת סְפוֹד וְעֵת רְקוֹד:

A time to cast away stones,   עֵת לְהַשְׁלִיךְ אֲבָנִים

and a time to gather stones together;   וְעֵת כְּנוֹס אֲבָנִים

a time to embrace,   עֵת לַחֲבוֹק

and a time to refrain from embracing;   וְעֵת לִרְחֹק מֵחַבֵּק:

A time to seek, and a time to lose;   עֵת לְבַקֵּשׁ וְעֵת לְאַבֵּד

a time to keep, and a time to cast away;   עֵת לִשְׁמוֹר וְעֵת לְהַשְׁלִיךְ:

A time to rend, and a time to sew;   עֵת לִקְרוֹעַ וְעֵת לִתְפּוֹר

a time to keep silence, and a time to speak;   עֵת לַחֲשׁוֹת וְעֵת לְדַבֵּר:

A time to love, and a time to hate;   עֵת לֶאֱהֹב וְעֵת לִשְׂנֹא

a time of war, and a time of peace.   עֵת מִלְחָמָה וְעֵת שָׁלוֹם:

To everything there is a season, and a time to every demand under heaven

What profit has the worker from his toil?

10 I have seen the task which God has given to the sons of men to be exercised in it. 11 He has made everything beautiful in His time, also He has set the mystery of the world in their heart, so that no man can find out the work which God has made from the beginning to the end. 12 I know that there is nothing better for them than to rejoice, and to do good in his life: 13 also that it is the gift of God that every man should eat and drink and enjoy the good of all his labour. 14 I know that, whatever God does, it shall be forever: nothing can be added to it, nor anything taken from it; and God does it, so that men should fear before Him. 15 That which is, already has been; and that which is to be, has already been; and only God can find the fleeting moment.

מַה־יִּתְרוֹן הָעוֹשֶׂה בַּאֲשֶׁר הוּא עָמֵל:

יּ רָאִיתִי אֶת־הָעִנְיָן אֲשֶׁר נָתַן אֱלֹהִים לִבְנֵי הָאָדָם לַעֲנוֹת בּוֹ: אֶת־הַכֹּל

עָשָׂה יָפֶה בְעִתּוֹ גַּם אֶת־הָעֹלָם נָתַן בְּלִבָּם מִבְּלִי אֲשֶׁר לֹא־יִמְצָא הָאָדָם

אֶת־הַמַּעֲשֶׂה אֲשֶׁר־עָשָׂה הָאֱלֹהִים מֵרֹאשׁ וְעַד־סוֹף: יָדַעְתִּי כִּי אֵין

טוֹב בָּם כִּי אִם־ לִשְׂמוֹחַ וְלַעֲשׂוֹת טוֹב בְּחַיָּיו: וְגַם כָּל־הָאָדָם שֶׁיֹּאכַל

וְשָׁתָה וְרָאָה טוֹב בְּכָל־עֲמָלוֹ מַתַּת אֱלֹהִים הִיא: יָדַעְתִּי כִּי כָּל־אֲשֶׁר

יַעֲשֶׂה הָאֱלֹהִים הוּא יִהְיֶה לְעוֹלָם עָלָיו אֵין לְהוֹסִיף וּמִמֶּנּוּ אֵין לִגְרֹעַ

וְהָאֱלֹהִים עָשָׂה שֶׁיִּרְאוּ מִלְּפָנָיו: מַה־שֶּׁהָיָה כְּבָר הוּא וַאֲשֶׁר לִהְיוֹת

כְּבָר הָיָה וְהָאֱלֹהִים יְבַקֵּשׁ אֶת־ נִרְדָּף:

And moreover I saw under the sun in the place of judgment that wickedness was there, and in the place of righteousness, that iniquity was there. [17]I said in my heart, God shall judge the righteous and the wicked; for there is a time there for every purpose and for every work. [18]I said in my heart after the speech of the sons of men, that God has chosen them out, but only to see that they themselves are but as beasts; [19]that that which befalls the sons of men befalls the beasts; even one thing befalls them both; as the one dies, so the other dies; yea, they have all one breath; so that a man has no preeminence over a beast: for all is vapour. [20]All go to one place; all are of the dust and all return to dust. [21]Who knows whether the spirit of man goes upwards, and th' spirit of the beast goes downwards to the earth? [22]So I saw that there is nothing better than that a man should rejoice in his work; for that is his portion: for who shall bring him to see what shall be after him?

רָאִיתִי תַּחַת הַשֶּׁמֶשׁ מְקוֹם הַמִּשְׁפָּט **וְעוֹד**

שָׁמָּה הָרֶשַׁע וּמְקוֹם הַצֶּדֶק שָׁמָּה

הָרָשַׁע: אָמַרְתִּי אֲנִי בְּלִבִּי אֶת-הַצַּדִּיק וְאֶת-הָרָשָׁע יִשְׁפֹּט

הָאֱלֹהִים כִּי-עֵת לְכָל-חֵפֶץ וְעַל כָּל-הַמַּעֲשֶׂה שָׁם: אָמַרְתִּי

אֲנִי בְּלִבִּי עַל-דִּבְרַת בְּנֵי הָאָדָם לְבָרָם הָאֱלֹהִים וְלִרְאוֹת

שְׁהֶם-בְּהֵמָה הֵמָּה לָהֶם: כִּי מִקְרֶה בְנֵי-הָאָדָם וּמִקְרֶה

הַבְּהֵמָה וּמִקְרֶה אֶחָד לָהֶם כְּמוֹת זֶה כֵּן מוֹת זֶה וְרוּחַ אֶחָד

לַכֹּל וּמוֹתַר הָאָדָם מִן-הַבְּהֵמָה אָיִן כִּי הַכֹּל הָבֶל: הַכֹּל

הוֹלֵךְ אֶל-מָקוֹם אֶחָד הַכֹּל הָיָה מִן-הֶעָפָר וְהַכֹּל שָׁב אֶל-

הֶעָפָר: מִי יוֹדֵעַ רוּחַ בְּנֵי הָאָדָם הָעֹלָה הִיא לְמָעְלָה

וְרוּחַ הַבְּהֵמָה הַיֹּרֶדֶת הִיא לְמַטָּה לָאָרֶץ:

וְרָאִיתִי כִּי אֵין טוֹב מֵאֲשֶׁר

יִשְׂמַח הָאָדָם בְּמַעֲשָׂיו כִּי-הוּא חֶלְקוֹ

כִּי מִי יְבִיאֶנּוּ לִרְאוֹת בְּמֶה שֶׁיִּהְיֶה אַחֲרָיו:

I returned and considered all the oppressions that are done under the sun; and behold the tears of such as were oppressed, and have had no comforter; and on the side of their oppressors there was power, but they had no comforter. [2]So I praised the dead that are already dead more than the living that are yet alive: [3]but better than both of them is he who has not yet been, who has not seen the evil work that is done under the sun. [4]Again, I considered all labour, and every skill in work that it comes from a man's rivalry with his neighbour: This also is vapour and a striving after wind. [5]The fool folds his hands together, and eats his own flesh. [6]Better is a handful with quietness, than both the hands full of labour and striving after wind. [7]Then I returned and I saw vapour under the sun.

עַל־אֵלֶּה אֲנִי בוֹכְיָּה שֵׂעִי עֵינִי יָרְדָה בַיָּם כִּי־רָחַק מִמֶּנִּי פָּנָס בֵּית נֶפֶשׁ הֵו בְּנֵי שֶׁבְכִיס כִּי גָבְרָאוּב פִּרְשָׂה צִיּוֹן בִּידֵיהָ אֵין מְנַחֵם לָה צִוָּה יְיָ לְיַעֲקֹב סְבִיבָ

אֲנִי וָאֶרְאֶה אֶת־כָּל־הָעֲשֻׁקִים

אֲשֶׁר נַעֲשִׂים תַּחַת הַשָּׁמֶשׁ וְהִנֵּה דִּמְעַת

הָעֲשֻׁקִים וְאֵין לָהֶם מְנַחֵם וּמִיַּד

עֹשְׁקֵיהֶם כֹּחַ וְאֵין לָהֶם מְנַחֵם: וְשַׁבֵּחַ אֲנִי אֶת־הַמֵּתִים שֶׁכְּבָר

מֵתוּ מִן־הַחַיִּים אֲשֶׁר הֵמָּה חַיִּים עֲדֶנָה: וְטוֹב מִשְּׁנֵיהֶם אֵת

אֲשֶׁר־עֲדֶן לֹא הָיָה אֲשֶׁר לֹא־רָאָה אֶת־הַמַּעֲשֶׂה הָרָע אֲשֶׁר

נַעֲשָׂה תַּחַת הַשָּׁמֶשׁ: וְרָאִיתִי אֲנִי אֶת־כָּל־עָמָל וְאֵת כָּל־כִּשְׁרוֹן הַמַּעֲשֶׂה כִּי

הִיא קִנְאַת־אִישׁ מֵרֵעֵהוּ גַּם־זֶה הֶבֶל וּרְעוּת רוּחַ: הַכְּסִיל חֹבֵק אֶת־יָדָיו

וְאֹכֵל אֶת־בְּשָׂרוֹ: טוֹב מְלֹא כַף נָחַת מִמְּלֹא חָפְנַיִם עָמָל וּרְעוּת רוּחַ:

וְשַׁבְתִּי אֲנִי וָאֶרְאֶה הֶבֶל תַּחַת הַשָּׁמֶשׁ:

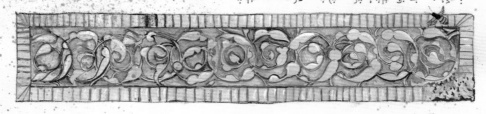

אֵיכָה יֹשְׁבָה בָדָד הָעִיר רַבָּתִי עָם נֶפֶשׁ יָשׂוֹבֵב

⁸There is one alone, without a companion; yea, he has neither son nor brother, yet is there no end of all his labour; neither is his eye satisfied with riches: he may say, For whom then do I labour, and bereave my soul of good? This also is vapour; indeed, it is a sorry business. ⁹Two are better than one: because they have a good reward for their labour. ¹⁰For if they fall, the one will lift up his fellow: but woe to him that is alone when he falls: for he has not another to help him up. ¹¹Again, if two lie together, then they have warmth, but how can one be warm alone? ¹²And if one prevail against him, two shall withstand him: but a threefold cord is not quickly broken. ¹³Better is a poor and a wise child than an old and foolish king, who no longer knows how to take care of himself. ¹⁴For out of prison one came forth to reign: whilst another in his royal power may become poor. ¹⁵I saw all the living who wander under the sun – they were with the second child who was to rise up in his stead. ¹⁶There is no end of all the people who come to acclaim the one who goes before them: yet they who come after shall not rejoice in him. Surely this also is vapour and a striving after wind. ¹⁷Keep thy foot when thou goest to the house of God; to draw near to hearken is better than to give the sacrifice of fools: for they consider not that they do evil.

יֵשׁ אֶחָד וְאֵין שֵׁנִי גַּם בֵּן וָאָח אֵין-לוֹ וְאֵין קֵץ לְכָל-עֲמָלוֹ גַּם-עֵינָיו (עֵינוֹ) לֹא-תִשְׂבַּע

עֹשֶׁר וּלְמִי אֲנִי עָמֵל וּמְחַסֵּר אֶת-נַפְשִׁי מִטּוֹבָה גַּם-זֶה הֶבֶל וְעִנְיַן רָע הוּא: ⁹טוֹבִים

הַשְּׁנַיִם מִן-הָאֶחָד אֲשֶׁר יֵשׁ-לָהֶם שָׂכָר טוֹב בַּעֲמָלָם: ¹⁰כִּי אִם-יִפֹּלוּ הָאֶחָד יָקִים

אֶת-חֲבֵרוֹ וְאִילוֹ הָאֶחָד שֶׁיִּפּוֹל וְאֵין שֵׁנִי לַהֲקִימוֹ: ¹¹גַּם אִם-יִשְׁכְּבוּ שְׁנַיִם וְחַם לָהֶם

וּלְאֶחָד אֵיךְ יֵחָם: ¹²וְאִם-יִתְקְפוֹ הָאֶחָד הַשְּׁנַיִם יַעַמְדוּ נֶגְדּוֹ וְהַחוּט הַמְשֻׁלָּשׁ לֹא

בִמְהֵרָה יִנָּתֵק: ¹³טוֹב יֶלֶד מִסְכֵּן וְחָכָם מִמֶּלֶךְ זָקֵן וּכְסִיל אֲשֶׁר

לֹא-יָדַע לְהִזָּהֵר עוֹד: ¹⁴כִּי-מִבֵּית הָסוּרִים יָצָא לִמְלֹךְ כִּי גַּם

בְּמַלְכוּתוֹ נוֹלַד רָשׁ: ¹⁵רָאִיתִי אֶת-כָּל-הַחַיִּים הַמְהַלְּכִים תַּחַת

הַשֶּׁמֶשׁ עִם הַיֶּלֶד הַשֵּׁנִי אֲשֶׁר יַעֲמֹד תַּחְתָּיו: ¹⁶אֵין-קֵץ

לְכָל-הָעָם לְכֹל אֲשֶׁר-הָיָה לִפְנֵיהֶם גַּם הָאַחֲרוֹנִים לֹא יִשְׂמְחוּ-בוֹ

כִּי-גַם-זֶה הֶבֶל וְרַעְיוֹן רוּחַ: ¹⁷שְׁמֹר רַגְלְךָ (רַגְלֶיךָ) כַּאֲשֶׁר תֵּלֵךְ

אֶל-בֵּית הָאֱלֹהִים וְקָרוֹב לִשְׁמֹעַ מִתֵּת הַכְּסִילִים זָבַח כִּי-אֵינָם

יוֹדְעִים לַעֲשׂוֹת רָע:

Be not rash with thy mouth and let not thy heart be hasty to utter anything before God, for God is in heaven, and thou upon earth: therefore let thy words be few. [2] For a dream comes through a multitude of business; and a fools voice is known by a multitude of words. [3] When thou vowest a vow to God, do not defer to pay it: for He has no pleasure in fools: pay that which thou hast vowed. [4] Better is it that thou shouldst not vow, than that thou shouldst vow and not pay. [5] Do not let thy mouth cause thy flesh to sin: nor say before the angel, that it was an error: why should God be angry at thy voice and destroy the work of thy hand? [6] For this comes from the multitude of dreams and vapours and many words; but fear thou God.

Keep thy foot when thou goest to the house of God; to draw near to hear then

⁷If you seest the oppression of the poor, and the violent perverting of judgment and justice in a province, do not marvel at the matter, for there is a high one who watches over him that is high; and there are yet higher ones over them. ⁸Moreover, land has an advantage for everyone: he who tills a field is a king. ⁹He who loves silver shall not be satisfied with silver, nor he that loves abundance with increase: this is also vapour. ¹⁰When goods increase, they who eat them are increased and what good is there to their owner, saving the beholding of them with his eyes? ¹¹The sleep of a labouring man is sweet, whether he eat little or much: but the repletion of the rich will not suffer them to sleep.

¹²There is a sore evil which I have seen under the sun, namely, riches kept for their owner to his hurt. ¹³But those riches perish by evil adventure: and he begets a son, and there is nothing in his hand. ¹⁴As he came forth from his mother's womb, naked and shall he return to go as he came, and he shall take nothing for his labour, which he may carry away in his hand. ¹⁵And this also is a sore evil, that in all points as he came, so shall he go, and what profit has he that labours for the wind? ¹⁶All his days also he eats in darkness, and he has much sorrow and sickness and wrath.

אִם־עֹשֶׁק רָשׁ וְגֵזֶל מִשְׁפָּט וָצֶדֶק תִּרְאֶה בַמְּדִינָה אַל־תִּתְמַהּ עַל־הַחֵפֶץ

כִּי גָבֹהַּ מֵעַל גָּבֹהַּ שֹׁמֵר וּגְבֹהִים עֲלֵיהֶם: ⁸וְיִתְרוֹן אֶרֶץ בַּכֹּל הִיא (הוּא)

מֶלֶךְ לְשָׂדֶה נֶעֱבָד: ⁹אֹהֵב כֶּסֶף לֹא־יִשְׂבַּע כֶּסֶף וּמִי־אֹהֵב בֶּהָמוֹן

לֹא תְבוּאָה גַּם־זֶה הָבֶל: ¹⁰בִּרְבוֹת הַטּוֹבָה רַבּוּ אוֹכְלֶיהָ וּמַה־כִּשְׁרוֹן

לִבְעָלֶיהָ כִּי אִם־רְאִית (רְאוּת) עֵינָיו: ¹¹מְתוּקָה שְׁנַת הָעֹבֵד אִם־מְעַט

וְאִם־הַרְבֵּה יֹאכֵל וְהַשָּׂבָע לֶעָשִׁיר אֵינֶנּוּ מַנִּיחַ לוֹ לִישׁוֹן:

¹²יֵשׁ רָעָה חוֹלָה רָאִיתִי תַּחַת הַשָּׁמֶשׁ עֹשֶׁר שָׁמוּר לִבְעָלָיו לְרָעָתוֹ: ¹³וְאָבַד הָעֹשֶׁר הַהוּא

בְּעִנְיָן רָע וְהוֹלִיד בֵּן וְאֵין בְּיָדוֹ מְאוּמָה: ¹⁴כַּאֲשֶׁר יָצָא מִבֶּטֶן אִמּוֹ עָרוֹם יָשׁוּב לָלֶכֶת כְּשֶׁבָּא

וּמְאוּמָה לֹא־יִשָּׂא בַעֲמָלוֹ שֶׁיֹּלֵךְ בְּיָדוֹ: ¹⁵וְגַם־זֹה רָעָה חוֹלָה כָּל־עֻמַּת שֶׁבָּא כֵּן יֵלֵךְ

וּמַה־יִּתְרוֹן לוֹ שֶׁיַּעֲמֹל לָרוּחַ: ¹⁶גַּם כָּל־יָמָיו בַּחֹשֶׁךְ יֹאכֵל וְכָעַס הַרְבֵּה וְחָלְיוֹ וָקָצֶף:

¹⁷Behold that which I have seen: It is good and comely for one to eat and to drink and to enjoy the good for all his labour in which he toils under the sun all the days of his life, which God gives him: for it is his portion. ¹⁸Every man also to whom God has given riches and wealth, and has given him power to eat of it, and to take his portion, and to rejoice in his labour: this is the gift of God. ¹⁹For he shall remember that the days of his life are not many, in which God provides him with the joy of his heart.

CHAPTER 5:17–19

There is an evil which I have seen under the sun and it is heavy upon men: [2]a man to whom God has given riches, wealth and honour, so that he lacks nothing for his soul of all that he desires, yet God does not give him power to eat of it, but a stranger eats it: this is vapour, and it is an evil disease. [3]If a man begets a hundred children, and lives many years, so that the days of his years are many, and his soul is not content with the good, and also that he has no burial: I say that an untimely birth is better than he. [4]For it comes in vapour, and departs in darkness, and its name is covered with darkness. [5]Moreover it has not seen the sun, nor known anything: this has more comfort than the other. [6]For though he live a thousand years twice-told, yet he has seen no good: do not all go to one place? [7]All the labour of man is for his mouth and yet the appetite is not filled. [8]For what advantage has the wise more than the fool? what has the poor man who knows how to make his way among the living? [9]Better is the sight of the eyes than the wandering of the desire, this is also vapour and a striving after wind. [10]That which has been was named long ago, and it is known that it is but man: nor may he contend with one who is mightier than he. [11]Seeing there are many things that increase vapour, what is man the better? [12]For who knows what is good for man in this life: all the days of his misty life which he spends like a shadow? for who can tell a man what shall be after him under the sun?

GATHER YE ROSEBUDS WHILE YE MAY

CHAPTER 6

רֵ֫שׁ רָעָה אֲשֶׁר רָאִיתִי תַּחַת הַשֶּׁמֶשׁ וְרַבָּה הִיא עַל־הָאָדָם:

אִישׁ אֲשֶׁר יִתֶּן־לוֹ הָאֱלֹהִים עֹשֶׁר וּנְכָסִים וְכָבוֹד

וְאֵינֶנּוּ חָסֵר לְנַפְשׁוֹ ׀ מִכֹּל אֲשֶׁר־יִתְאַוֶּה וְלֹא־יַשְׁלִיטֶנּוּ הָאֱלֹהִים

לֶאֱכֹל מִמֶּנּוּ כִּי אִישׁ נָכְרִי יֹאכְלֶנּוּ זֶה הֶבֶל וָחֳלִי רָע הוּא:

אִם־יוֹלִיד אִישׁ מֵאָה וְשָׁנִים רַבּוֹת יִחְיֶה וְרַב ׀ שֶׁיִּהְיוּ יְמֵי־שָׁנָיו

וְנַפְשׁוֹ לֹא־תִשְׂבַּע מִן־הַטּוֹבָה וְגַם־קְבוּרָה לֹא־הָיְתָה לּוֹ אָמַרְתִּי

טוֹב מִמֶּנּוּ הַנָּפֶל: כִּי־בַהֶבֶל בָּא וּבַחֹשֶׁךְ יֵלֵךְ וּבַחֹשֶׁךְ שְׁמוֹ יְכֻסֶּה:

גַּם־שֶׁמֶשׁ לֹא־רָאָה וְלֹא יָדָע נַחַת לָזֶה מִזֶּה: וְאִלּוּ חָיָה אֶלֶף

שָׁנִים פַּעֲמַיִם וְטוֹבָה לֹא רָאָה הֲלֹא אֶל־מָקוֹם אֶחָד הַכֹּל הוֹלֵךְ:

כָּל־עֲמַל הָאָדָם לְפִיהוּ וְגַם־הַנֶּפֶשׁ לֹא תִמָּלֵא: כִּי מַה־יּוֹתֵר

לֶחָכָם מִן־הַכְּסִיל מַה־לֶּעָנִי יוֹדֵעַ לַהֲלֹךְ נֶגֶד הַחַיִּים: טוֹב מַרְאֵה

עֵינַיִם מֵהֲלָךְ־נָפֶשׁ גַּם־זֶה הֶבֶל וּרְעוּת רוּחַ: מַה־שֶּׁהָיָה כְּבָר

נִקְרָא שְׁמוֹ וְנוֹדָע אֲשֶׁר־הוּא אָדָם וְלֹא־יוּכַל לָדִין עִם שהתקיף

(שֶׁתַּקִּיף) מִמֶּנּוּ: כִּי יֵשׁ־דְּבָרִים הַרְבֵּה מַרְבִּים הָבֶל מַה־יֹּתֵר

לָאָדָם: כִּי מִי־יוֹדֵעַ מַה־טּוֹב לָאָדָם בַּחַיִּים מִסְפַּר יְמֵי־חַיֵּי

הֶבְלוֹ וְיַעֲשֵׂם כַּצֵּל אֲשֶׁר מִי־יַגִּיד לָאָדָם מַה־יִּהְיֶה אַחֲרָיו תַּחַת הַשָּׁמֶשׁ:

A good name is better than precious ointment: and the day of death than the day of one's birth. ² It is better to go to the house of mourning, than to go to the house of feasting: for that is the end of all humans, and the living will lay it to his heart. ³ Sorrow is better than laughter for by the sadness of the countenance the heart is made glad. ⁴ The heart of the wise is in the house of mourning: but the heart of fools is in the house of mirth. ⁵ It is better to hear the rebuke of the wise than for one to hear the song of fools. ⁶ For as the crackling of thorns under a pot so is the laughter of the fool: this also is vapour. ⁷ Surely oppression makes a wise person mad; and a bribe destroys the heart. ⁸ Better is the end of a thing than the beginning of it and the patient in spirit is better than the proud in spirit ⁹ Be not hasty in thy spirit to be angry for anger rests in the bosom of fools.

אֵטוֹב שֵׁם מִשֶּׁמֶן טוֹב וְיוֹם הַמָּוֶת מִיּוֹם הִוָּלְדוֹ:

בּטוֹב לָלֶכֶת אֶל־בֵּית־אֵבֶל מִלֶּכֶת אֶל־בֵּית מִשְׁתֶּה בַּאֲשֶׁר הוּא סוֹף כָּל־הָאָדָם וְהַחַי יִתֵּן אֶל־לִבּוֹ: גּטוֹב כַּעַס מִשְּׂחֹק כִּי־בְרֹעַ פָּנִים יִיטַב לֵב: דּלֵב חֲכָמִים בְּבֵית אֵבֶל וְלֵב כְּסִילִים בְּבֵית שִׂמְחָה: הטוֹב לִשְׁמֹעַ גַּעֲרַת חָכָם מֵאִישׁ שֹׁמֵעַ שִׁיר כְּסִילִים: וכִּי כְקוֹל הַסִּירִים תַּחַת הַסִּיר כֵּן שְׂחֹק הַכְּסִיל וְגַם־זֶה הָבֶל: זכִּי הָעֹשֶׁק יְהוֹלֵל חָכָם וִיאַבֵּד אֶת־לֵב מַתָּנָה: חטוֹב אַחֲרִית דָּבָר מֵרֵאשִׁיתוֹ טוֹב אֶרֶךְ־רוּחַ מִגְּבַהּ־רוּחַ: טאַל־תְּבַהֵל בְּרוּחֲךָ לִכְעוֹס כִּי כַעַס בְּחֵיק כְּסִילִים יָנוּחַ: ——

¹⁰Do not say, How, was it that the former days were better than these? for thou dost not inquire wisely concerning this. ¹¹Wisdom is good with an inheritance: and by it there is profit to them that see the sun. For wisdom is a defence, and money is a defence: but the excellency of knowlede is, that wisdom gives life to those who have it. ¹³Consider the work of God: for who can make that straight, which has been made crooked? ¹⁴in the day of prosperity be joyful, but in the day of adversity consider: God has made the one as well as the other, to the end that man should find nothing after him.

י אַל־תֹּאמַר מֶה הָיָה שֶׁהַיָּמִים הָרִאשֹׁנִים הָיוּ טוֹבִים מֵאֵלֶּה כִּי לֹא מֵחָכְמָה

שָׁאַלְתָּ עַל־זֶה: יא טוֹבָה חָכְמָה עִם־נַחֲלָה וְיֹתֵר לְרֹאֵי הַשָּׁמֶשׁ: יב כִּי בְּצֵל

הַחָכְמָה בְּצֵל הַכֶּסֶף וְיִתְרוֹן דַּעַת הַחָכְמָה תְּחַיֶּה בְעָלֶיהָ: יג רְאֵה אֶת־מַעֲשֵׂה

הָאֱלֹהִים כִּי מִי יוּכַל   לְתַקֵּן אֵת אֲשֶׁר

עִוְּתוֹ: יד בְּיוֹם   טוֹבָה הֱיֵה בְטוֹב

וּבְיוֹם רָעָה רְאֵה גַּם   אֶת־זֶה לְעֻמַּת־זֶה

עָשָׂה הָאֱלֹהִים   עַל־דִּבְרַת שֶׁלֹּא

יִמְצָא הָאָדָם אַחֲרָיו   מְאוּמָה:

¹⁵All things have I seen in the days of my vapour: there is a just man who perishes in his righteousness, and there is a wicked man who prolongs his life in his wickedness. ¹⁶Be not righteous overmuch; nor make thyself overwise: why shouldst thou destroy thyself? ¹⁷Be not wicked overmuch, nor be foolish: why shouldst thou die before thy time? ¹⁸It is good that thou shouldst take hold of this: but do not withdraw thy hand from that either for he that fears God, performs them all. ¹⁹Wisdom strengthens the wise more than ten rulers who are in a city. ²⁰For there is not a just man upon earth that does good, and sins not. ²¹Also take no heed to all words that are spoken; lest thou hear thy servant curse thee: ²²for oftentimes also thy own heart knows that thou thyself hast likewise cursed others. ²³All this have I proved by wisdom; I said I will be wise; but it was far from me. ²⁴That which is far off, and exceeding deep, who can find it out? ²⁵I cast about in my mind to know, and to search, and to seek out wisdom, and the reason of things and to know the wickedness of folly and foolishness which is madness: ²⁶and I find more bitter than death the woman, whose heart is snares and nets, and her hands are fetters: he who pleases God shall escape from her; but the sinner shall be caught by her. ²⁷Behold, this have I found, says Qobelet, counting one thing to another, to find out the sum. ²⁸which yet my soul seeks, but I have not found it: One man among a thousand I have found; but a woman among all those I have not found. ²⁹Lo, this only have I found, that God has made man upright; but they have sought out many inventions.

אֶת-הַכֹּל רָאִיתִי בִּימֵי הֶבְלִי יֵשׁ צַדִּיק אֹבֵד

בְּצִדְקוֹ וְיֵשׁ רָשָׁע מַאֲרִיךְ בְּרָעָתוֹ:אַל-תְּהִי

צַדִּיק הַרְבֵּה וְאַל-תִּתְחַכַּם יוֹתֵר לָמָּה תִּשּׁוֹמֵם:

אַל-תִּרְשַׁע הַרְבֵּה וְאַל-תְּהִי סָכָל לָמָּה תָמוּת

בְּלֹא עִתֶּךָ:טוֹב אֲשֶׁר תֶּאֱחֹז בָּזֶה וְגַם-מִזֶּה

אַל-תַּנַּח אֶת-יָדֶךָ כִּי-יְרֵא אֱלֹהִים יֵצֵא אֶת-כֻּלָּם:

הַחָכְמָה תָּעֹז לֶחָכָם מֵעֲשָׂרָה שַׁלִּיטִים אֲשֶׁר הָיוּ בָּעִיר:כִּי אָדָם אֵין צַדִּיק בָּאָרֶץ

אֲשֶׁר יַעֲשֶׂה-טּוֹב וְלֹא יֶחֱטָא:גַּם לְכָל-הַדְּבָרִים אֲשֶׁר יְדַבֵּרוּ אַל-תִּתֵּן לִבֶּךָ אֲשֶׁר

לֹא-תִשְׁמַע אֶת-עַבְדְּךָ מְקַלְלֶךָ:כִּי גַּם-פְּעָמִים רַבּוֹת יָדַע לִבֶּךָ אֲשֶׁר גַּם-אַתְּ

(אַתָּה) קִלַּלְתָּ אֲחֵרִים:כָּל-זֹה נִסִּיתִי בַחָכְמָה אָמַרְתִּי אֶחְכָּמָה וְהִיא רְחוֹקָה מִמֶּנִּי:

רָחוֹק מַה-שֶּׁהָיָה וְעָמֹק ׀ עָמֹק מִי יִמְצָאֶנּוּ:סַבּוֹתִי אֲנִי וְלִבִּי לָדַעַת וְלָתוּר

וּבַקֵּשׁ חָכְמָה וְחֶשְׁבּוֹן וְלָדַעַת רֶשַׁע כֶּסֶל וְהַסִּכְלוּת הוֹלֵלוֹת:וּמוֹצֵא אֲנִי מַר מִמָּוֶת

אֶת-הָאִשָּׁה אֲשֶׁר-הִיא מְצוֹדִים וַחֲרָמִים לִבָּהּ אֲסוּרִים יָדֶיהָ טוֹב לִפְנֵי הָאֱלֹהִים יִמָּלֵט

מִמֶּנָּה וְחוֹטֵא יִלָּכֶד בָּהּ:רְאֵה זֶה מָצָאתִי אָמְרָה קֹהֶלֶת אַחַת לְאַחַת לִמְצֹא

חֶשְׁבּוֹן:אֲשֶׁר עוֹד-בִּקְשָׁה נַפְשִׁי וְלֹא מָצָאתִי אָדָם אֶחָד מֵאֶלֶף מָצָאתִי וְאִשָּׁה וְאִשָּׁה

בְּכָל-אֵלֶּה לֹא מָצָאתִי:לְבַד רְאֵה-זֶה מָצָאתִי אֲשֶׁר

עָשָׂה הָאֱלֹהִים אֶת-הָאָדָם יָשָׁר וְהֵמָּה בִקְשׁוּ חִשְּׁבֹנוֹת רַבִּים:

Who is like the wise man? and who knows the interpretation of a thing? a man's wisdom makes his face to shine, and the boldness of his face is changed. [2] I counsel thee to keep the king's commandment, and that in the manner of an oath of God. [3] Be not hasty to go out of his presence; stand not in an evil thing; for he does whatever pleases him. [4] For the word of a king has authority: and who may say to him, What doest thou? [5] He who keeps the commandment shall feel no evil thing: and a wise man's heart discerns both time and method. [6] For every matter has its time and method, though the misery of man is great upon him. [7] For he knows not that which shall be, for who can tell him when it shall be? [8] There is no man who has power over the wind to retain the wind: nor has he power over the day of death: and there is no discharge in that war; nor shall wickedness deliver those who are given up to it. [9] All this have I seen, and have appointed my heart to every work that is done under the sun: there is a time when one man rules over another to his own hurt. [10] And so I saw the wicked buried, and come to their rest: but those who had done right were gone from the holy place, and were forgotten in the city: this also is vapour.

מִי כְּהֶחָכָם וּמִי יוֹדֵעַ פֵּשֶׁר

דָּבָר חָכְמַת אָדָם תָּאִיר פָּנָיו וְעֹז

פָּנָיו יְשֻׁנֶּא׃ אֲנִי פִּי־מֶלֶךְ שְׁמוֹר וְעַל

דִּבְרַת שְׁבוּעַת אֱלֹהִים׃ אַל־תִּבָּהֵל

מִפָּנָיו תֵּלֵךְ אַל־תַּעֲמֹד בְּדָבָר רָע כִּי

כָּל־אֲשֶׁר יַחְפֹּץ יַעֲשֶׂה׃ בַּאֲשֶׁר דְּבַר־מֶלֶךְ שִׁלְטוֹן וּמִי יֹאמַר־לוֹ

מַה־תַּעֲשֶׂה׃ שׁוֹמֵר מִצְוָה לֹא יֵדַע דָּבָר רָע וְעֵת וּמִשְׁפָּט יֵדַע לֵב

חָכָם׃ כִּי לְכָל־חֵפֶץ יֵשׁ עֵת וּמִשְׁפָּט כִּי־רָעַת הָאָדָם רַבָּה עָלָיו׃

כִּי־אֵינֶנּוּ יֹדֵעַ מַה־שֶּׁיִּהְיֶה כִּי כַּאֲשֶׁר יִהְיֶה מִי יַגִּיד לוֹ׃ אֵין אָדָם

שַׁלִּיט בָּרוּחַ לִכְלוֹא אֶת־הָרוּחַ וְאֵין שִׁלְטוֹן בְּיוֹם הַמָּוֶת וְאֵין

מִשְׁלַחַת בַּמִּלְחָמָה וְלֹא־יְמַלֵּט רֶשַׁע אֶת־בְּעָלָיו׃ אֶת־כָּל־זֶה

רָאִיתִי וְנָתוֹן אֶת־לִבִּי לְכָל־מַעֲשֶׂה אֲשֶׁר נַעֲשָׂה תַּחַת הַשָּׁמֶשׁ עֵת

אֲשֶׁר שָׁלַט הָאָדָם בְּאָדָם לְרַע לוֹ׃ וּבְכֵן רָאִיתִי וּשְׁעָיִם קְבֻרִים

וָבָאוּ וּמִמְּקוֹם קָדוֹשׁ יְהַלֵּכוּ וְיִשְׁתַּכְּחוּ בָעִיר אֲשֶׁר

כֵּן־עָשׂוּ גַּם־זֶה הָבֶל׃

15 So I commend mirth, because a man has no better thing under the sun, than to eat, and to drink and to be merry for that shall accompany him in his labour during the days of his life, which God gives him under the sun. 16 When I applied my heart to know wisdom, and to see the business that is done upon the earth: (how one sees no sleep with one's eyes either by day or by night:) 17 then I beheld all the work of God, that a man cannot find out the work that is done under the sun: because though a man labour to seek it out, yet he shall not find it: furthermore; though a wise man think to know it, yet he shall not be able to find it.

טו וְשִׁבַּחְתִּי אֲנִי אֶת־הַשִּׂמְחָה
אֲשֶׁר אֵין־טוֹב לָאָדָם תַּחַת
הַשֶּׁמֶשׁ כִּי אִם־לֶאֱכֹל וְלִשְׁתּוֹת
וְלִשְׂמוֹחַ וְהוּא יִלְוֶנּוּ בַעֲמָלוֹ יְמֵי
חַיָּיו אֲשֶׁר־נָתַן־לוֹ הָאֱלֹהִים תַּחַת
הַשָּׁמֶשׁ: טז כַּאֲשֶׁר נָתַתִּי אֶת־לִבִּי
לָדַעַת חָכְמָה וְלִרְאוֹת אֶת־הָעִנְיָן
אֲשֶׁר נַעֲשָׂה עַל־הָאָרֶץ כִּי גַם
בַּיּוֹם וּבַלַּיְלָה שֵׁנָה בְּעֵינָיו אֵינֶנּוּ
רֹאֶה: יז וְרָאִיתִי אֶת־כָּל־מַעֲשֵׂה
הָאֱלֹהִים כִּי לֹא יוּכַל הָאָדָם
לִמְצוֹא אֶת־הַמַּעֲשֶׂה אֲשֶׁר נַעֲשָׂה
תַחַת־הַשֶּׁמֶשׁ בְּשֶׁל אֲשֶׁר יַעֲמֹל
הָאָדָם לְבַקֵּשׁ וְלֹא יִמְצָא וְגַם
אִם־יֹאמַר הֶחָכָם לָדַעַת
לֹא יוּכַל לִמְצֹא:

"Because sentence against an evil work is not executed speedily, therefore the heart of the sons of men is fully set in them to do evil.

¹²A sinner do evil a hundred times, and his days are prolonged, yet surely I know that it shall be well with those who fear God, who fear before him: ¹³but it shall not be well with the wicked, and, like the shadow, he will not prolong his days; because he does not fear before God. ¹⁴There is a vapour which is done upon the earth; that there are just men to whom it happens according to the deeds of the wicked: again, there are wicked men to whom it happens according to the deeds of the righteous: I said that this also is vapour.

יא אֲשֶׁר אֵין־נַעֲשָׂה פִתְגָם

מַעֲשֵׂה הָרָעָה מְהֵרָה עַל־כֵּן

מָלֵא לֵב בְּנֵי־הָאָדָם בָּהֶם

לַעֲשׂוֹת רָע: יב אֲשֶׁר חֹטֶא

עֹשֶׂה רַע מְאַת וּמַאֲרִיךְ לוֹ כִּי

גַם־יוֹדֵעַ אָנִי אֲשֶׁר יִהְיֶה־טּוֹב

לְיִרְאֵי הָאֱלֹהִים אֲשֶׁר יִירְאוּ

מִלְּפָנָיו: יג וְטוֹב לֹא־יִהְיֶה

לָרָשָׁע וְלֹא־יַאֲרִיךְ יָמִים כַּצֵּל

אֲשֶׁר אֵינֶנּוּ יָרֵא מִלִּפְנֵי

אֱלֹהִים: יד יֶשׁ־הֶבֶל אֲשֶׁר

נַעֲשָׂה עַל־הָאָרֶץ אֲשֶׁר יֵשׁ

צַדִּיקִים אֲשֶׁר מַגִּיעַ אֲלֵהֶם

כְּמַעֲשֵׂה הָרְשָׁעִים וְיֵשׁ רְשָׁעִים

שֶׁמַּגִּיעַ אֲלֵהֶם כְּמַעֲשֵׂה

הַצַּדִּיקִים אָמַרְתִּי שֶׁגַּם־זֶה

הָבֶל:

all this I laid to my heart and sought to clarify all this, that the righteous and the wise, and their deeds, are in the hand of God; no man knows whether love or hatred is in store: all is before them. ²All things come alike to all; there is one event to the righteous, and to the wicked, to the good and to the clean, and to the unclean: to him who sacrifices, and to him who does not sacrifice: as is the good, so is the sinner: and he who swears, as he who fears an oath. ³This is an evil in all things that are done under the sun, that there is one event to all: yea, also the heart of the sons of men is full of evil, and madness is in their heart while they live, and after that they go to the dead. ⁴For to him that is joined to all the living there is hope, for a living dog is better than a dead lion.⁵ For the living know that they shall die, but the dead know nothing, nor do they have any more a reward: for the memory of them is forgotten. ⁶Also their love and their hatred and their envy, is now long perished: nor have they any more a portion forever in any thing that is done under the sun.

אֶת־כָּל־זֶה נָתַתִּי אֶל־לִבִּי וְלָבוּר אֶת־כָּל־זֶה אֲשֶׁר הַצַּדִּיקִים וְהַחֲכָמִים וַעֲבָדֵיהֶם

בְּיַד הָאֱלֹהִים גַּם־אַהֲבָה גַם־שִׂנְאָה אֵין יוֹדֵעַ הָאָדָם הַכֹּל לִפְנֵיהֶם: ²הַכֹּל כַּאֲשֶׁר

לַכֹּל מִקְרֶה אֶחָד לַצַּדִּיק וְלָרָשָׁע לַטּוֹב וְלַטָּהוֹר וְלַטָּמֵא וְלַזֹּבֵחַ וְלַאֲשֶׁר אֵינֶנּוּ זֹבֵחַ

כַּטּוֹב כַּחֹטֶא הַנִּשְׁבָּע כַּאֲשֶׁר שְׁבוּעָה יָרֵא: ³זֶה רָע בְּכֹל אֲשֶׁר־נַעֲשָׂה תַּחַת

הַשֶּׁמֶשׁ כִּי־מִקְרֶה אֶחָד לַכֹּל וְגַם לֵב בְּנֵי־הָאָדָם מָלֵא־רָע וְהוֹלֵלוֹת בִּלְבָבָם

בְּחַיֵּיהֶם וְאַחֲרָיו אֶל־הַמֵּתִים: ⁴כִּי־מִי אֲשֶׁר (יְבֻחָר) יְחֻבַּר אֶל כָּל־הַחַיִּים יֵשׁ

בִּטָּחוֹן כִּי־לְכֶלֶב חַי הוּא טוֹב מִן־הָאַרְיֵה הַמֵּת: ⁵כִּי הַחַיִּים יוֹדְעִים שֶׁיָּמֻתוּ

וְהַמֵּתִים אֵינָם יוֹדְעִים מְאוּמָה וְאֵין־עוֹד לָהֶם שָׂכָר כִּי נִשְׁכַּח זִכְרָם: ⁶גַּם אַהֲבָתָם

גַּם־שִׂנְאָתָם גַּם קִנְאָתָם כְּבָר אָבָדָה וְחֵלֶק אֵין־לָהֶם עוֹד לְעוֹלָם בְּכֹל אֲשֶׁר־נַעֲשָׂה

תַּחַת הַשָּׁמֶשׁ:

⁷Go thy way, eat thy bread with joy, and drink thy wine with a merry heart; for God has already accepted thy works. ⁸Let thy garments be always white, and let thy head lack no oil. ⁹Live joyfully with the wife whom thou lovest all the days of the life of thy vapour, which He has given thee under the sun, all the days of thy vapour: for that is thy portion in life and in thy labour in which thou dost labour under the sun. ¹⁰Whatever thy hand finds to do, do it with thy strength, for there is no work, nor device, nor knowledge, nor wisdom in Sheol, whither thou goest.

¹¹I returned, and saw under the sun, that the race is not to the swift, nor the battle to the strong, nor yet bread to the wise, nor yet riches to men of understanding, nor yet favour to men of skill; but time and chance happens to them all. ¹²For man also knows not his time: like the fishes that are taken in an evil net, and like the birds that are caught in the snare; so are the sons of men snared in an evil time, when it falls suddenly upon them. ¹³This wisdom have I seen also under the sun, and it seemed great to me. ¹⁴There was a little city and few men within it; and came a great king against it and besieged it, and built great siegeworks against it: ¹⁵now there was found in it a poor wise man, and he by his wisdom saved the city; yet no man remembered that same poor man. ¹⁶Then said I, Wisdom is better than strength; nevertheless the poor man's wisdom is despised, and his words are not heard. ¹⁷The words of wise men heard in quiet are better than the cry of him who rules among fools. ¹⁸Wisdom is better than weapons of war: but one sinner destroys much good.

יא שַׁבְתִּי וְרָאֹה תַחַת־הַשֶּׁמֶשׁ כִּי לֹא לַקַּלִּים הַמֵּרוֹץ וְלֹא לַגִּבּוֹרִים הַמִּלְחָמָה וְגַם לֹא לַחֲכָמִים לֶחֶם וְגַם לֹא לַנְּבֹנִים עֹשֶׁר וְגַם לֹא לַיֹּדְעִים חֵן כִּי־עֵת וָפֶגַע יִקְרֶה אֶת־כֻּלָּם: יב כִּי גַם לֹא־יֵדַע הָאָדָם אֶת־עִתּוֹ כַּדָּגִים שֶׁנֶּאֱחָזִים בִּמְצוֹדָה רָעָה וְכַצִּפֳּרִים הָאֲחֻזוֹת בַּפָּח כָּהֵם יוּקָשִׁים בְּנֵי הָאָדָם לְעֵת רָעָה כְּשֶׁתִּפּוֹל עֲלֵיהֶם פִּתְאֹם:

יג גַּם־זֹה רָאִיתִי חָכְמָה תַּחַת הַשָּׁמֶשׁ וּגְדוֹלָה הִיא אֵלָי: יד עִיר קְטַנָּה וַאֲנָשִׁים בָּהּ מְעָט וּבָא־אֵלֶיהָ מֶלֶךְ גָּדוֹל וְסָבַב אֹתָהּ וּבָנָה עָלֶיהָ מְצוֹדִים גְּדֹלִים: טו וּמָצָא בָהּ אִישׁ מִסְכֵּן חָכָם וּמִלַּט־הוּא אֶת־הָעִיר בְּחָכְמָתוֹ וְאָדָם לֹא זָכַר אֶת־הָאִישׁ הַמִּסְכֵּן הַהוּא:

טז וְאָמַרְתִּי אָנִי טוֹבָה חָכְמָה מִגְּבוּרָה וְחָכְמַת הַמִּסְכֵּן בְּזוּיָה וּדְבָרָיו אֵינָם נִשְׁמָעִים: יז דִּבְרֵי חֲכָמִים בְּנַחַת נִשְׁמָעִים מִזַּעֲקַת מוֹשֵׁל בַּכְּסִילִים: יח טוֹבָה חָכְמָה מִכְּלֵי קְרָב וְחוֹטֶא אֶחָד יְאַבֵּד טוֹבָה הַרְבֵּה:

Dead flies cause the perfumer's ointment to give off a foul odour: so does a little folly outweigh wisdom and honour. ²A wise man's heart inclines him to his right hand: but a fool's heart to his left. ³Yea also, when a fool walks by the way, his understanding fails him, and he reveals to everyone that he is a fool. ⁴If the spirit of the ruler rise up against thee, do not leave thy place, for deference appeases great offences. ⁵There is an evil which I have seen under the sun, when an error proceeds from the ruler: ⁶folly is set in great dignity, and the rich sit in low place. ⁷I have seen servants upon horses, and princes walking as servants upon the earth. ⁸He who digs a pit shall fall into it: and whoever breaks through a hedge, a snake shall bite him. ⁹He who removes stones shall be hurt by them: and he who chops wood shall be endangered by that. ¹⁰If the iron is blunt and one does not whet the edge, then he must put to more strength but wisdom increases skill. ¹¹If the serpent bites and cannot be charmed, then there is no advantage in a charmer. ¹²The words of a wise man's mouth are gracious, but the lips of a fool will swallow up himself. ¹³The beginning of the words of his mouth is foolishness: and the end of his talk is grievous madness. ¹⁴A fool also multiplies words: yet no man can tell what shall be: and what shall be after him, who can tell him? ¹⁵The labour of fools wearies himself: for he does not know to get to the city.

זְבוּבֵי מָוֶת יַבְאִישׁ יַבִּיעַ שֶׁמֶן רוֹקֵחַ יָקָר מֵחָכְמָה מִכָּבוֹד

סִכְלוּת מְעָט: ²לֵב חָכָם לִימִינוֹ וְלֵב כְּסִיל

לִשְׂמֹאלוֹ: ³וְגַם־בַּדֶּרֶךְ כְּשֶׁהַסָּכָל (כְּשֶׁסָּכָל) הֹלֵךְ לִבּוֹ חָסֵר וְאָמַר לַכֹּל סָכָל

הוּא: ⁴אִם־רוּחַ הַמּוֹשֵׁל תַּעֲלֶה עָלֶיךָ מְקוֹמְךָ אַל־תַּנַּח כִּי מַרְפֵּא יַנִּיחַ

חֲטָאִים גְּדוֹלִים: ⁵יֵשׁ רָעָה רָאִיתִי תַּחַת הַשָּׁמֶשׁ כִּשְׁגָגָה שֶׁיֹּצָא מִלִּפְנֵי

הַשַּׁלִּיט: ⁶נִתַּן הַסֶּכֶל בַּמְּרוֹמִים רַבִּים וַעֲשִׁירִים בַּשֵּׁפֶל יֵשֵׁבוּ: ⁷רָאִיתִי עֲבָדִים

עַל־סוּסִים וְשָׂרִים הֹלְכִים כַּעֲבָדִים עַל־הָאָרֶץ: ⁸חֹפֵר גּוּמָּץ בּוֹ יִפּוֹל וּפֹרֵץ

גָּדֵר יִשְּׁכֶנּוּ נָחָשׁ: ⁹מַסִּיעַ אֲבָנִים יֵעָצֵב בָּהֶם בּוֹקֵעַ עֵצִים יִסָּכֶן בָּם:

¹⁰אִם־קֵהָה הַבַּרְזֶל וְהוּא לֹא־פָנִים קִלְקַל וַחֲיָלִים יְגַבֵּר וְיִתְרוֹן

הַכְשֵׁיר חָכְמָה: ¹¹אִם־יִשֹּׁךְ הַנָּחָשׁ בְּלוֹא־לָחַשׁ וְאֵין יִתְרוֹן לְבַעַל

הַלָּשׁוֹן: ¹²דִּבְרֵי פִי־חָכָם חֵן וְשִׂפְתוֹת כְּסִיל תְּבַלְּעֶנּוּ: ¹³תְּחִלַּת

דִּבְרֵי־פִיהוּ סִכְלוּת וְאַחֲרִית פִּיהוּ הוֹלֵלוּת רָעָה: ¹⁴וְהַסָּכָל יַרְבֶּה

דְבָרִים לֹא־יֵדַע הָאָדָם מַה־שֶׁיִּהְיֶה וַאֲשֶׁר יִהְיֶה

מֵאַחֲרָיו מִי יַגִּיד לוֹ: ¹⁵עֲמַל הַכְּסִילִים תְּיַגְּעֶנּוּ

אֲשֶׁר לֹא־יָדַע לָלֶכֶת אֶל־עִיר:

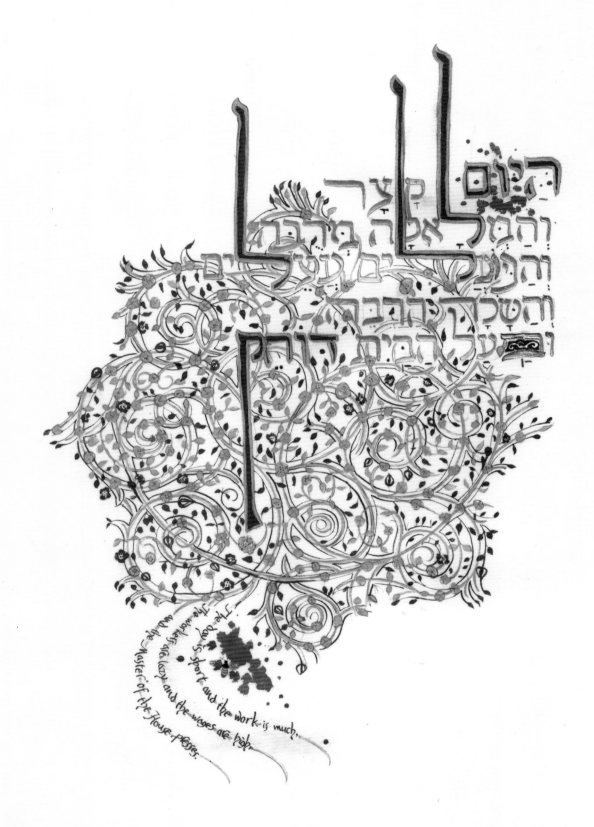

Woe to thee, O land, when thy king is a child, and thy princes dine in the morning! 17 Happy art thou, O land when thy king is a man of dignity and thy princes eat in due season, for strength and not for drunkenness! 18 By much slothfulness the beams collapse: and through idleness of the hands, the house leaks. 19 A feast is made for laughter, and wine makes life joyful and money answers all things. 20 Do not curse the king, no, not even in thy thought; and do not curse the rich, even in thy bedchamber: for a bird of the sky shall carry the sound, and that which has wings shall tell the matter.

אִי־לָךְ אֶרֶץ שֶׁמַּלְכֵּךְ נָעַר וְשָׂרַיִךְ בַּבֹּקֶר יֹאכֵלוּ׃ 17 אַשְׁרֵיךְ אֶרֶץ שֶׁמַּלְכֵּךְ בֶּן־חוֹרִים וְשָׂרַיִךְ בָּעֵת יֹאכֵלוּ בִּגְבוּרָה וְלֹא בַשְּׁתִי׃ 18 בַּעֲצַלְתַּיִם יִמַּךְ הַמְּקָרֶה וּבְשִׁפְלוּת יָדַיִם יִדְלֹף הַבָּיִת׃ 19 לִשְׂחוֹק עֹשִׂים לֶחֶם וְיַיִן יְשַׂמַּח חַיִּים וְהַכֶּסֶף יַעֲנֶה אֶת־הַכֹּל׃ 20 גַּם בְּמַדָּעֲךָ מֶלֶךְ אַל־תְּקַלֵּל וּבְחַדְרֵי מִשְׁכָּבְךָ אַל־תְּקַלֵּל עָשִׁיר כִּי עוֹף הַשָּׁמַיִם יוֹלִיךְ אֶת־הַקּוֹל וּבַעַל הכנפים (כְּנָפַיִם) יַגֵּיד דָּבָר׃

לַחְמְךָ עַל־פְּנֵי הַמָּיִם כִּי־בְרֹב הַיָּמִים תִּמְצָאֶנּוּ:

² תֶּן־חֵלֶק לְשִׁבְעָה וְגַם לִשְׁמוֹנָה כִּי לֹא תֵדַע מַה־יִּהְיֶה רָעָה
עַל־הָאָרֶץ: ³ אִם־יִמָּלְאוּ הֶעָבִים גֶּשֶׁם עַל־הָאָרֶץ יָרִיקוּ
וְאִם־יִפּוֹל עֵץ בַּדָּרוֹם וְאִם בַּצָּפוֹן מְקוֹם שֶׁיִּפּוֹל הָעֵץ שָׁם יְהוּא: ⁴ שֹׁמֵר רוּחַ לֹא יִזְרָע וְרֹאֶה
בֶעָבִים לֹא יִקְצוֹר: ⁵ כַּאֲשֶׁר אֵינְךָ יוֹדֵעַ מַה־דֶּרֶךְ הָרוּחַ כַּעֲצָמִים בְּבֶטֶן הַמְּלֵאָה כָּכָה לֹא תֵדַע
אֶת־מַעֲשֵׂה הָאֱלֹהִים אֲשֶׁר יַעֲשֶׂה אֶת־הַכֹּל: ⁶ בַּבֹּקֶר זְרַע אֶת־זַרְעֶךָ וְלָעֶרֶב אַל־תַּנַּח יָדֶךָ כִּי
אֵינְךָ יוֹדֵעַ אֵי זֶה יִכְשָׁר הֲזֶה אוֹ־זֶה וְאִם שְׁנֵיהֶם כְּאֶחָד טוֹבִים: ⁷ וּמָתוֹק הָאוֹר וְטוֹב לַעֵינַיִם
לִרְאוֹת אֶת־הַשָּׁמֶשׁ: ⁸ כִּי אִם־שָׁנִים הַרְבֵּה יִחְיֶה הָאָדָם בְּכֻלָּם יִשְׂמָח וְיִזְכֹּר אֶת־יְמֵי הַחֹשֶׁךְ
כִּי־הַרְבֵּה יִהְיוּ כָּל־שֶׁבָּא הָבֶל: ⁹ שְׂמַח בָּחוּר בְּיַלְדוּתֶיךָ וִיטִיבְךָ לִבְּךָ בִּימֵי בְחוּרוֹתֶךָ וְהַלֵּךְ
בְּדַרְכֵי לִבְּךָ וּבְמַרְאֵי עֵינֶיךָ וְדַע כִּי עַל־כָּל־אֵלֶּה יְבִיאֲךָ הָאֱלֹהִים בַּמִּשְׁפָּט: ¹⁰ וְהָסֵר כַּעַס מִלִּבֶּךָ
וְהַעֲבֵר רָעָה מִבְּשָׂרֶךָ כִּי־הַיַּלְדוּת וְהַשַּׁחֲרוּת הָבֶל:

thy bread upon the waters: for thou shalt find it after many days.
²Give a portion to seven, and even to eight; for thou knowest not what
evil shall be upon the earth.³If the clouds are full of rain, they empty
themselves upon the earth: and if the tree falls toward the south, or towards the north in the place where
the tree falls, there it shall lie.⁴He who observes the wind shall not sow and he who regards the clouds shall
not reap.⁵As thou knowst not what is the way of the wind, nor how the bones grow in the womb of her that
is with child, even so thou knowst not the works of God who makes all.⁶In the morning sow thy seed, and in
the evening do not withold thy hand: for thou knowst not which shall prosper, whether this or that, or
whether they both shall be alike good.⁷Truly the light is sweet, and a pleasant thing it is for the eyes to
behold the Sun:⁸for if a man live many years, let him rejoice in them all; yet let him remember the
days of darkness; for they shall be many. All that comes is vapour.⁹Rejoice, O young man in thy youth;
and let thy heart cheer thee in the days of thy youth, and walk in the ways of thy heart, and in
the sight of thy eyes: but know thou, that for all these things, God will bring thee into judgment.
¹⁰Therefore remove vexation from thy heart, and put away evil from thy flesh on account of childhood and youth
being vapour.

CHAPTER 11

CHAPTER 12:1–8   82

אֶת־בּוֹרְאֶיךָ בִּימֵי בְּחוּרֹתֶיךָ עַד אֲשֶׁר לֹא־יָבֹאוּ יְמֵי הָרָעָה

וְהִגִּיעוּ שָׁנִים אֲשֶׁר תֹּאמַר אֵין־לִי בָהֶם חֵפֶץ: עַד אֲשֶׁר

לֹא־תֶחְשַׁךְ הַשֶּׁמֶשׁ וְהָאוֹר וְהַיָּרֵחַ וְהַכּוֹכָבִים וְשָׁבוּ הֶעָבִים אַחַר

הַגָּשֶׁם: בַּיּוֹם שֶׁיָּזֻעוּ שֹׁמְרֵי הַבַּיִת וְהִתְעַוְּתוּ אַנְשֵׁי הֶחָיִל וּבָטְלוּ

הַטֹּחֲנוֹת כִּי מִעֵטוּ וְחָשְׁכוּ הָרֹאוֹת בָּאֲרֻבּוֹת: וְסֻגְּרוּ דְלָתַיִם בַּשּׁוּק בִּשְׁפַל קוֹל הַטַּחֲנָה

וְיָקוּם לְקוֹל הַצִּפּוֹר וְיִשַּׁחוּ כָּל־בְּנוֹת הַשִּׁיר: גַּם מִגָּבֹהַּ יִרָאוּ וְחַתְחַתִּים בַּדֶּרֶךְ וְיָנֵאץ

הַשָּׁקֵד וְיִסְתַּבֵּל הֶחָגָב וְתָפֵר הָאֲבִיּוֹנָה כִּי־הֹלֵךְ הָאָדָם אֶל־בֵּית עוֹלָמוֹ וְסָבְבוּ בַשּׁוּק

הַסֹּפְדִים: עַד אֲשֶׁר לֹא־יִרָחֵק (וְיֵרָתֵק) חֶבֶל הַכֶּסֶף וְתָרֻץ גֻּלַּת הַזָּהָב וְתִשָּׁבֶר

כַּד עַל־הַמַּבּוּעַ וְנָרֹץ הַגַּלְגַּל אֶל־הַבּוֹר: וְיָשֹׁב הֶעָפָר עַל־הָאָרֶץ כְּשֶׁהָיָה וְהָרוּחַ

תָּשׁוּב אֶל־הָאֱלֹהִים אֲשֶׁר נְתָנָהּ: הֲבֵל הֲבָלִים אָמַר הַקּוֹהֶלֶת הַכֹּל הָבֶל׃

Remember now thy Creator in the days of thy youth, before the evil days come and the years draw near, which thou shall say, I have no pleasure in them; [2] before the sun, or the light, or the moon, or the stars are darkened, and the clouds return after the rain: [3] in the day when the keepers of the house — tremble and the strong men bow themselves and the grinders cease because they are few, and those that look out of the windows are dimmed [4] and the doors are shut in the street, when the sound of the grinding is low, and one starts up at the voice of the bird, and all the daughters of music are brought low, [5] and when they are also afraid of that which is high, and terrors are in the way, and the almond tree blossoms, and the grasshopper drags itself along and the caper-berry fails; because the man goes to his eternal home, and the mourners go about the streets; [6] before the silver cord is loosed or the golden bowl is shattered, or the pitcher is broken at the fountain, or the wheel broken at the cistern; and the dust returns to the earth as it was [7] and the spirit returns to God who gave it. [8] Vapour* of vapours, says Qohelet; all is vapour.

NOTES

[1] The Hebrew, *amarti ani b'libi*, is much clearer in this regard. Most English translations, however, reduce the triple self-attribution to a doubled first person: "I said in my heart."

[2] To which, as noted in my general introduction, Martin Shuster's Heideggerian reading of Qohelet's premise adds an interesting philosophical dimension. See Shuster, "Being as Breath, Vapor as Joy," esp. 234ff.

[3] As noted in my general introduction, n. 27, R. B. Y. Scott offers a conjoined rendering of *hevel*, translating 1:2 as "A vapor of vapors! (says Qohelet). Thinnest of vapors! All is vapor!" but adding in a footnote: "*[H]evel* denotes a breath empty of substance and also transient. The writer's thesis is that everything in a man's experience in this world … is empty of meaning or worth…. Hence … his efforts to achieve something are ultimately futile."

[4] For a comprehensive survey of traditional and contemporary readings of the term, see Meek, "Twentieth- and Twenty-First-Century Readings of *Hebel* (הֶבֶל) in Ecclesiastes."

[5] See, e.g., Fox, "The Meaning of *Hebel* for Qohelet," which surveys the relevant literature on the term *hevel* and concludes: "For Qohelet the reliability of the causal nexus fails, leaving only fragmented sequences of events which, though divinely determined, must be judged random from the human perspective…. The belief in a reliable causal order fails, and with it human reason and self-confidence. But this failure is what God intends, for after it comes fear. And fear is the only emotion that Qohelet explicitly wants God to arouse."

[6] One is reminded both of the Greeks' notion of the perfectly cyclical perfection of the realm "above the moon" and of what Emile Meyerson famously dubbed "the elimination of time" characteristic of modern physics, namely, the way the seemingly temporal dynamics of physical systems is reduced mathematically to atemporal laws of conservation. See Emile Meyerson, *Identity & Reality*, trans. Katie Loewenberg (Mineola, N.Y.: Dover, 1965), chap. 6.

[7] E.g., Gen 45:3; 1 Kgs 18:21.

[8] E.g., Gen 30:33; Exod 20:12.

[9] E.g., Gen 15:13; Lev 23:27.

[10] E.g., Exod 10:3; Hos 5:5.

[11] E.g., Exod 3:7; 2 Kgs 14:26.

[12] On the important role played by the "two books" metaphor in the rise of modern science, see Kenneth J. Howell, *God's Two Books: Copernican Cosmology and Biblical Interpretation in Early Modern Science* (South Bend, Ind.: University of Notre Dame Press, 2004); Peter Harrison, *The Bible, Protestantism and the Rise of Natural Science* (Cambridge: Cambridge University Press, 2006); Menachem Fisch, "Judaism and the Religious Crisis of Modern Science," in *Nature & Scripture in the Abrahamic Religions: 1700–Present*, ed. Jitse M. van der Meer and Scott Mandelbrote (Leiden: Brill, 2008), 2:525–67.

[13] For a forceful rabbinic portrayal of how God's Word is inevitably refracted through the diversified lenses of human languages and experience, see Menachem Fisch, "God's Word and the Languages of Man: The Wisdom of Solomon and the Birth of Midrash," in *Interesse am Anderen: Interdisziplinäre Beiträge zum Verhältnis von Religion und Rationalität. Für Heiko Schulz zum 60*, ed. Gerhard Schreiber (Berlin: De Gruyter, 2019), 369–82.

loating in the golden bowl to which Qohelet will compare human life (12:7) is a vision of a royal castle, symbolizing humankind's dreams and illusions of immortality. The castle glowing on the mountain ridge is modeled on the fourteenth-century Alhambra, Qalat al-Hamra, on the heights of the Andalusian town of Granada, the once-grand home of the Nasrid emirs of Córdoba, home to the vibrant Muslim and Jewish court life of medieval Sepharad. Today, still regal, still robed in carvings, mosaics, and gardens bearing witness to its rulers' boundless wealth and its artisans' skills, the Alhambra seems to echo with the voices and footsteps of its once-vibrant court life. Yet its tiles and stones slowly crumble. In the painting, mists obscure the view of castle, orchards, vineyards, and fields, alluding to the transience of human life and the attendant difficulty of discerning the value of the individual's deeds here "under the heavens." The fresh green branch alludes to the joy of life, despite its inevitable brevity.

The richly chased handles of the bowl allude to a midrash characterizing Solomon's search for wisdom. R. Jose, imagined the Torah as

> a big basket full of produce without any handle, so that it could not be lifted, till one clever man came and made handles to it, and then it began to be carried by the handles. So till Solomon arose no one could properly understand the words of the Torah, but when Solomon arose, all began to comprehend the Torah.[1]

The waves of micrography surrounding this painting and the first Hebrew and English text pages include the full text of the book of Qohelet.

NOTE

[1] Freedman and Simon, *Midrash Rabbah*, 9:9.

אַ דִּבְרֵי קֹהֶלֶת בֶּן־דָּוִד מֶלֶךְ בִּירוּשָׁלָ͏ִם: בַּ הֲבֵל הֲבָלִים אָמַר קֹהֶלֶת הֲבֵל הֲבָלִים הַכֹּל הָבֶל: גַּ מַה־יִּתְרוֹן לָאָדָם בְּכָל־עֲמָלוֹ שֶׁיַּעֲמֹל תַּחַת הַשָּׁמֶשׁ:

¹The words of Qohelet, the son of David, king in Yerushalayim. ²Vapour of vapours, says Qohelet, vapour of vapours: all is vapour. ³What profit has a man of all his labour wherein he labours under the sun?

As Qohelet cries out that human life is as insubstantial and fleeting as vapor, the golden pattern of the frontispiece's golden bowl transforms to the blue filigreed letters of the first Hebrew and English words of the text. The individual's deeds, limited to the human sphere "under the sun," make no indelible mark on the world, bring the person no lasting benefit, and ultimately do not help him or her achieve wisdom.

On the Hebrew page, the philosopher's eye peers through the initial letter. The plain clay jar spilling the jewels that tumble down around the words describe, in midrash, Solomon's unsealing of wisdom of Torah. The rabbis compare the Torah

> to a cask which was full of precious stones and pearls, but which had a tight-fitting cover and was put away in a corner, so that no one knew what was in it, until someone came and emptied it and then everyone knew what was in it. So the heart of Solomon was full of wisdom but no one knew what was in it but when the holy spirit rested on him and he composed three books, all knew his wisdom…. *And I applied my heart to seek and to explore by wisdom.* (Qoh 1:13)[1]

The English page presents midrashic imagery about the transience of human life. Qohelet Rabbah suggests that the first verse of Solomon's Qohelet explains words uttered by his father, David, in Ps 144:4: "Humankind is like a breath; its days are like a passing shadow."[2] The same poem praises the beauty of Israel's vibrant youth, despite the fragility of life: "For our sons are like saplings, well-tended in their youth; our daughters are like cornerstones trimmed to give shape to a palace."[3] The midrash adds that R.

Huna, in the name of R. Aḥa, compared life to the transient shadow of a flying bird. The English page muses upon these images of transience. A budding sapling grows beside a decorated wall tiled with the words "Humankind is like a breath; its days are like a passing shadow," as the shadow of a flying dove floats across the scene.

Qohelet, wealthy, powerful, and worldly-wise, will probe and test the lasting value of life and humanity's access to lasting wisdom, completing Solomon's great works. The interlocking waves of micrography surrounding this pair of paintings and the frontispiece painting include the full text of Qohelet.

NOTES
[1] H. Freedman and Maurice Simon, trans. and eds., *Midrash Rabbah*: vol. 9, *Song of Songs* (London: Soncino, 1939), 8.
[2] Qohelet Rabbah 1:3. See Hillel Danziger et al., eds., *The Midrash: The Five Megillos—Koheles/Compact Size* (Brooklyn, N.Y.: Mesorah, 2015), 3^2. My trans. of Ps 144:4.
[3] Trans. from *JPS Hebrew-English Tanakh* (Philadelphia: Jewish Publication Society, 1999), 1591.

דּוֹר הֹלֵךְ וְדוֹר בָּא וְהָאָרֶץ לְעוֹלָם עֹמָדֶת: ⁴One generation passes away, and another generation comes: but the earth abides forever. ⁵The sun also rises, and the sun goes down, and hastens to its place where it rises again. ⁶The wind goes towards the south, and veers to the north; round and round goes the wind and on its circuits the wind returns. ⁷All the rivers run into the sea; yet the sea is not full; to the place where the rivers flow, thither they return. ⁸All things are full of weariness: man cannot utter it; the eye is not satisfied with seeing, nor the ear filled with hearing. ⁹That which has been, it is that which shall be; and that which has been done is that which shall be done; and there is nothing new under the sun. ¹⁰Is there a thing whereof it may be said, See, this is new; but it has already been in the ages before us. ¹¹There is no remembrance of former things; nor will there be any remembrance of things that are to come among those who shall come after.

וְזָרַח הַשֶּׁמֶשׁ וּבָא הַשָּׁמֶשׁ וְאֶל־מְקוֹמוֹ שׁוֹאֵף זוֹרֵחַ הוּא שָׁם: ⁶ הוֹלֵךְ אֶל־דָּרוֹם וְסוֹבֵב אֶל־צָפוֹן סוֹבֵב | סֹבֵב הֹלֵךְ הָרוּחַ וְעַל־סְבִיבֹתָיו שָׁב הָרוּחַ: ⁷ כָּל־הַנְּחָלִים הֹלְכִים אֶל־הַיָּם וְהַיָּם אֵינֶנּוּ מָלֵא אֶל־מְקוֹם שֶׁהַנְּחָלִים הֹלְכִים שָׁם הֵם שָׁבִים לָלָכֶת: ⁸ כָּל־הַדְּבָרִים יְגֵעִים לֹא־יוּכַל אִישׁ לְדַבֵּר לֹא־תִשְׂבַּע עַיִן לִרְאוֹת וְלֹא־תִמָּלֵא אֹזֶן מִשְּׁמֹעַ: ⁹ מַה־שֶּׁהָיָה הוּא שֶׁיִּהְיֶה וּמַה־שֶּׁנַּעֲשָׂה הוּא שֶׁיֵּעָשֶׂה וְאֵין כָּל־חָדָשׁ תַּחַת הַשָּׁמֶשׁ: ¹ יֵשׁ דָּבָר שֶׁיֹּאמַר רְאֵה־זֶה חָדָשׁ הוּא כְּבָר הָיָה לְעֹלָמִים אֲשֶׁר הָיָה מִלְּפָנֵנוּ: ¹¹ אֵין זִכְרוֹן לָרִאשֹׁנִים וְגַם לָאַחֲרֹנִים שֶׁיִּהְיוּ לֹא־יִהְיֶה לָהֶם זִכָּרוֹן עִם שֶׁיִּהְיוּ לָאַחֲרֹנָה:

---

he philosopher compares the immutable cycle of life to the daily journey of the sun and to the water cycle, all three beyond the reach of human will and action. For all Qohelet's frustration at the impermanence of an individual's mark on the world, biblical writers found beauty in the order of God's Creation. See, for instance, Psalm 104:

²¹The lions roar for prey,
   seeking their food from God.
²²When the sun rises, they come home
   and couch in their dens.

[23]Man then goes out to his work,
to his labor until the evening.
[24]How many are the things You have made, O LORD;
You have made them all with wisdom;
the earth is full of Your creations.[1]

We glimpse the philosopher standing at a window seeing these consistent cycles reflected in a mosaic-covered wall and in the sky and sea outside. The mosaic repeats its own complex, man-made pattern endlessly, in colors that echo the sea, sky, sunlight, and forests. Outside, mist—the same ephemeral vapor that the philosopher likens to human life—rises from the gardens below into the clouds, only to fall to land and sea again as rain. Across the two paintings, the sun rises and sets, and the moon appears in its crescent and full phases. The cloud of micrographic text in the Hebrew illumination includes passages of the eleventh-century Spanish Jewish philosopher and poet Solomon Ibn Gabirol's Neoplatonic philosophical tract in verse, *The Royal Crown*. The first passage expresses humankind's inability to comprehend God's eternity; the second laments the clouds of human imperfection that obscure humanity's view of divine wisdom, likened here to light:

III

Thou dost exist, we say, though never ear
Gathered report of Thee, nor mortal eye
Hath glimpsed Thee; what existence, then, is here,
Whereof we cannot ask whence, how, and why?
Exist Thou dost—a sole, unpartnered *Ens*:
Or e'er time did commence,
E'er space there was, didst Thou thy pitch select.
Thou art a hidden mystery, whom sense
Can reach not, thine existence to reflect,
Searching for what Itself must secret keep:
Shall any find? Nay, ours to sigh, 'tis, deep, too deep!

VII

Thou art that Light whose supramundane ray
The soul may look upon, so be she pure,
But intervening sin doth overlay
With clouds, till Thou dost lurk from her, obscure:
The light to which this world is as a screen,
But in God's City seen;
Eternal Light, the intellect for Thee
Yearns love-lorn whilst , myopic, she may glean
Naught but blurred vision—more she cannot see.[2]

NOTES
[1] Ellen F. Davis, *Proverbs, Ecclesiastes, and the Song of Songs* (Louisville, Ky.: Westminster John Knox, 2000), 172.
[2] Raphael Loewe, *Ibn Gabirol* (New York: Grove Weidenfeld, 1989), 121, 123.

יב אֲנִי קֹהֶלֶת הָיִיתִי מֶלֶךְ עַל־יִשְׂרָאֵל בִּירוּשָׁלָ͏ִם: יג וְנָתַתִּי אֶת־לִבִּי לִדְרוֹשׁ וְלָתוּר בַּחָכְמָה עַל כָּל־אֲשֶׁר נַעֲשָׂה תַּחַת הַשָּׁמָיִם הוּא | עִנְיַן רָע נָתַן אֱלֹהִים לִבְנֵי הָאָדָם לַעֲנוֹת בּוֹ: יד רָאִיתִי אֶת־כָּל־הַמַּעֲשִׂים שֶׁנַּעֲשׂוּ תַּחַת הַשָּׁמֶשׁ וְהִנֵּה הַכֹּל הֶבֶל וּרְעוּת רוּחַ: טו מְעֻוָּת לֹא־יוּכַל לִתְקֹן וְחֶסְרוֹן לֹא־יוּכַל לְהִמָּנוֹת: טז דִּבַּרְתִּי אֲנִי עִם־לִבִּי לֵאמֹר אֲנִי הִנֵּה הִגְדַּלְתִּי וְהוֹסַפְתִּי חָכְמָה עַל כָּל־אֲשֶׁר־הָיָה לְפָנַי עַל־יְרוּשָׁלָ͏ִם וְלִבִּי רָאָה הַרְבֵּה חָכְמָה וָדָעַת: יז וָאֶתְּנָה לִבִּי לָדַעַת חָכְמָה וְדַעַת הוֹלֵלוֹת וְשִׂכְלוּת יָדַעְתִּי שֶׁגַּם־זֶה הוּא רַעְיוֹן רוּחַ: יח כִּי בְּרֹב חָכְמָה רָב־כָּעַס וְיוֹסִיף דַּעַת יוֹסִיף מַכְאוֹב:

¹²I Qohelet was King over Yisra'el in Yerushalayim. ¹³And I gave my heart to seek and search out by wisdom concerning all things that are done under the heaven: it is a sore task that God has given to the son of man to be exercised with. ¹⁴I have seen all the works that are done under the sun; and, behold, all is vapour and a striving after wind. ¹⁵That which is crooked cannot be made straight: and that which is wanting cannot be numbered. I spoke to my own heart, saying. ¹⁶See, I have acquired great wisdom, surpassing all those who were before me in Yerushalayim: for my heart has seen much of wisdom and knowledge. ¹⁷And I gave my heart to know wisdom, and to know madness and folly: I perceived that this also was a striving after wind. ¹⁸For in much wisdom is much grief: and he that increases knowledge increases sorrow.

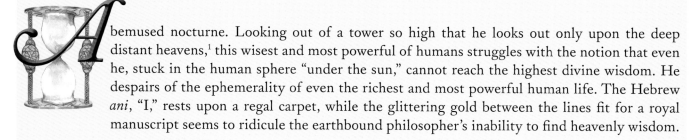

A bemused nocturne. Looking out of a tower so high that he looks out only upon the deep distant heavens,¹ this wisest and most powerful of humans struggles with the notion that even he, stuck in the human sphere "under the sun," cannot reach the highest divine wisdom. He despairs of the ephemerality of even the richest and most powerful human life. The Hebrew *ani*, "I," rests upon a regal carpet, while the glittering gold between the lines fit for a royal manuscript seems to ridicule the earthbound philosopher's inability to find heavenly wisdom.

95

The English pronoun "I" rests upon a clay bulla of the Judaean royal LeMeLeK ("by the King") seal. The balustrade upon which he rests is from the ruins of the Judaean palace at Ramat Raḥel,[2] hinting at the monumental palace that Qohelet inhabits.

NOTES

[1] The starry sky is based on the 2014 Hubble Space Telescope image of the Ultra Deep Field of space, showing lights in the sky stretching back to the early universe (https://apod.nasa.gov/apod/ap140605.html). In July 2022, the James Webb Space Telescope produced a new version of this image (https://apod.nasa.gov/apod/ap220713.html).

[2] Balustrade from Ramat Raḥel, late eighth–early seventh century B.C.E. See Yael Israeli et al., *Treasures of the Holy Land: Ancient Art from the Israel Museum* (New York: Metropolitan Museum of Art, 1986), 170.

INTRODUCTION TO CHAPTER TWO
DASHED DREAMS OF A LASTING ACHIEVEMENT

Chapter 1 ended with the heart-wrenching realization that because human understanding and judgment are forever historical, and hence inherently tentative, applying reason reflexively to better understand reason's constraints will never yield more than tentative conclusions. Even the wisest of humans is only humanly wise and therefore capable, at most, of better understanding, but not solving, the *hevel* predicament. Reason's intrinsic time-boundedness cannot be transcended by better human reasoning—a conclusion that renders it all the more worrying. In this regard, laments Qohelet, "much wisdom is much grief, and he that increases knowledge increases sorrow." Again, the Hebrew is far harsher: much wisdom is much anger, or frustration (*ka'as*), and he that increases knowledge increases pain (*makh'ov*).

But can one speak of lasting human accomplishment despite our inability to comprehend it? Can a wedge be somehow driven between the inevitably time-bound nature of our understanding and the actual mark we leave on reality—between our words and works, as it were? Qohelet devotes the first part of chapter 2 to the first of several discussions of the relevance of material achievement and enjoyment to the possible lasting meaning and worth of one's lifework.

However, his topic here is not hedonism. Choosing to enjoy the comforts and pleasures of carefree existence—whether out of despair of, or indifference to, grappling with Qohelet's problem—will be seriously raised and dealt with by him in chapter 9. Here, talking still as King Solomon, after realizing that even his supreme wisdom is incapable of transcending human reason's inherent transience, Qohelet turns to consider the king's equally unprecedented political achievement: the unmatched wealth that he accumulated (which was promised to him by God, together with the gift of wisdom),[1] the unprecedented building projects in Jerusalem, the kingdom's prosperous state commerce and international standing, and, of course, his highly animated and lavish court.

In chapter 8, Qohelet will consider material success—not as constituting one's life's worth but as a divine sign, in "Calvinist" spirit, that one is on the right track—and will deal with it deftly. Here in chapter 2, in the book's first consideration of the value of material gain, Qohelet considers the possibility of gauging life's worth itself, its *yitaron* (value, significance), by means of two related aspects of King Solomon's unrivaled success: the joy of achieving what one sets out to achieve; and what might be termed the "pleasure principle." It is not about indulgence, or pleasure for pleasure's sake. The depths of despair to which Qohelet is plunged when he realizes that life's worth cannot be lastingly gauged in this way clearly attests to it being a serious attempt to address the problem. And I shall read it as such.[2]

The key word is *simha*, which means "joy" or "happiness"; in Qohelet, it also connotes a sense of fulfillment or contentment. As, for instance, in 2:10: "I did not restrain my heart from any joy, for my heart *rejoiced in all my labor.*" I would therefore strongly recommend retaining such an understanding of *simha* throughout, at least when used by Qohelet to express his own position. The Jerusalem Bible follows KJV in translating *simha* in the chapter's opening verse as "mirth," which, I believe, undermines the force of Qohelet's argument. "I said in my heart come now I will try thee with mirth, therefore enjoy pleasure" (2:1) implies a very different approach from "I said in my heart, now I will try thee with *joyous fulfillment* [in] seeking to do good," or "with good in mind"—which also accords better with the Hebrew, which has no "therefore" linking the verse's two clauses. In our translation, we have substituted "joy" for "mirth."

Even if we can never comprehend God's world and will with absolute assurance, we can devote our efforts to laboring to achieve good, and when we can rejoice in our success, our life's work will be deemed worthy and meaningful.

Coupling success to the good is crucial. Rejoicing in one's success can apply equally to the righteous and the wicked. Calculated and premeditated evil can be the source of great satisfaction to its perverse perpetrator. But when geared to doing good, wickedness is left out. The problem is that from a human perspective, the good is as relative and time-bound as any other evaluative concept. No divinely sanctionable notion of value can be bestowed upon such a time-bounded thin notion as "good."[3] Qohelet, I suggest, therefore links the good to pleasure and happiness—to avoiding and countering harm, suffering, and pain, to which, he believes, a notion of worth can be attributed, in the serious sense of the term, just as it is used by moral philosophers of a utilitarian bent.

Solomon's Jerusalem, alluded to here in almost every verse, serves Qohelet as a paradigm of utilitarian morality: a royal lifework devoted to the common good as defined above, which achieved decades of lasting peace and prosperity for the kingdom unlike any other king, before or after him. This is not merely the story of an extraordinarily rich individual's success and enjoyment. It is explicitly that of a king (2:12) who had achieved more as a king than "all who were before" him in Jerusalem (2:7, 9), namely, all former kings.

Not even the decades of Israel's peaceful, blissful existence and immense prosperity that owed to Solomon's lifework, Qohelet realizes to his horror, begin to meet the demand of divinely defined lasting value. Human material and political achievement fares no better in the test of time than human understanding. Fleetingly transient, both are equally meaningless under the cruel scrutiny of absolute divine approval. From that point of view—the only point of view that counts for Qohelet, the religious philosopher, at this point—all, but "all is *hevel*" and, therefore, not more than "a striving after the wind," from which follows that "there is no profit under the sun" to speak of (2:11). The difference between the fool and the wise should be categorical. The advantage of wisdom over foolishness should be absolute. But it is not. Wisdom is as transitory as foolishness, death being the great leveler: for "as it happens to the fool, so it happens even to me; and why was I then more wise?... For of the wise man, as of the fool, there is no enduring remembrance; seeing that which now is, shall in the days to come, be entirely forgotten. And how does the wise man die? Just like the fool" (2:15–16).

Restating the *hevel* predicament from which he set forth in the religious terms of a God-given and divinely judged undertaking drives Qohelet to the utterly depressing conclusion that the transience of human life renders it irredeemably worthless in absolute divine terms. There is no limit to the depths of his despair. "Therefore I hated life … and I hated all my labor which I had labored under the sun.… Therefore I went about to cause my heart to despair of all the labor which I took under the sun."

And so it seems that even when *hevel* is read, as we propose to read it, as connoting transience rather than emptiness or nothingness, within the space of fewer than thirty verses, the two meanings are seen by Qohelet to converge in a way that would seem to eradicate the difference between the two notions of *hevel* that we have labored so hard to establish. It is certainly true that by the end of chapter 2, the transience of human life has come to be viewed by Qohelet as synonymous with emptiness and worthlessness. However, as chapter 3 will amply prove, it is an understanding that marks not the end of his discussion, as it does for most, but merely its starting point.

NOTES

[1] 1 Kgs 3:13.

[2] As we shall see in chapter 3, Qohelet alternates subtly between the first and third person. He uses the former exclusively to present the various stations of his own philosophical journey. The views, observations, and conclusions couched in the first person are always his own. He reserves the third person for two types of statement: those of his adversaries (such as the advocates of hedonism in chapter 9), which he goes on to refute; and observations and conclusions to which he believes all should agree, as in the first eleven verses of chapter 1.

[3] In philosophical parlance, thin evaluative terms such as "good," "bad," "improper," "unreasonable," "worthy," and "disgusting" carry no intrinsic meaning. They are mere shorthand—empty placeholders whose specific content is supplied without remainder for each community by means of its specific time-bound, culture-relative vocabulary of thick terms.

אָמַרְתִּי אֲנִי בְּלִבִּי לְכָה־נָּא אֲנַסְּכָה בְשִׂמְחָה וּרְאֵה בְטוֹב וְהִנֵּה גַם־הוּא הָבֶל: ^ב לִשְׂחוֹק אָמַרְתִּי מְהוֹלָל וּלְשִׂמְחָה מַה־זֹּה עֹשָׂה: ^ג תַּרְתִּי בְלִבִּי לִמְשׁוֹךְ בַּיַּיִן אֶת־בְּשָׂרִי וְלִבִּי נֹהֵג בַּחָכְמָה וְלֶאֱחֹז בְּסִכְלוּת עַד אֲשֶׁר־אֶרְאֶה אֵי־זֶה טוֹב לִבְנֵי הָאָדָם אֲשֶׁר יַעֲשׂוּ תַּחַת הַשָּׁמַיִם מִסְפַּר יְמֵי חַיֵּיהֶם:

[1]I said in my heart, Come now, l will try thee with mirth, therefore enjoy pleasure: and, behold, this also was vapour. [2]I said of laughter, it is mad: and of mirth, What does it achieve? [3]I sought in my heart to stimulate my body with wine (yet guiding my heart with wisdom) and to lay hold on folly: till it might see what was good for the sons of men, which they should do under the heaven all the days of their life.

ohelet begins to test various approaches to discovering wisdom. Each effort only strengthens his awareness of the evanescence of human life and accomplishments. The Hebrew illumination presents the grand portal of a palace rich with the mosaics and carving, commissioned by the ruler—yet it crumbles at its base. A graceful sapling offers its fruit, although both Qohelet and the viewer know that its fresh leaves will one day drop and that its lovely branches will one day dry and crack. On the English illumination, a wine set contemporary with Qohelet[1] blends wine with water, not only diluting the strong wine to a potable drink but perhaps reflecting the dilution of Qohelet's joy in his luxury. The midrash on this verse recounts numerous tales of celebrations ending in tragedy and relates the word *mehollal*, "mad," to the word *mahul*, "mixed," suggesting that "such laughter is inevitably mixed with sadness, for in the end it leads to mourning."[2]

The borders of the paintings offer other poets' comparisons of life to a fleeting dream. The Hebrew painting includes verses from the pen of the eleventh-century Spanish Jewish poet and grand vizier of Granada, Samuel the Nagid, warning that only God knows the mysteries of humanity's dream-like existence

My friend, we pass our lives as if in sleep;
    Our pleasures and our pains are merely dreams.
But stop your ears to all such things, and shut

> Your eyes—may Heaven grant you strength!—
> Don't speculate on hidden things; leave that
> To God, the Hidden One, whose eye sees all.[3]

In the English illumination, Shakespeare reflects upon the mysterious insubstantiality of life in *Hamlet* and *The Tempest*:[4]

> Which dreams indeed are ambition;
> for the very substance of the ambitious is merely the shadow of a dream.
> (Guildenstern, *Hamlet* 2.1)

> We are such stuff as dreams are made on, and our little life is rounded with a sleep.
> (Prospero, *The Tempest* 4.1)

NOTES

[1] Wine set found in Tel el-Farah, fifth–fourth century B.C.E. Michal Dayagi-Mendels and Silvia Rozenberg, eds., *Chronicles of the Land: Archaeology in the Israel Museum Jerusalem*, 2d ed. (Jerusalem: Israel Museum, 2011), 93.

[2] Danziger et al., eds., *The Midrash*, 2:1².

[3] Raymond P. Scheindlin, *Wine, Women, and Death: Medieval Poems on the Good Life* (Philadelphia: Jewish Publication Society, 1986), 54–55.

[4] A. L. Rowse, *The Annotated Shakespeare*, vol. 3: *The Tragedies and Romances* (New York: Clarkson N. Potter, 1978), 897.

דְּ הִגְדַּלְתִּי מַעֲשָׂי בָּנִיתִי לִי בָתִּים נָטַעְתִּי לִי כְּרָמִים׃
הֵ עָשִׂיתִי לִי גַּנּוֹת וּפַרְדֵּסִים וְנָטַעְתִּי בָהֶם עֵץ כָּל־
פֶּרִי׃ וֹ עָשִׂיתִי לִי בְּרֵכוֹת מָיִם לְהַשְׁקוֹת מֵהֶם יַעַר
צוֹמֵחַ עֵצִים׃

[4]I made great works for myself; I built houses; I planted vineyards: [5]I made gardens and orchards, and I planted trees in them of all kind of fruits; [6]I made pools of water, from which to water a forest of growing trees.

Qohelet meditates on the sensual joy and fulfillment that he sought by building and immersing himself in luxury.

The paintings present a meditation on the problem of attempting to find lasting meaning in life by immersing oneself in luxury. Qohelet's sensual pleasure and pride in his material achievement are clouded by his awareness that it evaporates, its beauties all the more poignant for their transience.

In the Hebrew illumination, Qohelet gazes upon the orderly orchards that display his power and his search for pleasure, irrigated by waterways and fountains modeled after the Alhambra and other Andalusian palaces, which he has constructed within his palace walls. Water not only enables life, such as his rich orchard, but this teacher of wisdom would already, by late biblical times, associate water within this arid land with the wisdom of Torah. The gazebo at right suggests the House of the Forest of Lebanon. Built of the fragrant wood that he imported from Lebanon—presumably, cedar and cypress trees, according to 1 Kgs 10:17—Jewish tradition suggests that Solomon used this structure to display his golden treasures.[1]

In the border, cherry branches—emblematic of the seat of American power in Washington, D.C., where these illuminations were painted—go through their annual cycle of bud, blossom, fruit, yellowing autumn foliage, and bare winter buds, bearing the buds promising the next season of growth, reminding him of the passing of generations. Despite Qohelet's pride in all the beauty that he has amassed, the drifting fog reminds him of the ephemerality of all his wealth here under the sun.

The English illumination shows the wealthy man contemplating the vine-covered hills, rising and falling away into the distance beyond the walls of his hilltop palace. The sensual pleasure of the ripe warm cluster resting in his hand, the anticipation of the wines to be pressed from his grapes, the taste of the wine in the fine cup,[2] and the sight of his vineyards stretching into the distance indulge his senses of pleasure and power; yet Qohelet cannot forget that all his works will drift away like vapor.

NOTES

[1] Danziger et al., eds., *The Midrash*, 3².

[2] The wine cup is modeled after the glass vessels from the workshop of Ennion, a well-known first-century C.E. glassworker near Sidon, many of whose molded glass cups and jugs have been found in Israel. See Yael Israeli, *Made by Ennion: Ancient Glass Treasures from the Shlomo Moussaieff Collection* (Jerusalem: Israel Museum, 2011), 72.

ז קָנִיתִי עֲבָדִים וּשְׁפָחוֹת וּבְנֵי-בַיִת הָיָה לִי גַּם מִקְנֶה בָקָר וָצֹאן הַרְבֵּה הָיָה לִי מִכֹּל שֶׁהָיוּ לְפָנַי בִּירוּשָׁלָ͏ִם: ח כָּנַסְתִּי לִי גַּם-כֶּסֶף וְזָהָב וּסְגֻלַּת מְלָכִים וְהַמְּדִינוֹת עָשִׂיתִי לִי שָׁרִים וְשָׁרוֹת וְתַעֲנוּגֹת בְּנֵי הָאָדָם שִׁדָּה וְשִׁדּוֹת: ט וְגָדַלְתִּי וְהוֹסַפְתִּי מִכֹּל שֶׁהָיָה לְפָנַי בִּירוּשָׁלָ͏ִם אַף חָכְמָתִי עָמְדָה לִּי: י וְכֹל אֲשֶׁר שָׁאֲלוּ עֵינַי לֹא אָצַלְתִּי מֵהֶם לֹא-מָנַעְתִּי אֶת-לִבִּי מִכָּל-שִׂמְחָה כִּי-לִבִּי שָׂמֵחַ מִכָּל-עֲמָלִי וְזֶה-הָיָה חֶלְקִי מִכָּל-עֲמָלִי: יא וּפָנִיתִי אֲנִי בְּכָל-מַעֲשַׂי שֶׁעָשׂוּ יָדַי וּבֶעָמָל שֶׁעָמַלְתִּי לַעֲשׂוֹת וְהִנֵּה הַכֹּל הֶבֶל וּרְעוּת רוּחַ וְאֵין יִתְרוֹן תַּחַת הַשָּׁמֶשׁ: יב וּפָנִיתִי אֲנִי לִרְאוֹת חָכְמָה וְהוֹלֵלוֹת וְסִכְלוּת כִּי | מֶה הָאָדָם שֶׁיָּבוֹא אַחֲרֵי הַמֶּלֶךְ אֵת אֲשֶׁר-כְּבָר עָשׂוּהוּ: יג וְרָאִיתִי אָנִי שֶׁיֵּשׁ יִתְרוֹן לַחָכְמָה מִן-הַסִּכְלוּת כִּיתְרוֹן הָאוֹר מִן-הַחֹשֶׁךְ: יד הֶחָכָם עֵינָיו בְּרֹאשׁוֹ וְהַכְּסִיל בַּחֹשֶׁךְ הוֹלֵךְ וְיָדַעְתִּי גַם-אָנִי שֶׁמִּקְרֶה אֶחָד יִקְרֶה אֶת-כֻּלָּם: טו וְאָמַרְתִּי אֲנִי בְּלִבִּי כְּמִקְרֵה הַכְּסִיל גַּם-אֲנִי יִקְרֵנִי וְלָמָּה חָכַמְתִּי אֲנִי אָז יֹתֵר וְדִבַּרְתִּי בְלִבִּי שֶׁגַּם-זֶה הָבֶל: טז כִּי אֵין זִכְרוֹן לֶחָכָם עִם-הַכְּסִיל לְעוֹלָם בְּשֶׁכְּבָר הַיָּמִים הַבָּאִים הַכֹּל נִשְׁכָּח וְאֵיךְ יָמוּת הֶחָכָם עִם-הַכְּסִיל: יז וְשָׂנֵאתִי אֶת-הַחַיִּים כִּי רַע עָלַי הַמַּעֲשֶׂה שֶׁנַּעֲשָׂה תַּחַת הַשָּׁמֶשׁ כִּי-הַכֹּל הֶבֶל וּרְעוּת רוּחַ: יח וְשָׂנֵאתִי אֲנִי אֶת-כָּל-עֲמָלִי שֶׁאֲנִי עָמֵל תַּחַת הַשָּׁמֶשׁ שֶׁאַנִּיחֶנּוּ לָאָדָם שֶׁיִּהְיֶה אַחֲרָי: יט וּמִי יוֹדֵעַ הֶחָכָם יִהְיֶה אוֹ סָכָל וְיִשְׁלַט בְּכָל-עֲמָלִי שֶׁעָמַלְתִּי וְשֶׁחָכַמְתִּי תַּחַת הַשָּׁמֶשׁ גַּם-זֶה הָבֶל:

[7]I acquired male and female servants, and had servants born in my house; also I had great possessions of herds and flocks, more than all who were in Yerushalayim before me: [8]I gathered also silver and gold, and the treasure of kings and of the provinces; I acquired men singers and women singers, and the delights of the sons of men, women very many. [9]So I was great, and increased more than all that were before me in Yerushalayim: also my wisdom remained with me, [10]And whatever my eyes desired I did not withhold from them; I did not restrain my heart from any joy; for my heart rejoiced in all my labour: and this was my portion of all my labour. [11]Then I looked at all the works that my hand had wrought, and at the labour that I had laboured to do: and behold, all was vapour and a striving after wind, and there was no profit under the sun. [12]And I turned myself to behold wisdom, and madness, and folly: for what can the man do who comes after the king? Even that which has been already done. [13]Then I saw that wisdom excels folly, as far as light excels darkness. [14]The wise man's eyes are in his head; but the fool walks in darkness: and I myself perceived also that one event happens to them all. [15]Then I said in my heart, As it happens to the fool, so it happens even to me; and why was I then more wise? Then I said in my heart, that this also is vapour. [16]For of the wise man as of the fool, there is no enduring remembrance; seeing that which now is, shall, in the days to come, be entirely forgotten. And how does the wise man die? Just like the fool. [17]Therefore I hated life; because the work that is done under the sun was grievous to me: for all is vapour and a striving after wind. [18]And I hated all my labour in which I had laboured under the sun: because I must leave it to the man who shall come after me. [19]And who knows whether he will be a wise man or a fool? Yet shall he have rule over all my labour in which I have laboured, and in which I have shown myself wise under the sun. This also is vapour.

ohelet plunges into despair and anger as he realizes that none of his power, none of his accomplishments and luxuries—not even their memory—will long outlast his finite life under the sun. How, then, should he live? Vanished is the lush flow of color and form of his vineyard and orchard views. The unbalanced and disoriented, bleached calligraphy tinged only with burning red reflects his hopeless fury. Even the golden chains and string of antique carnelian lotus-seed beads[1] that he might have given a lover lie broken across his words.

The number of potential pleasures that Qohelet has tested expresses the philosopher's despair—seven: houses, vineyards, gardens, parks, servants of both genders, precious gold and silver, and pleasure servants such as musicians and concubines. Ellen Davis observes that the number seven calls to mind the seven days of Creation, during which God summoned order from chaos.[2]

NOTES

[1] The beads are modeled on a string of twelfth-century B.C.E. carnelian lotus-seed beads found in Beth She'an. See Israeli et al., *Treasures of the Holy Land*, 133. The beads would have already been antique, and perhaps all the more prized, by the time Qohelet might have acquired them. In ancient Egypt, still an important cultural influence in Israel in Qohelet's day, the lotus was a symbol of rebirth.

[2] Davis, *Proverbs, Ecclesiastes, and the Song of Songs*, 178.

כ וְסַבּוֹתִי אֲנִי לְיַאֵשׁ אֶת־לִבִּי עַל כָּל־הֶעָמָל שֶׁעָמַלְתִּי תַּחַת הַשָּׁמֶשׁ: כא כִּי־יֵשׁ אָדָם שֶׁעֲמָלוֹ בְּחָכְמָה וּבְדַעַת וּבְכִשְׁרוֹן וּלְאָדָם שֶׁלֹּא עָמַל־בּוֹ יִתְּנֶנּוּ חֶלְקוֹ גַּם־זֶה הֶבֶל וְרָעָה רַבָּה: כב כִּי מֶה־הֹוֶה לָאָדָם בְּכָל־עֲמָלוֹ וּבְרַעְיוֹן לִבּוֹ שֶׁהוּא עָמֵל תַּחַת הַשָּׁמֶשׁ: כג כִּי כָל־יָמָיו מַכְאֹבִים וָכַעַס עִנְיָנוֹ גַּם־בַּלַּיְלָה לֹא־שָׁכַב לִבּוֹ גַּם־זֶה הֶבֶל הוּא: כד אֵין־טוֹב בָּאָדָם שֶׁיֹּאכַל וְשָׁתָה וְהֶרְאָה אֶת־נַפְשׁוֹ טוֹב בַּעֲמָלוֹ גַּם־זֹה רָאִיתִי אָנִי כִּי מִיַּד הָאֱלֹהִים הִיא: כה כִּי מִי יֹאכַל וּמִי יָחוּשׁ חוּץ מִמֶּנִּי: כו כִּי לְאָדָם שֶׁטּוֹב לְפָנָיו נָתַן חָכְמָה וְדַעַת וְשִׂמְחָה וְלַחוֹטֶא נָתַן עִנְיָן לֶאֱסוֹף וְלִכְנוֹס לָתֵת לְטוֹב לִפְנֵי הָאֱלֹהִים גַּם־זֶה הֶבֶל וּרְעוּת רוּחַ:

[20]Therefore I went about to cause my heart to despair of all the labour which I took under the sun. [21]For there is a man whose labour is with wisdom, and with knowledge, and with skill; yet he must leave it for a portion to a man who has not laboured in it. This also is a vapor and a great evil. [22]For what has a man of all his labour, and of the striving of his heart, in which he labours under the sun? [23]For all his days are pains, and his work is a vexation; even in the night his heart takes no rest. This also is vapour. [24]There is nothing better for a man, than that he should eat and drink, and that he should make his soul enjoy good in his labour; but this also I saw, that it was from the hand of God. [25]For who can eat, or who can enjoy pleasure, more than I? [26]Surely he gives to a man that is good in his sight, wisdom, and knowledge, and joy: but to the sinner he gives the task of gathering and heaping up, that he may give it to one who is good before God. This also is vapour and a striving after wind.

ohelet's rage dulls to a dark malaise as he contemplates the evident arbitrariness of divine reward for human effort. He sees the incipient decay of his architectural masterpiece, he watches his fragrant leaves and blossoms fall and shrivel, knowing that his own life will do the same. After a lifetime devoted to striving for divine wisdom and building worldly beauty, he is pained at the inscrutable fate that would enable a worthless man to inherit all that he has struggled to build. The micrographic borders, using a pattern from a tenth-century Tanakh in the British Library, incorporate the text of the Unetana Tokef prayer from the High Holiday liturgy. According to legend,[1] this moving poem was composed by Rabbi Amnon of Mainz in 1020 as he lay dying from torture inflicted by an archbishop infuriated by his refusal to convert to

Christianity. The prayer stresses—as has Qohelet—the inability of humanity to discern, much less control, human fate, and our ultimate vulnerability to divine judgment.

> Let us now relate the power of this day's holiness, for it is awesome and frightening, On it Your Kingship will be exalted; Your throne will be firmed with kindness and You will sit upon it in truth. It is true that You alone are the One Who judges, proves, knows, and bears witness; Who writes and seals, counts and calculates; Who remembers all that was forgotten. You will open the Book of Chronicles—it will read itself, and everyone's signature is in it. The great shofar will be sounded and a still, thin sound will be heard. Angels will hasten, a trembling and terror will seize then—and they will say, "Behold, it is the Day of Judgment, to muster the heavenly host for judgment!"—for they cannot be vindicated in Your eyes in judgment. All mankind will pass before You like members of the flock. Like a shepherd pasturing his flock, making sheep pass under his staff, so shall You cause to pass, count, calculate, and consider the soul of all the living; and You shall apportion the fixed needs of all Your creatures and inscribe their verdict.

> On Rosh Hashanah will be inscribed and on Yom Kippur will be sealed how many will pass from the earth and how many will be created; who will live and who will die, who will die at his predestined time and who before his time; who by water and who by fire, who by sword, who by beast, who by famine, who by thirst, who by storm, who by plague, who by strangulation, and who by stoning. Who will rest and who will wander, who will live in harmony and who will be harried, who will enjoy tranquility and who will suffer, who will be impoverished and who will be enriched, who will be degraded and who will be exalted.[2]

Whereas the prayer promises that "repentance, prayer, and charity remove the evil of the decree," Qohelet expresses no confidence in visible forgiveness or reward. It is noteworthy that the targum, rabbinic commentaries, and midrash on Qohelet read and interpolate divine justice *into* the biblical text, suggesting that while God's reward may not be visible in the course of human life, a life devoted to obeying divine law will meet with reward in the World to Come.

NOTES

[1] See https://www.geni.com/people/Rabbi-Amnon-ben-Gershom/6000000025428895408 for the details and sources for this legend. Translation of Unetana Tokef from Nosson Scherman et al., eds. and trans., *The Complete Artscroll Machzor: Yom Kippur* (New York: Mesorah, 1986), 531.

[2] Scherman, *The Complete Artscroll*, 533.

Introduction to Chapter Three
Qohelet's Great Turning Point

As I noted in my general introduction, it is hard to imagine a sharper contrast than that between the depths of morbid despair and loathing of life reached by Qohelet at the end of chapter 2, and the burst of buoyant optimism of the "Song of Seasons" with which he opens chapter 3. The change of mood and rhythm is dramatic, as are some highly suggestive turns of phrase. In realizing that "for everything there is a season and a time for every demand under heaven" (3:1), Qohelet clearly appears to have reached a profoundly new understanding that allows him to reembrace life and revisit almost verbatim the heart-gripping quandary from which he set forth in 1:12–13, yet without any trace of the bitterness and frustration he expressed there. He has come to understand the task that God has given us to contend with, he declares, but he no longer describes it as a painful or evil task, no longer deeming it an *inyan ra* (3:9–10).

But what is the nature of his new understanding? What has Qohelet suddenly realized that could make such a difference? And why only now? What could have prevented him from realizing it from the start?

To understand the new insight that sets chapter 3 in motion, as well as its late arrival on the scene, we need to look more closely at Qohelet's theology. As we have seen, the marked transition in 1:12 from third to first person signals what might be termed the religious turn in Qohelet's discourse, the transition from framing the question of the possible worth of human knowledge and achievement in detached philosophical terms, to profoundly engaged religious terms—from discerning its possible value per se to deliberating its possible value in the eyes of God. Qohelet's God is not an abstract idea. He is the perfect creator and perfect judge,[1] but his ways are unknowable.[2] He is, in this sense, remote and transcendent. But at the same time, he is immanently present in each of our lives, holding us meticulously accountable[3] for meeting his demands and living up to his expectations.[4] Yet even after the religious turn in his argument, Qohelet's reasoning remains wholly philosophical. From 1:12 onward, the master idea of God's intervening ever-presence in all human life joins Qohelet's other two master ideas—that of life's *hevel*, its time-bound impermanence; and that of life's *yitaron*, its possible worth and value—as the third taken-for-granted premise or axiom of his fervent deliberations. Qohelet's added "God axiom," if I be permitted the term, lends the other two an anxious urgency, but it is drained of all religious emotion. In Qohelet, divine transcendence adds a major epistemological dimension to the *hevel* premise but nothing of the *mysterium tremendum* or *fascinans* that Rudolf Otto famously associates with religiously experiencing "the numinous."[5] The same goes for divine immanence, which, in Qohelet, lends intense urgency to arriving at a viable notion of *yitaron* but comes accompanied by nothing of the love, grace, mercy, warm sense of security, or intimacy of prayer that we normally associate with divine closeness. Qohelet's God axiom lends his original philosophical quandary alarm, urgency, and profound religious relevance to all believers in the kind of God it portrays. Yet the God axiom, as well as the religious turn that it generates in Qohelet's thinking, has little to do with religiosity proper. Qohelet's undertaking is about how best to shoulder our "horizontal" responsibilities to the world that we inhabit and the society to which we belong. It remains unconcerned with our "vertical" religious obligations to God, such as worship, prayer, ritual purity, and sacrifice—not because he denies them or deems them unimportant but because he believes that they beg the more general epistemological question of our perpetually uncertain knowledge and the normative problem of deeming its application meaningful and worthy, which must therefore be dealt with first. More on this in a moment.

The only religious emotion triggered in Qohelet by the God axiom is fear.[6] But fear, too, is associated far more with the problem that he deems most basic, an anxious awareness of the *hevel* premise and of the need for *yitaron*, than with anything resembling the awe, dread, or submissive compliance normally associated with fear of God. Qohelet's theology is impassioned yet universal. It speaks, as we shall see, of chosenness (3:18), but universally, as applying not to a chosen people but to all humankind. Nor is it religion-specific; it is addressed to all forms of God-conscious religiosity. If Qohelet initially presented his problem in terms of the unbreachable gulf between what the world in reality is and how we portray it, adding the God axiom to the mix lends it a cruel normative twist. It is no longer a question of making a meaningful difference in a world that we can never claim to fully understand but of being held punctiliously accountable by a perfect judge whose transcendent standards we can never know. Qohelet thus emerges as what might be termed a "pre-revelatory" work of religious philosophy. It nowhere denies or dismisses divine revelation, as R. B. Y. Scott could be taken to imply. God's divine Word is irrelevant to Qohelet's discourse because the problem he raises has to be addressed before any attempt to make sense of it. In this sense, by adding the God axiom to the mix, the initial perplexing tension between Qohelet's *hevel* premise and the *yitaron* prerequisite is elevated to a contradiction of terms and aggravated to the point of devastation, so powerfully expressed toward the end of chapter 2.

What Qohelet realizes with a jolt at the opening of chapter 3 is that the God axiom harbors a contradiction in terms, bordering on the oxymoronic. God stands above time, and his ways and divine norms are indeed unknowable, but to hold humankind accountable to standards that they are incapable of knowing would constitute a violation of God's perfect justice. Because God cannot but be aware of the inherent time-boundedness of his creatures, it is unthinkable that he will hold them to his absolute standards.

The biblical term *ḥefets* means "will" or "desire";[7] in Qohelet, it is consistently applied to God's will.[8] I therefore read the opening verse thus: *Because* there is a season for everything under the heaven, *therefore*, there is [also] a time for every [divine] demand and purpose. God will measure and judge us not by his own perfect timeless standards, of which we can never be aware, but by the quality of our local and *tentative* decisions. Because we are inherently time-bound, so will be the standards to which God will hold us accountable. We cannot, and therefore shall not be expected to, form absolute universal criteria regarding planting, building, war, or peace, nor shall we be expected to recognize and endorse such criteria. What is expected of us is to make good temporary, time-bound rulings as to whether the changing times merit, for example, planting or uprooting, killing or healing, mourning or rejoicing, seeking or losing, waging war or making peace (2–8).

It is in such time-bound terms that the worth of human endeavor, the *yitaron* prerequisite, needs to be contended with locally (9). Qohelet now understands, with a great sigh of relief, the task that we face. It is no longer devastating (10). God has created everything beautifully set in time and "has also set the mystery of the world in their heart," but in a way that no man can comprehensively comprehend his work "from the beginning to the end" (11). We can, and should be content in doing the best we can (12), knowing that God will not hold us accountable to standards of which we can never be aware (14).[9]

Only by seriously contemplating—and allowing his readers to seriously contemplate—the full distressing force of the alternative could Qohelet have convincingly reached this radical conclusion, which jars with all accepted forms of revelatory God-fearing religiosity. For Qohelet, the idea that as recipients of divine revelation, we become privy to absolute, timeless God-given normative truths, is absurd (although he nowhere says so in those words). His *hevel* premise asserts that our knowledge and judgment are forever temporary and fallible, not because we happen to lack reliable sources of information but because our very language and understanding, the concepts and norms with which we form and evaluate our thoughts and conclusions, are irredeemably time-bound and transient. As much as God's revealed Word may be as timeless and absolute as the laws of his Creation, being the time-bound creatures that we are, we are incapable of understanding them as such—which is another way of explaining why, for Qohelet, the problem of *yitaron* in conditions of human *hevel* has to come before all questions of religiosity. The rabbinic literature of late antiquity is the only large-scale religious undertaking of which I am aware that was self-consciously composed along such lines.

Returning to Qohelet: under his new understanding of divine judgment, the problem of leading a worthy life has morphed into that of making good tentative normative choices. Alluding back to our inability to fully grasp nature's timeless laws (11) allows modern readers to better grasp Qohelet's change of heart (and why virtually all his interpreters miss it). The very idea of scientifically proved truth, we now realize, is a conceit. No general statement about the world can be proved. Scientists form hypotheses, test them as best they can, and replace them when they are refuted or otherwise found wanting. Science, at its best, remains inherently tentative and fallible. Yet no one would deem science to be therefore meaningless or worthless. Well-formed tentative hypotheses about the world can be as highly meaningful as they are of priceless practical utility, as long as we continue to suspect that they are probably wrong and to continue testing them to the best of our ability. Qohelet will extend this insight to all serious human judgment: scientific, political, moral, and religious—forever tentative, yet nonetheless meaningful.

However, the scientific analogy can be misleading. Because much can be learned from mistakes and little from justifications, Karl Popper, the modern father of scientific fallibilism,[10] encourages scientists to hypothesize boldly and refute their conjectures in quick succession to enhance the learning process. But with regard to social experimentation, he proposed the opposite—hesitant piecemeal social engineering, as he termed it—in order to minimize the risks of unintended and unforeseen human suffering.[11] Qohelet's main concern has less to do with science and technology than with social and political action. Because we are irredeemably fallible and certain to make mistakes, attempts to do justice will produce an inevitable measure of unintended suffering and injustice (that God, the perfect judge, will surely mend) (16–17).

Qohelet's concern here with the unavoidable suffering and injustice that fallible human social action is apt to produce is different from, and more basic than, Popper's. It has to do not with how best to minimize it—which, for Qohelet, goes without saying—but how to counter the pious renouncement of responsibility for the world by God-fearing individuals who, for fear of doing wrong, prefer to do nothing. We can count on God to perfectly mend all wrongs, they claim (15). Qohelet understands, yet forcefully condemns, those tempted to meet the *hevel* premise by remaining piously passive, refusing to exercise their judgment and act, preferring to keep their hands clean and leave things to God. Their attitude represents the first of two categories of foolishness that he will combat repeatedly in chapters to come. To adopt such a position, he rages here, is to deny humankind's very divine chosenness. To choose to remain piously inactive and indifferent to the world because we are fallible is to live no better than a beast (18–19). We are not only required to assume responsibility and do our knowingly imperfect best, but to rejoice in doing so (22).

[1] Qohelet does not formulate a theology of perfection and does not employ the term. However, he clearly premises ideas of divine omniscience and all-goodness but, again, without using the terms. See, e.g., 3:14–5; 5:1; 8:12–13.

[2] Regarding the laws of nature, see, esp., 3:12; with respect to his perfect norms of judgment, see 5:7 and, esp., 8:12–13.

[3] E.g., 3:17; 5:5; 8:6; 11:9; 12:14.

[4] See 1:12–13; 3:9; 12:13. As I shall argue below, I take this verse not to be part of a later apologetic add-on but an integral component of Qohelet's summarizing argument.

[5] Rudolf Otto, *The Idea of the Holy: An Inquiry into the Non-Rational Factor in the Idea of the Divine and Its Relation to the Rational*, trans. J. W. Harvey (Oxford: Oxford University Press, 1958).

[6] See 3:14; 5:6; 7:18; 8:12–13; 9:2; 12:13.

[7] Both as verb (e.g., Isa 58:13; Ezek 18:23) or noun (e.g., 1 Kgs 10:13; Jer 22:28).

[8] See 3:17; 5:3, 7; 8:6.

[9] For a diametrically opposed reading of the "Song of Seasons" as a parody of proverbial poems, rather than as a major turning point in Qohelet's argument, see Simeon Chavel's ingenious "The Utility and Futility of Poetry in Qohelet," in *Biblical Poetry and the Art of Close Reading*, ed. J. B. Couey and E. T. James (Cambridge: Cambridge University Press, 2018), 93–110. Reading *hevel* as futile absurdity, and, therefore, the question of the value of human toil, as rhetorical (109), leaves him with no choice but to read the song as continuing and concluding, rather than awakening from the nightmarish "line of thought" of 2:18-26.

[10] See, e.g., Karl R. Popper, *Conjectures and Refutations: The Growth of Scientific Knowledge* (New York: Harper & Row, 1963).

[11] Karl R. Popper, *The Poverty of Historicism* (New York: Harper & Row, 1957), esp. chap. 3.

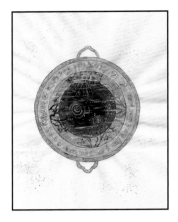

אלַכֹּל זְמָן וְעֵת לְכָל־חֵפֶץ תַּחַת הַשָּׁמָיִם:

[1]To everything there is a season, and a time to every demand under heaven.

ohelet arrives at the turning point in his struggle to perceive the individual's ability—indeed, responsibility—to find wisdom, to lead a meaningful life in the face of the transience of human achievement. He realizes that every human moment has its place in cosmic time, whether or not the individual can perceive that place. He meditates on a garden pond, in his imagination the golden bowl to which he will compare human life (12:6). The still water, disturbed only by fleeting ripples, reflects the distant heavens and trees reflecting every season.

עֵת לָלֶדֶת וְעֵת לָמוּת עֵת לָטַעַת וְעֵת לַעֲקוֹר נָטוּעַ: ‏ב

עֵת לַהֲרוֹג וְעֵת לִרְפּוֹא עֵת לִפְרוֹץ וְעֵת לִבְנוֹת: ‏ג

עֵת לִבְכּוֹת וְעֵת לִשְׂחוֹק עֵת סְפוֹד וְעֵת רְקוֹד: ‏ד

עֵת לְהַשְׁלִיךְ אֲבָנִים וְעֵת כְּנוֹס אֲבָנִים עֵת לַחֲבוֹק וְעֵת לִרְחֹק מֵחַבֵּק: ‏ה

עֵת לְבַקֵּשׁ וְעֵת לְאַבֵּד עֵת לִשְׁמוֹר וְעֵת לְהַשְׁלִיךְ: ‏ו

עֵת לִקְרוֹעַ וְעֵת לִתְפּוֹר עֵת לַחֲשׁוֹת וְעֵת לְדַבֵּר: עֵת לֶאֱהֹב וְעֵת לִשְׂנֹא עֵת מִלְחָמָה וְעֵת שָׁלוֹם: ‏ז ‏ח

²A time to be born, and a time to die;
   a time to plant, and a time to pluck up that
      which is planted.
³A time to kill, and a time to heal;
   a time to break down, and a time to build up.
⁴A time to weep, and a time to laugh;
   a time to mourn, and a time to dance.
⁵A time to cast away stones, and a time to gather
      stones together;
   a time to embrace, and time to refrain from
      embracing.
⁶A time to seek, and a time to lose;
   a time to keep, and a time to cast away.
⁷A time to rend, and a time to sew;
   a time to keep silence, and a time to speak.
⁸A time to love, and a time to hate;
   a time of war, and a time of peace.

Qohelet meditates further on how every aspect and moment of life has its converse moment; the destined time for each is unknowable to any but God, the master of all existence. Gazing at his garden, he perceives life as a river, its origin unknowable, its endpoint obscure, each mirage-like moment subject to fluctuations and eddies that he cannot anticipate. The wall through which the stream emerges is capped by a mosaic bearing a fragment of the musical notation of Pete Seeger's famous 1965 setting of the poem "Turn, Turn, Turn."

ט מַה־יִּתְרוֹן הָעוֹשֶׂה בַּאֲשֶׁר הוּא עָמֵל: י רָאִיתִי אֶת־הָעִנְיָן אֲשֶׁר נָתַן אֱלֹהִים לִבְנֵי הָאָדָם לַעֲנוֹת בּוֹ: יא אֶת־הַכֹּל עָשָׂה יָפֶה בְעִתּוֹ גַּם אֶת־הָעֹלָם נָתַן בְּלִבָּם מִבְּלִי אֲשֶׁר לֹא־יִמְצָא הָאָדָם אֶת־הַמַּעֲשֶׂה אֲשֶׁר־עָשָׂה הָאֱלֹהִים מֵרֹאשׁ וְעַד־סוֹף: יב יָדַעְתִּי כִּי אֵין טוֹב בָּם כִּי אִם־לִשְׂמוֹחַ וְלַעֲשׂוֹת טוֹב בְּחַיָּיו: יג וְגַם כָּל־הָאָדָם שֶׁיֹּאכַל וְשָׁתָה וְרָאָה טוֹב בְּכָל־עֲמָלוֹ מַתַּת אֱלֹהִים הִיא: יד יָדַעְתִּי כִּי כָּל־אֲשֶׁר יַעֲשֶׂה הָאֱלֹהִים הוּא יִהְיֶה לְעוֹלָם עָלָיו אֵין לְהוֹסִיף וּמִמֶּנּוּ אֵין לִגְרֹעַ וְהָאֱלֹהִים עָשָׂה שֶׁיִּרְאוּ מִלְּפָנָיו: טו מַה־שֶׁהָיָה כְּבָר הוּא וַאֲשֶׁר לִהְיוֹת כְּבָר הָיָה וְהָאֱלֹהִים יְבַקֵּשׁ אֶת־נִרְדָּף:

[9]What profit has the worker from his toil? [10]I have seen the task, which God has given to the sons of men to be exercised in it. [11]He has made everything beautiful in his time: also he has set the mystery of the world in their heart, so that no man can find out the work which God has made from the beginning to the end. [12]I know that there is nothing better for them than to rejoice, and to do good in his life: [13]also that it is the gift of God that every man should eat and drink, and enjoy the good of all his labour. [14]I know that, whatever God does, it shall be forever: nothing can be added to it, nor anything taken from it; and God does it, so that men should fear before him. [15]That which is, already has been; and that which is to be has already been; and only God can find the fleeting moment.

Qohelet meditates on the inexorable passage of time and life. He considers how the individual should use his or her unpredictable lifetime in the light of the mystery of divine intent.

The sun crosses the sky tracking the course of the day, and the moon's phases track the course of the month, against the deep sky. A maple branch floats along a garden stream; its leaves transform with age from fresh green to gold to dry brown. Ripe grapes, fallen before their time, bob and sink below the water's surface.

טז וְעוֹד רָאִיתִי תַּחַת הַשֶּׁמֶשׁ מְקוֹם הַמִּשְׁפָּט שָׁמָּה הָרֶשַׁע וּמְקוֹם הַצֶּדֶק שָׁמָּה הָרָשַׁע: יז אָמַרְתִּי אֲנִי בְּלִבִּי אֶת־הַצַּדִּיק וְאֶת־הָרָשָׁע יִשְׁפֹּט הָאֱלֹהִים כִּי־עֵת לְכָל־חֵפֶץ וְעַל כָּל־הַמַּעֲשֶׂה שָׁם: יח אָמַרְתִּי אֲנִי בְּלִבִּי עַל־דִּבְרַת בְּנֵי הָאָדָם לְבָרָם הָאֱלֹהִים וְלִרְאוֹת שְׁהֶם־בְּהֵמָה הֵמָּה לָהֶם: יט כִּי מִקְרֶה בְנֵי־הָאָדָם וּמִקְרֶה הַבְּהֵמָה וּמִקְרֶה אֶחָד לָהֶם כְּמוֹת זֶה כֵּן מוֹת זֶה וְרוּחַ אֶחָד לַכֹּל וּמוֹתַר הָאָדָם מִן־הַבְּהֵמָה אָיִן כִּי הַכֹּל הָבֶל: כ הַכֹּל הוֹלֵךְ אֶל־מָקוֹם אֶחָד הַכֹּל הָיָה מִן־הֶעָפָר וְהַכֹּל שָׁב אֶל־הֶעָפָר: כא מִי יוֹדֵעַ רוּחַ בְּנֵי הָאָדָם הָעֹלָה הִיא לְמָעְלָה וְרוּחַ הַבְּהֵמָה הַיֹּרֶדֶת הִיא לְמַטָּה לָאָרֶץ: כב וְרָאִיתִי כִּי אֵין טוֹב מֵאֲשֶׁר יִשְׂמַח הָאָדָם בְּמַעֲשָׂיו כִּי־הוּא חֶלְקוֹ כִּי מִי יְבִיאֶנּוּ לִרְאוֹת בְּמֶה שֶׁיִּהְיֶה אַחֲרָיו:

16And moreover I saw under the sun in the place of judgment, that wickedness was there; and in the place of righteousness, that iniquity was there. 17I said in my heart, God shall judge the righteous and the wicked; for there is a time there for every purpose and for every work. 18I said in my heart, after the speech of the sons of men, that God has chosen them out, but only to see that they themselves are but as beasts; 19that that which befalls the sons of men befalls the beasts; even one thing befalls them both; as the one dies, so the other dies; yea, they have all one breath; so that a man has no preeminence over a beast: for all is vapour. 20All go to one place; all are of the dust, and all return to dust. 21Who knows whether the spirit of man goes upward, and the spirit of the beast goes downward to the earth? 22So I saw that there is nothing better than that a man should rejoice in his work; for that is his portion: for who shall bring him to see what shall be after him?

The illuminations express the inescapable passing of each of the Earth's living creatures in poetry and image. The Hebrew page bears verses from Psalm 49:

7They that trust in their wealth, and boast themselves in the multitude of their riches;

8none of them can by any means redeem his brother, nor give to God a ransom for him....

11When he sees that wise men die, that the fool and the brutish person perish together, and leave their wealth to others:

¹²their inward thought is, that their houses shall continue forever, and their dwelling places to all generations; they call their lands after their own names.

¹³Nevertheless man abides not in honour: he is like the beasts that perish.

Under the starry sky behind the initial word, the elegant palace wall crumbles to dust. The mosaic's pattern is adapted from masonry remaining in the Sinagoga de Santa María la Blanca in Toledo, built in 1180, then appropriated and converted to a church by the Catholic Church following the expulsion of the Jews from Spain in 1492.

The English page offers verses from "Elegy Written in a Country Churchyard," by Thomas Gray (1716–71):[1]

> The boast of heraldry, the pomp of pow'r,
>   And all that beauty, all that wealth e'er gave,
>   Awaits alike th' inevitable hour.
>   The paths of glory lead but to the grave....
>
> Can storied urn or animated bust
>   Back to its mansion call the fleeting breath?
>   Can Honour's voice provoke the silent dust,
>   Or Flatt'ry soothe the dull cold ear of Death?

Broken branches and dry leaves of a pomegranate tree surrounded their trunk, now covered in moss; a single branch lies with a fallen dried fruit behind the wall shown on the adjacent page. Amid the decay, a fallen seed has sprouted, promising a new individual, a new life to succeed the one that passes.

NOTE

[1] Found at https://www.poetryfoundation.org/poems/44299/elegy-written-in-a-country-churchyard.

ohelet ended chapter 3 urging us not to lean passively on God but to assume personal responsibility for the world, despite our inherent fallibility and time-boundedness. How to do so? What can render a life worthy of living in conditions of perpetual doubt? What counts as doing one's best in such conditions? These are the questions to which Qohelet devotes the remainder of his book, taking a first important step in chapter 4.

Perhaps surprisingly, he chooses to begin the constructive portion of his argument with politics. "But for fear of the authorities, people would swallow one another alive," states the well-known mishna in Avot.[1] Chapter 4 sets forth from a dark vision of an ungoverned society in which each man is to himself and might is right; in which the many oppressed "had no comforter, and on the side of their oppressors there was power, but they had no comforter" (4:1). Into such a world, Qohelet declares, it is better not to be born (2–3). But unlike Avot (or, for that matter, Hobbes's much later vision of humankind's unruly "state of nature"),[2] Qohelet is far less concerned with the pitiful and wretched state of unchecked brute human nature than with the inescapable variability of human normativity and culture.

To claim with Qohelet that the culture-specific, thick content that we lend to our thin notions of, say, true, false, right, and wrong is forever *hevel*—forever the transient children of our particular time and place[3]—is to accept that different people's descriptive and normative vocabularies will be as radically diverse as the different life trajectories in which they were honed. Qohelet describes the normative chaos as owing to "rivalry" and "envy" between diverse life plans of labor and skill (4), which he attributes explicitly to our *hevel* existence (7).[4] The problem of political cooperation for Qohelet has therefore nothing to do with curbing our brutish animal nature but with the unavoidable contrastive plurality of conceptions of the good, even among the most civilized people. It is a problem that cannot be evaded by refraining from acting, or by acting alone. Only fools sit idly on their hands and "eat their own flesh" (5). Although the motivation, in this case, to sit back and refuse responsibility to judge and act is different from the type of pious passivity condemned by Qohelet in the previous chapter, the two forms of passivity amount to the same betrayal of what Qohelet takes to be our very destiny as agents of reasoned intervention. Qohelet has extremely little patience for either. To hazard a speculation, I believe that for the same reason, Qohelet would have objected to the Hobbesian idea of achieving political stability and civility by surrendering all agency—civic and religious—to the monarch. I shall return to this point below.

Slightly better, perhaps, but equally pointless, is to withdraw from society and attempt to act alone. Such a strategy is not classified as foolish by Qohelet but is nonetheless rejected. The relevant verse (8) is worth attending to closely, especially its closing clause. Because of the rivalry and envy between conflicting conceptions of the good that arise due to our *hevel* existence (7), some people choose to live their lives alone, "without a companion, yea … neither son nor brother." The problem is that even if they mean to do good and are not driven by mere greed (8), their efforts lack an "end"[5]—or, as Qohelet puts it: "yet there is no end of all his labor … he may say: For whom then do I labor, and bereave my soul of good?" Human endeavor is pointless and can have no purpose outside a social context. Withdrawal from the social world we inhabit, even when we remain active, can never boast *yitaron* because, as it now emerges, a life can be deemed profitable only if others can profit from it. But under the inevitable *hevel* conditions of normative diversity, human society is unlivable.

In other words, because a livable, properly governed, society is a prerequisite for living a life of worth, the question of how social cooperation can be achieved under conditions of such normative diversity has to be dealt with before anything else. This is why Qohelet sets it as the first big question on his philosophical agenda, following the great turning point of chapter 3 and the one to which he devotes chapter 4.

His answer is no less than ingenious. Social cooperation does not require normative agreement and need not presuppose it. (Indeed, as he will argue in chapter 7, nonviolent normative *dis*agreement and the mutual normative critique that it generates are invaluable assets in conditions of uncertainty.) Stable social cohesion can and should be achieved not by cooperating to promote a shared form of life, on which broad agreement is impossible (and certainly not by accepting, even willingly, the dictated form of life enforced by an all-powerful Leviathan), but by agreeing to cooperate in order to maximize safekeeping and minimize suffering.[6] Standing together, Qohelet argues emphatically, whether in the face of natural hazards or of human menace, is always preferable to standing alone (9–12).

> Two are better than one because they have a good reward for their labour. For if they fall, the one will lift up his fellow; but woe to him that is alone when he falls; for he has not another to help him up. Again, if two lie together, then they have warmth; but how can one be warm alone? And if one prevail against him, two shall withstand him. (9–12)

By the same logic, three, of course, are preferable to two (12), and so forth. This, argues Qohelet, is incentive enough for people to form and maintain stable societies, while remaining faithful to their very different, even contrasting, ideas of the good life, and, most important, to tolerate,[7] rather than combat, other people's different, even contradictory, choices.

Such societies need to be governed, but as in modern ideas of political liberalism,[8] the regime's obligation is to ensure a just distribution of duty and freedom while refraining resolutely from enforcing an obligatory, shared form of life. Qohelet's great political idea is that the undeniable advantage of facing life's perils together is enough to furnish a sufficiently robust fraternity of mutual dependency to prevent the plurality of normative choices contained within it from reverting to violence and exploding it from within.

The question of government is not a simple one for Qohelet because the only form of government he knew was monarchy. Lacking the checks and balances of modern parliamentarism, ancient monarchs (not unlike Hobbes's Leviathan) tended to amass far more power than was necessary for administering the kind of regulation of basic need and social and state security that Qohelet envisioned. They tended to view themselves as embodiments of the good of their subjects, to see their destiny in fashioning the nation in their image and their liking, and to lay down the law in areas that Qohelet insisted had to be left to personal choice and commitment. Facing life's natural and human perils, while ensuring the natural diversity of normative commitment,[9] requires a king who is wise in Qohelet's emerging sense of the term, namely, humbly aware of the essential time-boundedness and fallibility of all human experience and achievement and of the consequently broad and inevitable variety of conflicting ideas of the good and the need to preserve it. This runs hard against the grain of how the monarchs of his time and their subjects perceived the monarch's role. This explains Qohelet's seemingly strange comments regarding the type of king best suited to govern the kind of human society that he envisages. The combination of arrogance, self-importance, enormous wealth, and unchecked power in the hands of an old, respected king can be detrimental to the fundamental aims of such a society. As will become clearer in chapters to come, the main task of the monarch is not to appease his people or to tell them what is good for them but to imagine and prepare for the worst. It is far better, Qohelet advises, to elect a young, poor lad of questionable background than to keep on an old and distinguished, overconfident fool, even if the former "came out of prison to reign" (13–15)—someone who is sensitive and no stranger to the possible and unpredictable hazards of life, human suffering, and social diversity. Here, in passing, the second category of fools with which Qohelet will contend—already at the outset of chapter 5—makes its first quick appearance in the form of the old arrogant king who is recklessly incautious because he is certain that he has seen and heard it all.

NOTES

[1] Attributed to R. Ḥanina, "Deputy High Priest," Mishna, Avot 2:3.

[2] "Hereby it is manifest that during the time men live without a common power to keep them all in awe, they are in that condition which is called war; and such a war as is of every man against every man"; Thomas Hobbes, *Leviathan or the Matter, Forme and Power of a Commonwealth Ecclesiasticall and Civil* (London: Andrew Crooke, 1651), 77.

[3] Although they often use the same words, the fact that normatively diverse communities share "thin" concepts such as "reasonable" and "repugnant" is but apparent because of the different, even contrasting, meanings that they give them. What might be considered highly reasonable for one could well be deemed to be wholly unwarranted by the other. On the impossibility, therefore, of normatively ranking the quality of two sufficiently diverse communities in a manner acceptable to both, see Fisch and Benbaji, *The View from Within*, esp. chap. 2.

[4] Interestingly, Hobbes explains the state of "war" that characterizes humans in the state of nature as owing to different people desiring the same things and locates the key to civilized peace in joint willingness to relinquish their ideas of the good and grant the Leviathan absolute authority to decide for them. Qohelet goes in the opposite direction. He views the problem, as we shall see immediately, as owing to the fact that different people harbor different and contrasting ideas of the good, and he insists that stable political corporation is reachable in a way that ensures, rather than undermines, normative diversity.

[5] Many are likely to deem my reading here of the phrase *eyn ketz*—"no end," as "aimless" or "pointless," rather than "endless"—as philologically forced, especially in the context of biblical Hebrew. (Although it sounds less far-fetched, perhaps, against the backdrop of Qohelet's near-contemporary Daniel's several eschatological employments of the term—e.g., Dan 8:17–19; 11:27; 12:4, 8; esp. 12:13.) From a hermeneutical, rather than purely philological, perspective, the latter part of v. 8 clearly implies that had the lone laborer others for whom to labor *for*, his endless toiling would not have been for nothing—thus transforming the endlessness of the first clause to aimlessness.

[6] Needless to say, different conceptions of the good inevitably generate different conceptions of evil and suffering. Qohelet, I believe, as his examples amply prove, refers here to *agreed* suffering: disease, poverty, shelter, natural disasters, deception, and threats to body and soul that constitute what Michael Walzer dubs "a kind of minimal and universal code" that is "recognized and accepted in virtually every human society"; Michael Walzer, *Interpretation and Social Criticism* (Cambridge, Mass.: Harvard University Press, 1987), 24.

[7] As noted, Qohelet's move from merely tolerating normative diversity, to viewing it as a desired blessing, will come later.

[8] The founding work in this regard is that of John Rawls, who coined the term "political liberalism." See his *Political Liberalism*, expanded ed. (New York: Columbia University Press, 2005).

[9] Not because Qohelet might have believed that people have the right to live in accord with their various conceptions of the good—that would be a wildly inappropriate anachronism—but because he believed that it was their duty before God to do so.

אֹ וְשַׁבְתִּי אֲנִי וָאֶרְאֶה אֶת־כָּל־הָעֲשֻׁקִים אֲשֶׁר נַעֲשִׂים תַּחַת הַשָּׁמֶשׁ וְהִנֵּה ׀ דִּמְעַת הָעֲשֻׁקִים וְאֵין לָהֶם מְנַחֵם וּמִיַּד עֹשְׁקֵיהֶם כֹּחַ וְאֵין לָהֶם מְנַחֵם: בֹּ וְשַׁבֵּחַ אֲנִי אֶת־הַמֵּתִים שֶׁכְּבָר מֵתוּ מִן־הַחַיִּים אֲשֶׁר הֵמָּה חַיִּים עֲדֶנָה: גֹּ וְטוֹב מִשְּׁנֵיהֶם אֵת אֲשֶׁר־עֲדֶן לֹא הָיָה אֲשֶׁר לֹא־רָאָה אֶת־הַמַּעֲשֶׂה הָרָע אֲשֶׁר נַעֲשָׂה תַּחַת הַשָּׁמֶשׁ: דֹּ וְרָאִיתִי אֲנִי אֶת־כָּל־עָמָל וְאֵת כָּל־כִּשְׁרוֹן הַמַּעֲשֶׂה כִּי הִיא קִנְאַת־אִישׁ מֵרֵעֵהוּ גַּם־זֶה הֶבֶל וּרְעוּת רוּחַ: ה הַכְּסִיל חֹבֵק אֶת־יָדָיו וְאֹכֵל אֶת־בְּשָׂרוֹ: ו טוֹב מְלֹא כַף נַחַת מִמְּלֹא חָפְנַיִם עָמָל וּרְעוּת רוּחַ: ז וְשַׁבְתִּי אֲנִי וָאֶרְאֶה הֶבֶל תַּחַת הַשָּׁמֶשׁ:

[1]So I returned, and considered all the oppressions that are done under the sun: and behold the tears of such as were oppressed, and have had no comforter; and on the side of their oppressors there was power; but they had no comforter. [2]So I praised the dead that are already dead more than the living that are yet alive; [3]but better than both of them is he who has not yet been, who has not seen the evil work that is: done under the sun. [4]Again, I considered all labour, and every skill in work, that it comes from a man's rivalry with his neighbor. This also is vapour and a striving after wind. [5]The fool folds his hands together, and eats his own flesh. [6]Better is a handful with quietness, than both the hands full of labour and striving after wind. [7] Then I returned, and I saw vapour under the sun.

Behind the illuminated first word of the Hebrew painting, a simply dressed skilled artisan perches on a scaffold as he labors to carve an ornate frieze, while a luxuriously clad prince purports to direct him from below. In the small painting near the bottom of the English page, the horse, an exotic symbol of wealth and military power in preexilic Israel, becomes an allegory of the stages of human life and labor. A carefree filly cavorts near her pregnant mother, who awaits another birth. A richly caparisoned mare may be exquisitely groomed and maintained, yet lives at the end of a tether, awaiting her rider's whim. Finally, on the rough road outside the paddock, a broken-down cart horse plods along hopelessly, with no expectation of comfort or relief in sight.

The micrography associates these passages from Qohelet with the first chapter of the book of Lamentations, Jeremiah's tragic poem mourning the oppression and humiliation that Jerusalem suffered in 586 B.C.E. at the hands and swords of the conquering Babylonian Empire. The braided cord symbolizes the mutual support offered by companionship amid oppression, mentioned in verse 12, shown in the next paintings.

יֵשׁ אֶחָד וְאֵין שֵׁנִי גַּם בֵּן וָאָח אֵין־לֹו וְאֵין ח קֵץ לְכָל־עֲמָלֹו גַּם־עֵינֹו לֹא־תִשְׂבַּע עֹשֶׁר וּלְמִי ׀ אֲנִי עָמֵל וּמְחַסֵּר אֶת־נַפְשִׁי מִטּוֹבָה גַּם־זֶה הֶבֶל וְעִנְיַן רָע הוּא: ט טוֹבִים הַשְּׁנַיִם מִן־הָאֶחָד אֲשֶׁר יֵשׁ־לָהֶם שָׂכָר טוֹב בַּעֲמָלָם: י כִּי אִם־יִפֹּלוּ הָאֶחָד יָקִים אֶת־חֲבֵרֹו וְאִילֹו הָאֶחָד שֶׁיִּפֹּול וְאֵין שֵׁנִי לַהֲקִימֹו: יא גַּם אִם־יִשְׁכְּבוּ שְׁנַיִם וְחַם לָהֶם וּלְאֶחָד אֵיךְ יֵחָם: יב וְאִם־יִתְקְפֹו הָאֶחָד הַשְּׁנַיִם יַעַמְדוּ נֶגְדֹּו וְהַחוּט הַמְשֻׁלָּשׁ לֹא בִמְהֵרָה יִנָּתֵק: יג טֹוב יֶלֶד מִסְכֵּן וְחָכָם מִמֶּלֶךְ זָקֵן וּכְסִיל אֲשֶׁר לֹא־יָדַע לְהִזָּהֵר עֹוד: יד כִּי־מִבֵּית הָסוּרִים יָצָא לִמְלֹךְ כִּי גַּם בְּמַלְכוּתֹו נֹולַד רָשׁ: טו רָאִיתִי אֶת־ כָּל־הַחַיִּים הַמְהַלְּכִים תַּחַת הַשָּׁמֶשׁ עִם הַיֶּלֶד הַשֵּׁנִי אֲשֶׁר יַעֲמֹד תַּחְתָּיו: טז אֵין־קֵץ לְכָל־הָעָם לְכֹל אֲשֶׁר־הָיָה לִפְנֵיהֶם גַּם הָאַחֲרֹונִים לֹא יִשְׂמְחוּ־בֹו כִּי־גַם־זֶה הֶבֶל וְרַעְיֹון רוּחַ:

[8]There is one alone, without a companion; yea, he has neither son nor brother; yet is there no end of all his labour; neither is his eye satisfied with riches: he may say, For whom then do I labour, and bereave my soul of good! This is also vapour; indeed, it is a sorry business. [9]Two are better than one: because they have a good reward for their labour. For if they fall, the one will lift up his fellow: [10]but woe to him that is alone when he falls; for he has not another to help him up. [11]Again, if two lie together, then they have warmth: but how can one be warm alone? [12]And if one prevail against him, two shall withstand him: but a threefold cord is not quickly broken. [13]Better is a poor and a wise child than an old and foolish king, who no longer knows how to take care of himself. [14]For out of prison one came forth to reign; whilst another lo his royal power may become poor. [15]I saw all the living who wander under the sun—they were with the second child who was to rise up in his stead. [16]There is no end of all the people who come to acclaim the one who goes before them; yet they who come after shall not rejoice in him. Surely this also is vapour and a striving after wind. [17]Keep thy foot when thou goest to the house of God; to draw near to hearken is better than to give the sacrifice of fools: for they consider not that they do evil.

The illuminations dwell upon the contrast that Qohelet paints between the strength of people who live with integrity and companionship despite poverty and insignificance, and the danger of those who live in empty narcissism and vainglory. Atop the Hebrew illumination, a frieze of storks, whose Hebrew name shares the same letters as the word *ḥesed* ("lovingkindness") and which are noted in midrash for their loving care of their chicks, hints at the kindness below. The painting at left presents two women in a scene reminiscent of Ruth and Naomi. Resting on a crumbling wall outside the grounds of the great palace, the young woman comforts the older one; the caper bush springing from the stones suggests the courage to persevere that they will find through their joint effort and divine providence.[1]

In contrast, the English illumination riffs on Hans Christian Andersen's tale of the emperor's new clothes, comparing a foolish and narcissistic ruler who preens at the adulation of his court, to the fairy tale's vain and gullible emperor. Off at the side, two small children gape and point in amazement at his bizarre nakedness. The ruler's narcissism threatens dangers far beyond his individual fate, portending fearful consequences for his people. In contrast to the kindness expressed at the top of the Hebrew page, the (classical Chinese) swastika pattern painted here warns all who recognize the fatal symbols of World War II of the danger of foolish rulers and those who follow them.

Please note that verse 4:17 is treated in the illuminations and commentary for the beginning of Chapter 5.

NOTE

[1] The association between the caper plant and the quality of perseverance is recorded in the Babylonian Talmud, Beitsa 25b: " 'As R. Shimon the son of Lakish said: Three persevere: Israel among the nations; a dog among the animals; and a chicken among fowl.' And there are those who add a goat among the beasts. And there are those who add a caper among trees."

The Tosafot, followers of the essential eleventh-century French rabbi and commentator Rashi, comment on the passage above: "And the caper among trees: Rashi commented, 'and I don't know what is its perseverance,' and the Tosefta commented that because it makes three fruits—the leaves, the fruit, and the buds—and because it puts on fruit every day, as opposed to all other trees. And also Rabbi Isaac of Dampierre commented that its perseverance comes from putting the buds into wine to preserve it."

FOOLISHNESS MULTIPLIED
THE RELIGIOUS DIMENSION

ith a political vision of a livable society in place, sufficiently cohesive to accommodate broad normative diversity and to enable people to pursue their conflicting chosen lifeworks and to flourish unthreatened by others, Qohelet turns in chapter 5 to look closer at the place of religion in our lives. Again, similar to the political question addressed in the previous chapter, it is a preliminary question that requires attending to before the main task of tackling the concept of worthwhileness can be addressed. He does so by considering the two types of foolishness with which he contends throughout the book—that of the overly overwhelmed and that of the overly confident—to which he returns here from a different angle. This time, his topic is religion more specifically, to the extent that for one brief moment, the thrust of his argument ceases to be universal.

In my introduction to chapter 3, I introduced what I called Qohelet's God axiom, which, taken together with his *hevel* premise and *yitaron* prerequisite, serves as the grounding premise of his entire discussion. The God axiom consists of two main claims: first, that God's ways, both as legislator of nature's laws and judge of humankind, are unknowable to us with any certainty—which constitutes the theological version of the *hevel* principle; and second, that we are nonetheless charged by God with responsibility for our world, for which he holds us accountable—which amounts to the theological version of the *yitaron* prerequisite. The first kind of fool—the overly overwhelmed—whom we encountered in chapter 3, fully endorses the *hevel* premise, the claim that our convictions regarding the true and the good, however firm, are forever time-bound conjectures that we can never prove, but to the point of paralysis. Because we can never know for certain what we are up against and what should be done, he argues, it is better to refrain from acting altogether and rely on God's providence to right the world's wrongs. Taking the *hevel* premise seriously, he maintains, renders the *yitaron* prerequisite empty and void.

In chapter 3, Qohelet objected to such a position on the grounds that the religious piety that it supposedly expresses is groundless. According to the second clause of the God axiom, it is our religious obligation to act to better the world as best we can. Refusing to do so on religious grounds is hence, for Qohelet, a heretical contradiction in terms.

In chapter 5, Qohelet sets his sights on another disturbing dimension of foolish pious apathy, one in which the two categories of folly momentarily converge. Withdrawing from playing an active role in the world for religious reasons comes invariably accompanied by ardent religious observance. We are all familiar with such forms of self-directed, narcissistic religious zeal that shrivel the space and scope of human responsibility to the realm of personal perfection and ritual observance. Writing long before the rabbinic transformation of Judaism, in which prayer and Torah study became central, and the birth of monastic Christianity, Qohelet understandably identifies the realm of personal compliance and ritual observance with the Temple-centered cult of voluntary pledge and sacrifice.

Guard your feet from[1] frequenting the House of God, he cautions, for it is preferable to seek understanding—limited as it may be—than to sacrifice like clueless fools who refrain from judging because they cannot know what it is to do bad (4:17). On one level, Qohelet is obviously complaining against those who, overwhelmed by the unbridgeable chasm between human uncertainty and divine perfection, foolishly opt for pious inaction, while investing all their energy in religious reverence and appeasing rituals.

The second type of fool with whom Qohelet contends repeatedly would seem to occupy the exact opposite position. Rather than endorse the *hevel* premise, he dismisses it, claiming arrogantly to know the truth and what is good for him. We shall have a chance to examine this category of foolishness more closely in chapter 7. However, when it comes to fools of the first kind finding refuge from the uncertainties of life in the seeming certainty of religious observance, the two categories merge. Only at the end of the book, when "all is said and done," and Qohelet has solved the problem of living a divinely approvable life worth living to his satisfaction, will he make explicit reference to the words of the wise and the sayings of the masters of assemblies with explicit reference to what is "given by the one shepherd" (12:11), clearly implying that what is true of our inherent uncertainty concerning the laws of nature and proper norms of conduct is equally true of our capacity to comprehend divine revelation. However, as we have seen, there is much to imply that from the beginning (i.e., from 1:12 onward), Qohelet's *hevel* premise, as to the temporary and fallible nature of all human understanding, was meant to apply to comprehending not only God's world but also God's Word.[2] But if that be case, there is no refuge to be found in the seeming certainties of religious observance because our knowledge of them, too, can be no more certain than any other.

Thus, when he cautions against undertaking rash commitments to God, he is addressing both categories of fools:

> Be not rash with thy mouth, and let not thy heart utter anything before God: For God is in heaven, and thou upon earth: Therefore let thy words be few. For … a fool's voice is known by a multitude of words. When thou vowest a vow to God, do not defer to pay it; for he has no pleasure in fools: pay that which thou hast vowed. Better is it that thou shouldst not vow, than that thou shouldst vow and not pay. Do not let thy mouth cause thy flesh to sin; nor say before the angel, that it was an error: why should God be angry at thy voice and destroy the work of thy hands?[3]

Equally cocksure of themselves, fools of both categories shoot their mouths in foolhardy, long-term ritual commitment, unreflectively oblivious to the good chance that they will be proved wrong: the first, foolishly believing that the paralyzing *hevel* premise does not apply to the realm of worship; the second, foolishly believing that it does not apply at all.

The necessary corrective to such loudmouthed hubris, argues Qohelet, is to fear God (6)—which, as noted, is perhaps his main religious concept.[4] For Qohelet, fear of God has far less to do with dreading the harshness of his judgment, or agonizing over finding favor in his eyes. Fear of God, for Qohelet, is a far more self-directed and reflective religious category—one that steers closer to humility than to dread. Fear of God is a form of disposition, of standing in God's ever-presence, fully aware that "God is in heaven and thou upon earth" (1) in sobering realization that in comparison to him, all things human are radically mist-like, even if deemed highly appropriate in the short term.

To toe the delicate line between stupid hubris and foolish submission (married to stupid hubris in the realm of ritual law) requires acting in awareness of our imperfection, knowing that even the most prudently run societies will witness some measure of injustice and perverted judgment (7). But to do so as committed believers requires extending that awareness to our religious outlook. The fact that the injustice and suffering that we unwittingly cause are temporarily allowed to prevail should not diminish our faith in God's perfect judgment (7). The fact that divine retribution is rarely transparent or immediate should not cause us to doubt the first clause of Qohelet's God axiom: that in the long run, he is the perfect judge. God is likely to allow people to enjoy material success temporarily, in order to punish them by causing that success to vanish (12–13). Material gain should therefore always be considered a (temporary) "gift of God" (18), never as a reward and never as our endeavor's final end and measure (9–15). We should act to better the world to our satisfaction as best we can, while humbly acknowledging our shortsightedness as far as God's response to our efforts is concerned. Judging him on the basis of a person's short-term success or failure is the source of great evil because we never see the larger picture (15).

The paradigm of a profitable life, he notes in enigmatic brevity (8), is that of the farmer who, as he will explain later in detail (11:1–6), makes the most of the land that he commands, precisely by acknowledging his limitations.

NOTES

[1] I have rendered the verse "Guard your feet *from*," rather than "*when* frequenting the House of God," in line with the reading attributed to Shmuel bar Naḥmani in b. Berakhot 21a.

[2] Which makes all the more sense for those who read Qohelet as part of that very revelatory canon. Read thus, and in the spirit proposed here, Qohelet's *hevel* premise could not *but* apply to the revelatory portions of the Bible that detail the Law, both ritual and civic.

[3] See 5:1–5.

[4] See 3:14; 7:18; 8:12–13; 9:2; 12:13.

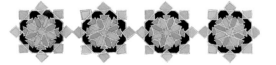

ד' י״זשָׁמֹ֤ר רַגְלְךָ֙ כַּאֲשֶׁ֤ר תֵּלֵךְ֙ אֶל־בֵּ֣ית הָֽאֱלֹהִ֔ים וְקָר֣וֹב לִשְׁמֹ֔עַ מִתֵּ֥ת הַכְּסִילִ֖ים זָ֑בַח כִּֽי־אֵינָ֥ם יֽוֹדְעִ֖ים לַעֲשׂ֥וֹת רָֽע׃

א אַל־תְּבַהֵ֨ל עַל־פִּ֜יךָ וְלִבְּךָ֧ אַל־יְמַהֵ֛ר לְהוֹצִ֥יא דָבָ֖ר לִפְנֵ֣י הָאֱלֹהִ֑ים כִּ֣י הָאֱלֹהִ֤ים בַּשָּׁמַ֨יִם֙ וְאַתָּ֣ה עַל־הָאָ֔רֶץ עַל־כֵּ֛ן יִהְי֥וּ דְבָרֶ֖יךָ מְעַטִּֽים׃ ב כִּ֣י בָּ֤א הַחֲלוֹם֙ בְּרֹ֣ב עִנְיָ֔ן וְק֥וֹל כְּסִ֖יל בְּרֹ֥ב דְּבָרִֽים׃ ג כַּאֲשֶׁר֩ תִּדֹּ֨ר נֶ֜דֶר לֵֽאלֹהִ֗ים אַל־תְּאַחֵר֙ לְשַׁלְּמ֔וֹ כִּ֣י אֵ֥ין חֵ֖פֶץ בַּכְּסִילִ֑ים אֵ֥ת אֲשֶׁר־תִּדֹּ֖ר שַׁלֵּֽם׃ ד ט֖וֹב אֲשֶׁ֣ר לֹֽא־תִדֹּ֑ר מִשֶּׁתִּדּ֖וֹר וְלֹ֥א תְשַׁלֵּֽם׃ ה אַל־תִּתֵּ֤ן אֶת־פִּ֨יךָ֙ לַחֲטִ֣יא אֶת־בְּשָׂרֶ֔ךָ וְאַל־תֹּאמַר֙ לִפְנֵ֣י הַמַּלְאָ֔ךְ כִּ֥י שְׁגָגָ֖ה הִ֑יא לָ֣מָּה יִקְצֹ֤ף הָֽאֱלֹהִים֙ עַל־קוֹלֶ֔ךָ וְחִבֵּ֖ל אֶת־מַעֲשֵׂ֥ה יָדֶֽיךָ׃ ו כִּ֣י בְרֹ֤ב חֲלֹמוֹת֙ וַהֲבָלִ֔ים וּדְבָרִ֖ים הַרְבֵּ֑ה כִּ֥י אֶת־הָאֱלֹהִ֖ים יְרָֽא׃

4:17Keep thy foot when thou goest to the house of God; to draw near to hearken is better than to give the sacrifice of fools: for they consider not that they do evil.

5:1Be not rash with thy mouth, and let not thy heart be hasty to utter anything before God: for God is in heaven, and thou upon earth: therefore let thy words be few. 2For a dream comes through a multitude of business; and a fool's voice is known by a multitude of words. 3When thou vowest a vow to God, do not defer to pay it; for he has no pleasure in fools; pay that which thou hast vowed. 4Better is it that thou shouldst not vow, than that thou shouldst vow and not pay. 5Do not let thy mouth cause thy flesh to sin; nor say before the angel, that it was an error; why should God be angry at thy voice and destroy the work of thy hands? 6For this comes from the multitude of dreams and vapours and many words; but fear thou God.

On the Hebrew page, the philosopher-king gazes into his fields, considering the impact of his personal ethics and decisions on his agricultural lands and laborers. He reflects upon the consequences of humankind's actions taken in the shadow of God, anticipating the issues that he will confront throughout this fifth chapter. The texts begin with the last verse of chapter 4, in which Qohelet begins this train of thought; in the Hebrew painting, the verse floats in the night sky; in the English painting, it becomes the posts of the sukkah.

The borders of the paintings present a passage from the small mishnaic ethical tract, *Pirke Avot*, expressing the king's caution:

> Which is the right path that you should choose for yourself? One that is admirable in your eyes, and admirable in the eyes of others. Be as careful with a minor commandment as with a major one, for you do not know the rewards of the commandments. Weigh the losses in doing the right thing against the gains, and the gains in committing a sin against the losses. Reflect on three things and you will not come into the grip of sin: know that above you are an eye that sees, an ear that hears, and all your deeds are written in a book.[1]

As an unseen servant cools him with a peacock-feather fan, he imagines the possible consequences of his management of his lands and, by extension, kingdom and life. Careful personal conduct and moral guidance of his lands, carefully guided by God's law, may persuade God to enable his lands to thrive; the burgeoning fields and unsupervised workers bringing home baskets heavy with new grain symbolize the divine favor promised in Torah. An eagle, symbolizing God's protection of Israel,[2] as well as the Davidic dynasty, soars overhead. In contrast, at left, he imagines that he has allowed oppression and viciousness to dominate the society. A foreman beats a collapsed worker with a flail—and the land lies dry and cracked, yielding only weeds instead of lush grains and fruit. As carefully as he attempts to discern divine demand, the philosopher-king cannot forget that an impenetrable firmament of cloud separates him, "under the sun," from God's view of the world.

The English page, edged with the same verse from *Pirke Avot* (minus the middle sentence), expresses Qohelet's sense of the uncertainty and fragility, the danger of careless words in human life "under the sun." Micrography composed of the words of the Kol Nidre[3] proclamation, annulling vows between God and humankind, traces the outlines of a sukkah. The sukkah's fragile and temporary structure, open and vulnerable to the elements despite our cleverest designs, stands as Judaism's most lasting symbol of the ephemeral nature of life.

NOTES

[1] William Berkson, trans., with Menachem Fisch, *Pirke Avot: Timeless Wisdom for Modern Life* (Philadelphia: Jewish Publication Society, 2010), 54, 56.

[2] Midrash Tanḥuma, commenting on God's protection of Israel at the Red Sea, "How I bore you on eagle's wings," Exod 19:4. How is the eagle different from all other birds? All other birds carry their young between their feet because they are afraid of birds flying above them. But the eagle is afraid only of man, who might shoot an arrow at him. [Therefore the eagle carries his young upon his wings], saying, 'I would rather have the arrow lodge in me than in my young.' " Quoted from H. N. Bialik and Y. H. Ravnitzky, eds., *The Book of Legends: Sefer ha-Aggadah*, trans. William G. Braude (New York: Schocken, 1992), 72.

[3] Kol Nidre is the prayer service that begins Yom Kippur, the Jewish Day of Atonement. The service draws its name from its opening proclamation, which dissolves all oaths between individuals and God.

ז אִם־עֹשֶׁק רָשׁ וְגֵזֶל מִשְׁפָּט וָצֶדֶק תִּרְאֶה בַמְּדִינָה אַל־
תִּתְמַהּ עַל־הַחֵפֶץ כִּי גָבֹהַּ מֵעַל גָּבֹהַּ שֹׁמֵר וּגְבֹהִים
עֲלֵיהֶם: ח וְיִתְרוֹן אֶרֶץ בַּכֹּל הִיא [הוּא] מֶלֶךְ לְשָׂדֶה
נֶעֱבָד: ט אֹהֵב כֶּסֶף לֹא־יִשְׂבַּע כֶּסֶף וּמִי־אֹהֵב בֶּהָמוֹן
לֹא תְבוּאָה גַּם־זֶה הָבֶל: י בִּרְבוֹת הַטּוֹבָה רַבּוּ אוֹכְלֶיהָ
וּמַה־כִּשְׁרוֹן לִבְעָלֶיהָ כִּי אִם־רְאִית [רְאוּת] עֵינָיו:
יא מְתוּקָה שְׁנַת הָעֹבֵד אִם־מְעַט וְאִם־הַרְבֵּה יֹאכֵל
וְהַשָּׂבָע לֶעָשִׁיר אֵינֶנּוּ מַנִּיחַ לוֹ לִישׁוֹן: יב יֵשׁ רָעָה
חוֹלָה רָאִיתִי תַּחַת הַשָּׁמֶשׁ עֹשֶׁר שָׁמוּר לִבְעָלָיו לְרָעָתוֹ:
יג וְאָבַד הָעֹשֶׁר הַהוּא בְּעִנְיַן רָע וְהוֹלִיד בֵּן וְאֵין בְּיָדוֹ
מְאוּמָה: יד כַּאֲשֶׁר יָצָא מִבֶּטֶן אִמּוֹ עָרוֹם יָשׁוּב לָלֶכֶת
כְּשֶׁבָּא וּמְאוּמָה לֹא־יִשָּׂא בַעֲמָלוֹ שֶׁיֹּלֵךְ בְּיָדוֹ: טו
וְגַם־זֹה רָעָה חוֹלָה כָּל־עֻמַּת שֶׁבָּא כֵּן יֵלֵךְ וּמַה־יִּתְרוֹן
לוֹ שֶׁיַּעֲמֹל לָרוּחַ: טז גַּם כָּל־יָמָיו בַּחֹשֶׁךְ יֹאכֵל וְכָעַס
הַרְבֵּה וְחָלְיוֹ וָקָצֶף:

7If thou seest the oppression of the poor, and the violent perverting of judgment and justice in a province, do not marvel at the matter; for there is a high one who watches over him that is high; and there are yet higher ones over them, 8Moreover, land has an advantage for everyone; he who tills a field is a king. 9He who loves silver shall not be satisfied with silver; nor he that loves abundance with increase: this is also vapour. 10When goods increase, they who eat them are increased: and what good is there to their owner, saving the beholding of them with his eyes? 11The sleep of a laboring man is sweet, whether he eat little or much: but the repletion of the rich will not suffer him to sleep. 12There is a sore evil which I have seen under the sun, namely, riches kept for their owner to his hurt. 13But those riches perish by evil adventure: and he begets a son, and there is nothing in his hand. 14As he came forth from his mother's womb, naked shall he return to go as he came, and he shall take nothing for his labour. which he may carry away in his hand, 15And this also is a sore evil, that in all points as he came, so shall he go: and what profit has he that labours for the wind? 16All his days also he eats in darkness, and he has much sorrow and sickness and wrath. Behold that which I have seen.

Qohelet turns to consider the foolishness of oppressors and the selfish wealthy in the face of both human and divine authority. In the human world, civil authorities answer to higher levels of government; and even the highest rulers finally answer to the unseen and unknowable God. Consequently, neither wealth nor power guarantees wisdom or reliable joy as securely as careful ethical behavior. In this passage, Qohelet prefigures his discussion of the wise farmer in chapter 11:

[4]He who observes the wind shall not sow; and he who regards the clouds shall not reap. [5]As thou knowst not what is the way of the wind, nor how the bones grow in the womb of her that is with child: even so thou knowst not the works of God who makes all. [6]In the morning sow thy seed, and in the evening do not withhold thy hand: for thou knowst not which shall prosper, whether this or that, or whether they both shall be alike good.

The Hebrew illumination presents the flail and the sword, weapons of state oppression typical of Qohelet's day, while the English illumination begins with an image of the taser used and abused by modern police forces across the world. The column of coins tips over to spill across both paintings. The starlit heavens show lights that reprocess every molecule throughout eternity and symbolize the all-suffusing divine presence; yet the heavenly lights, however we try to understand them, are obscured from human view by clouds of mist.

הַנֵּ֣ה אֲשֶׁר־רָאִ֣יתִי אָ֗נִי ט֤וֹב אֲשֶׁר־יָפֶ֣ה לֶֽאֱכוֹל־וְלִשְׁתּ֣וֹת וְלִרְא֣וֹת טוֹבָ֡ה בְּכָל־עֲמָל֣וֹ ׀ שֶׁיַּעֲמֹ֣ל תַּֽחַת־הַשֶּׁ֗מֶשׁ מִסְפַּ֧ר יְמֵי־חַיָּ֛ו [חַיָּ֖יו] אֲשֶׁר־נָֽתַן־ל֥וֹ הָאֱלֹהִ֖ים כִּי־ה֥וּא חֶלְקֽוֹ׃ יח גַּ֣ם כָּֽל־הָאָדָ֡ם אֲשֶׁ֣ר נָֽתַן־ל֣וֹ הָאֱלֹהִים֩ עֹ֨שֶׁר וּנְכָסִ֜ים וְהִשְׁלִיט֨וֹ לֶאֱכֹ֤ל מִמֶּ֙נּוּ֙ וְלָשֵׂ֣את אֶת־חֶלְק֔וֹ וְלִשְׂמֹ֖חַ בַּעֲמָל֑וֹ זֹ֕ה מַתַּ֥ת אֱלֹהִ֖ים הִֽיא׃ יט כִּ֚י לֹ֣א הַרְבֵּ֔ה יִזְכֹּ֖ר אֶת־יְמֵ֣י חַיָּ֑יו כִּ֣י הָאֱלֹהִ֥ים מַעֲנֶ֖ה בְּשִׂמְחַ֥ת לִבּֽוֹ׃

[17]It is good and comely for one to eat and to drink, and to enjoy the good of all his labour in which he toils under the sun all the days of his life, which God gives him: for it is his portion. [18]Every man also to whom God has given riches and wealth, and has given him power to eat of it, and to take his portion, and to rejoice in his labour; this is the gift of God. [19]For he shall remember that the days of his life are not many, in which God provides him with the joy of his heart.

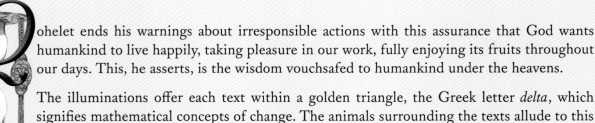

Qohelet ends his warnings about irresponsible actions with this assurance that God wants humankind to live happily, taking pleasure in our work, fully enjoying its fruits throughout our days. This, he asserts, is the wisdom vouchsafed to humankind under the heavens.

The illuminations offer each text within a golden triangle, the Greek letter *delta*, which signifies mathematical concepts of change. The animals surrounding the texts allude to this exhortation in the talmudic ethical tract, *Pirke Avot* (Ethics of the Fathers):

> Be bold as a leopard, as light as an eagle, as swift as a gazelle, and as brave as a lion to do the will of your Father in heaven.[1]

NOTE
[1] Berkson, *Pirke Avot*, 142.

Introduction to Chapter Six
The Futility of Hindsight

The big question that animates the book of Qohelet would by now seem clear enough: how to live a life worth living in the eyes of God in conditions of perpetual uncertainty. Having dealt with the political framework most conducive to the last clause—the *hevel* premise, with its necessary theological extensions—Qohelet devotes chapter 6 to looking closer at the second of his two main concepts: *yitaron*, variably translated as "worth," "gain," "profit," or "value."[1] All three renderings harbor the same semantic ambiguity—jointly designating blatantly material, alongside higher spiritual, meanings. The temptation to reduce the worthy to worth in the material sense is enormous. For one thing, as modern readers can well appreciate, economic value is tangible and can be calculated and measured, creating the illusion that worthwhileness in general is calculable. This temptation is most apparent in the stark reduction of propriety to (maximizing) utility in current economy-based, game-theoretic accounts of rationality.[2] Few would deny the great value of game-theoretic models to articulating rational decision-making in market-like scenarios where maximizing utility is indeed the sole objective. But in the pretentious attempt to extend the approach to all manner of reasoned action, something vital is lost. Normative value outside the marketplace, doing something because one deems it the right thing to do or to be one's duty to perform, has little to do with the dynamics of utility or economic gain.[3] In attempting to articulate the concept of *yitaron*, Qohelet clearly steers closer to propriety and decidedly away from profit. Indeed, he seems adamant to free it from all "marketplace" connotations.

It is wrong, he insists (6:2), to measure the value of our lifework, the *yitaron* of human labor, by means of its practical outcomes. First, success is a retroactive measure.[4] Qohelet seeks prospective criteria for deeming action to be of value. A worthy project is a project for which we have good reasons to embark on, not one judged to have been profitable after the event. Material gain is an inherently retroactive measure. Taking the *hevel* principle seriously is to acknowledge our fallibility. We are bound to make mistakes and to be proved wrong by hindsight. No conception of the worthwhileness of human effort under conditions of thoroughgoing *hevel* can afford to ignore our inherent liability to err. It is hence unthinkable to identify the value, the *yitaron* of embarking on a project, with the fact that it ended up being successful. Consider the (grossly anachronistic) example of a mathematician working for years on an exceptionally thorny problem without success. Could we deem his work meaningless?

Second, it is wrong to define *yitaron* retroactively in terms of actual outcome, even when our reasoning proves by hindsight to have been sound. Success and failure inevitably owe to factors beyond our control, for which we can never be held accountable: unpredictable natural causes, human and divine intervention, unpredictable political events, and so forth. Allowing one's self-esteem and the value of one's lifework to depend on the precariousness of success in general, and material profit in particular, is therefore not merely wrongheaded but "an evil" that lies "heavy upon men" (6:1).

What distinguishes the wise from the foolish cannot be gauged by the contingencies of eventual gain or loss (8). What only the wise can claim is to have done their reasonable best, regardless of whether they end up gaining or losing in retrospect—which brings Qohelet back from criticizing ill-conceived, materialist conceptions of *yitaron* to framing the question positively for the first time, from his own preferred perspective.

The question is daunting, if easily formulated: given our perpetual uncertainty and shortsightedness, how can we ever claim to set out to do our reasonable best? What is it to embark wisely on inherently tentative and fallible projects, in ways we can justifiably claim to be worthy at the outset? Qohelet devotes the second part of chapter 6 and the first part of chapter 7 to answering the question in some detail, thus rendering these verses fundamental to his entire project.

To act is to introduce change into our world. We have good reason to do so, when, to the best of our knowledge, we find some aspect of it sufficiently amiss, lacking, wanting, or flawed to warrant such intervention. Reasoned, deliberated action is hence action taken to right a perceived wrong, or to mend a perceived deficiency. To act wisely therefore consists first of taking keen critical stock of our domains of responsibility, on the lookout for possible problems or potential trouble spots and to determine how best to confront them—whether they give reason to plant or to uproot the planted, to break down or to build up (3:2–3).

Here, for the first time, Qohelet's sharp critical eye is deployed not to denigrate or disprove a rival position but to set the cornerstone to his own undertaking. His imagery is riveting, but to appreciate the full force of his words requires attending to the original Hebrew. The wise person's advantage over the fool, he says, resembles, according to the English rendition, "the poor man who knows how to make his way among the living" (6:8).[5] However, one important word in the Hebrew original is obscured to the point of distortion. What the poor man is reputed to know is in the Hebrew: *lahalokh* <u>*neged*</u> *ha-ḥa'im*—not "among" or even "before,"[6] so much as "against" or "in opposition to"[7] *ha-ḥa'im*. The second word to consider is *ha-ḥa'im*, which, in biblical Hebrew, can mean "the living" but can equally denote life itself.[8] Reading *neged* as "among" or "before" commits one to reading *ha-ḥa'im* as "the living"; but if *neged* is taken to mean "against" or "in opposition to," it makes far better sense to describe the poor man as knowing how to "make his way" or to "go *against* life" rather than "in opposition to the living."

The poor man who knows how to make his way against life offers a rich and layered metaphor for the wise person's advantage over the fool. First, the poor man is someone well aware of what he lacks and what he would prefer his world to be. Second, although aware of what he lacks, he refuses to surrender and succumb to his fate. Rather, he knowingly makes his way against what life has dealt him, determined to change reality for the better. His is the paradigm of critically motivated ameliorating action.

On another level, the image of the poor reformer powerfully signifies the difference between gauging meaningful action by means of the forward-looking motive force of a perceived deficiency that one is determined to right and by measuring its meaningfulness by the hindsight of eventual success or failure.

Such a combination of criticism and foresight (in diametrical opposition to judging retrospectively by outcome), Qohelet understands, requires vision and imagination: an ability and willingness not only to find fault in one's world but to imagine a better version of it, to envisage how things can and should be different from what they are. Taking critical stock of our situation, as I noted in my general introduction, is to issue a normative judgment as to its failings, shortcomings, and difficulties—all of which are breaches of the norms by which we abide—as is framing a plan to improve it. To use David Hume's famous idiom, it is to hold what *is*, accountable to what we believe it *ought* to be, and to undertake to transform that *ought* into a new *is*.[9]

From this follows Qohelet's neat and concise version of the naturalistic fallacy—claiming that it is both futile and stupid to stick to the facts and refrain from speculating. People who deem it preferable to wait and see how things turn out rather than to speculate and visualize imaginatively how things ought to be will never act in time. A situation that has rather been allowed to take form can no longer be prevented from doing so (9–10)—which is another way of saying that in conditions of thorough time-boundedness, wise, meaningful, worthy action has to be prospective, guided not by hindsight but by speculative foresight.

NOTES

[1] The Jerusalem Bible that we use here, like the JPS, follows the King James Version in translating *yitaron* as "profit," ESV and NIV as "gain," NAS as "advantage."

[2] See, e.g., Cristina Bicchieri, "Rationality and Game Theory," in *The Oxford Handbook of Rationality*, ed. Alfred R. Mele and Piers Rawling (Oxford: Oxford University Press, 2009), and the many references there.

[3] Maimonides' categorical differentiation between fulfilling one's religious duties out of fear of punishment or anticipation of reward, and doing so out of love, drives a powerful wedge between acting for self-serving ulterior motives (a desire to maximize utility) and being motivated by commitment to the true and the good. See his comments on Mishna Avot 1:3, and especially Mishne Torah, bk. 1, "Laws of Repentance," 10:1–2.

[4] Game-theoretical accounts are backward-looking in two respects. First, in measuring the rationality of a move by the extent to which it succeeds in maximizing the player's utility; to be considered rational on such a view, a move must succeed. Failed moves can therefore not be deemed rational. Second, what earns the title "rational," in these accounts, is the move made, not the deliberative process that yielded it, to the extent that a move that proves by hindsight to have been in the agent's interest will be considered rational even if it was performed wholly unawares.

[5] Or, as the King James Version has it: "the poor, that knoweth to walk before the living."

[6] Which fares better than many biblical uses of *neged*: e.g., Gen 21:17; Exod 10:10; 19:2; Deut 32:52.

[7] E.g., Gen 31:32, 37; Isa 40:17; 59:12; Amos 4:3; Ps 23:5; 29:20.

[8] As in Gen 2:9; Deut 30:15, 19; 1 Sam 25:29; Jer 21:8; Mal 2:5; Qoh 2:17.

[9] David Hume, *A Treatise of Human Nature* (1739), bk. 3, pt. 1, §1.

יֵ֣שׁ רָעָ֔ה אֲשֶׁ֥ר רָאִ֖יתִי תַּ֣חַת הַשָּׁ֑מֶשׁ וְרַבָּ֥ה הִ֖יא עַל־הָאָדָֽם: בּ אִ֣ישׁ אֲשֶׁ֣ר יִתֶּן־ל֣וֹ הָאֱלֹהִ֡ים עֹ֩שֶׁר֩ וּנְכָסִ֨ים וְכָב֜וֹד וְֽאֵינֶ֨נּוּ חָסֵ֥ר לְנַפְשׁ֣וֹ ׀ מִכֹּ֣ל אֲשֶׁר־יִתְאַוֶּ֗ה וְלֹֽא־יַשְׁלִיטֶ֤נּוּ הָֽאֱלֹהִים֙ לֶאֱכֹ֣ל מִמֶּ֔נּוּ כִּ֛י אִ֥ישׁ נָכְרִ֖י יֹֽאכְלֶ֑נּוּ זֶ֥ה הֶ֛בֶל וָחֳלִ֥י רָ֖ע הֽוּא: גּ אִם־יוֹלִ֣יד אִ֣ישׁ מֵאָ֡ה וְשָׁנִים֩ רַבּ֨וֹת יִֽחְיֶ֜ה וְרַ֣ב ׀ שֶׁיִּהְי֣וּ יְמֵֽי־שָׁנָ֗יו וְנַפְשׁוֹ֙ לֹא־תִשְׂבַּ֣ע מִן־הַטּוֹבָ֔ה וְגַם־קְבוּרָ֖ה לֹא־הָ֣יְתָה לּ֑וֹ אָמַ֕רְתִּי ט֥וֹב מִמֶּ֖נּוּ הַנָּֽפֶל: דּ כִּֽי־בַהֶ֥בֶל בָּ֖א וּבַחֹ֣שֶׁךְ יֵלֵ֑ךְ וּבַחֹ֖שֶׁךְ שְׁמ֥וֹ יְכֻסֶּֽה: הּ גַּם־שֶׁ֥מֶשׁ לֹא־רָאָ֖ה וְלֹ֣א יָדָ֑ע נַ֥חַת לָזֶ֖ה מִזֶּֽה: וּ וְאִלּ֣וּ חָיָ֗ה אֶ֤לֶף שָׁנִים֙ פַּעֲמַ֔יִם וְטוֹבָ֖ה לֹ֣א רָאָ֑ה הֲלֹ֛א אֶל־מָק֥וֹם אֶחָ֖ד הַכֹּ֥ל הוֹלֵֽךְ: זּ כָּל־עֲמַ֥ל הָאָדָ֖ם לְפִ֑יהוּ וְגַם־הַנֶּ֖פֶשׁ לֹ֥א תִמָּלֵֽא: חּ כִּ֣י מַה־יּוֹתֵ֤ר לֶֽחָכָם֙ מִן־הַכְּסִ֔יל מַה־לֶּעָנִ֣י יוֹדֵ֔עַ לַהֲלֹ֖ךְ נֶ֥גֶד הַחַיִּֽים: טּ ט֛וֹב מַרְאֵ֥ה עֵינַ֖יִם מֵֽהֲלָךְ־נָ֑פֶשׁ גַּם־זֶ֥ה הֶ֖בֶל וּרְע֥וּת רֽוּחַ: יּ מַה־שֶּֽׁהָיָ֗ה כְּבָר֙ נִקְרָ֣א שְׁמ֔וֹ וְנוֹדָ֖ע אֲשֶׁר־ה֣וּא אָדָ֑ם וְלֹֽא־יוּכַ֣ל לָדִ֔ין עִ֥ם שֶׁתַּקִּיף [שֶׁהַתַּקִּ֖יף] מִמֶּֽנּוּ: יאּ כִּ֛י יֵשׁ־דְּבָרִ֥ים הַרְבֵּ֖ה מַרְבִּ֣ים הָ֑בֶל מַה־יֹּתֵ֖ר לָאָדָֽם: יבּ כִּ֣י מִֽי־יוֹדֵעַ֩ מַה־טּ֨וֹב לָֽאָדָ֜ם בַּֽחַיִּ֗ים מִסְפַּ֛ר יְמֵי־חַיֵּ֥י הֶבְל֖וֹ וְיַעֲשֵׂ֣ם כַּצֵּ֑ל אֲשֶׁ֣ר מִֽי־יַגִּ֣יד לָֽאָדָ֗ם מַה־יִּהְיֶ֥ה אַחֲרָ֖יו תַּ֥חַת הַשָּֽׁמֶשׁ:

[1]There is an evil which I have seen under the sun, and it is heavy upon men: [2]a man to whom God has given riches, wealth, and honour, so that he lacks nothing for his soul of all that he desires, yet God does not give him power to eat of it but a stranger eats it: this is vapour, and it is an evil disease. [3]If a man begets a hundred children, and lives many years, so that the days of his years are many, and his soul is not content with the good, and also that he has no burial; I say, that an untimely birth is better than he. [4]For it comes in vapour, and departs in darkness, and its name is covered with darkness. [5]Moreover it has not seen the sun, nor known anything: this has more comfort than the other. [6]For though he live a thousand years twice told, yet he has seen no good: do not all go to one place? [7]All the labour of man is for his mouth, and yet the appetite is not filled. [8]For what advantage has the wise more than the fool? What has the poor man who knows how to make his way among the living? [9]Better is the sight of the eyes than the wandering of the desire: this is also vapour and a striving after wind. [10]That which has been was named long ago, and it is known that it is but man: nor may he contend with one who is mightier than he. [11]Seeing there are many things that increase vapour, what is man the better? [12]For who knows what is good for man in this life, all the days of his misty life which he spends like a shadow? For who can tell a man what shall be after him under the sun?

In some of his most jolting language, Qohelet builds his argument that people must deeply and intentionally relish the best qualities and moments of their lives. Without this consciousness, one risks a life without fulfillment. He raises the worst specters that he can imagine: that only others might enjoy the fruits of one's labors, the disappointment that follows unbounded greed, and the horrific notion that a miscarried fetus, which has died without experiencing the troubles of life, might be more fortunate than one who suffers disappointed expectations. Divine favor and personal security can never, he warns, be deduced from one's momentary wealth and status. Even the poor person who finds a path through the world may find greater happiness in life than a wealthy person who suffers a reversal of fortunes.

An exquisite mosaic wall within the palace and a budding, flowering, and fruiting rosebush climbing a decorated wall in a courtyard speak to the beauty and tentativeness of life.

The Hebrew page hints at the ruin that might result from careless actions. The palace wall is rich with mosaic, gleaming with the blues and purple associated with the biblical colors *tekhelet* and *argaman*, appointed for priestly fabrics and intricate carved masonry. A single crookedly set tile, however, breaks the serene symmetry of the pattern; and built on shifting sands, the wall has begun to crack and crumble.

A rosebush climbs the side of the English text, its buds, blossoms, and orange fruits suggesting the human life cycle. Yet the bush suggests the hazards of illness—disease has begun to wither its lower foliage and threatens its colorful life. The embossed ledge surrounding its roots urges those strolling in the garden to "gather ye rosebuds while ye may," in the words of the seventeenth-century British poet Robert Herrick, in his poem "To the Virgins, to Make Much of Time."

Bordering the two pages, verses from Psalm 39 echo Qohelet's somber apprehension at the unpredictable brevity of life:

> [5]Lord, make me to know my end, and the measure of my days, what it is: I will know how frail I am.

> [6]Behold, thou hast made my days like handbreadths; and my age is as nothing before thee: truly every man at his best state is altogether vapor.[1]

NOTE

[1] Ellen Davis points to the relevance of Psalm 39 to Qohelet's emotions in this passage. See Davis, *Proverbs, Ecclesiastes, and the Song of Songs*, 167.

Introduction to Chapter Seven
Breaching the Limits of Self-Critique

To discharge our duty to make the world a better place to the best of our ability is to adopt a keenly critical attitude toward our domains of responsibility with a view to righting the wrongs that we discover. But to do so wisely is to do so in full awareness of Qohelet's *hevel* premise: that all we know is tentative and fallible. The truly wise, therefore, extend the *hevel* premise reflexively to their own evaluations and plans for reform, to their data and to the standards that guide their deliberations and decisions. It is in this latter realm of self-assessment that a deeper problem presents itself.

As we have seen in the previous chapter, to undertake to improve our world requires holding it in critical review: seeking out its shortcomings and failings and seeking imaginative ways of putting them right. According to Qohelet, the wise—aware not only of their world's imperfections but also of their own epistemological shortcomings, their liability to misrepresent and misjudge their world—adopt the same keen critical attitude toward the picture that they form of it. They check and recheck their facts, interpret them with caution, and proceed warily. But the main epistemological tools by which they assess their situation and settle on a preferred course of reformative action are their very standards of right and wrong. To adopt a self-critical stance reflexively toward one's normative commitments might seem similarly straightforward, but it is not. For how can we possibly hold our norms in normative check, and change them for (what we deem to be) the better, if it is by means of those very norms that we perform such acts of normative appraisal? By what standard can we judge the standards we hold to be wrong and others to be preferable? Can it be that our very rationality is immune to rational self-review?

The problem of rationality's normative constraints is still very much with us today. Thomas Kuhn, whose study of scientific revolutions demonstrated how sciences undergo dramatic normative framework transitions (which he dubbed "paradigm shifts"), likened them not to reasoned decisions but to totally nonrational, near-involuntary gestalt switches.[1] This seems absurd—and not only with regard to science. Yet how can a person normatively evaluate the very norms by which he conducts such evaluations?

Qohelet was clearly not only aware of the problem but fully realized that, while it was absolutely essential to do justice to the *hevel* premise by holding one's normative commitments in critical check, it was humanly impossible to do so by merely talking to oneself. The image of the lone poor reformer of chapter 6 portrays the wise person's personal disposition. However, for a notion of *yitaron* to viably take the *hevel* premise properly on board, more is needed than personal awareness, dedication, and disposition.

Chapter 7 explores three main sobering ways of extending the limits of normative self-critique beyond the personal. Two involve humbly seeking criticism from without, and the third, being humbly wary of the limited practical significance of even our most heartfelt general normative principles. Qohelet seems to rightly assume—though without actually arguing the point—that exposure to normative criticism leveled at us from *without* is capable of destabilizing the commitments that it challenges sufficiently for us to hold them in critical review—a feat that no one can perform alone.

Read thus, chapter 7 constitutes the book of Qohelet's philosophical high point. The series of better-this-than-that statements listed in the chapter's first eleven verses urge active exposure—vexing as it may be, for indeed, "anger[2] is better than laughter" (3)—to negative feedback of two types.

First (as Karl Popper insisted), to assign priority to soberly reflect on calamity and failure rather than to bask in the warm, congratulating glow of success—real as it may be. Better to frequent "houses of mourning," rather than those of "merry feasting" (2, 4), and to study how things ended, rather than how they began (7)—which is not an argument in favor of retroactive reasoning, of course. On the contrary: in order to make better proactive plans, Qohelet urges us to look closely at the outcomes of similar past projects, for there is much to learn from them. The fact that our reasoning and actions are time-bound and tentative does not erase the past. Taking responsibility for what we think and do, aware of the *hevel* premise, does not mean that each generation must invent the wheel anew. On the other hand, Qohelet cautions us not to idealize the past but to hold it, too, in critical review: "Do not say, How was it that the former days were better than these? For thou dost not inquire wisely concerning this" (10). "Wisdom," he continues, "is good with an inheritance"—the past has much to teach us and should always be warily taken into account—for it embodies *yitaron* "to them who see the sun" (11).

The second, and more important, form of negative feedback that Qohelet urges us to actively seek is to expose ourselves to the critique of others: to pursue a good reputation rather than "precious ointment" (1), namely, to expose ourselves to the judgment of others and to take heed of the impression that we leave on them, rather than pursue material success—and to seek out especially the wise rebuke of those who think differently, rather than crave the praise and crackling laughter of those who agree (5–6). "Wise rebuke," or better, "the rebuke of the wise," is the rebuke of those whom Qohelet considers wise. These are not merely people who know better but people who share our endorsement of the *hevel* premise, realize our need for their criticism, and seek ours. They share with us the understanding (shared also, as I argued in my general introduction, with the talmudic literature's Hillelite voice) that exposure to the echo chamber of the trusted normative critique of people committed differently allows us to step back and see ourselves as they do—something that none of us can accomplish alone.

As they gradually take form, one cannot but marvel at the extent to which Qohelet's ideal of human wisdom and portrayal of the wise diverge from conventional understandings of both, even today. We still tend to associate wisdom with well-based knowledge and know-how. We consider wise those on whose judgment we can confidently rely. Institutions of learning are where we encounter the wise, acquire knowledge from them, and are able to leave wiser than when we entered. In most languages, the word "knowledge" and the verb "to know" are attributable only to truth. We can say that so-and-so thinks, or believes, or even is absolutely certain that 7 times 6 is 72, but it would be ungrammatical to assert that he *knows* that 7 times 6 is 72. Qohelet's notion of *hokhma*, human wisdom, is very different. If the wise can boast certain knowledge of anything, it is that their firmest convictions and taken-for-granted truths are, in all probability, wrong and will prove themselves to be wrong and that our sense of certitude and confidence is thoroughly time-bound and circumstantial and likely, like the mist, to evaporate at any moment in favor of different, equally transitory, certainties. Being wise, for Qohelet, has little to do with confidently knowing and everything to do with a perpetually restless doubt regarding everything we think that we know, suspicion of success, and keen awareness of our need for the critical input of others in order to transform our doubts into workable forms of criticism. There is satisfaction for the wise in knowing that they have done their best in conditions of thoroughgoing *hevel*, but doubt, self-critique, anxious epistemic restlessness, and a fixation on worst-case scenarios do not inspire the confidence or even the respect of others. In later chapters, Qohelet will have much to say about the inevitable lack of social standing of the wise and the high price with which it comes. Here, however, he is more interested in dealing with the opposition, right and left.

The more Qohelet's position acquires clarification and philosophical depth, the oppositions on either side of the ever-precarious line that it purports to toe between epistemic uncertainty and normative meaningfulness also assume a worrying and inviting clarity. By now, the two positions are familiar: on the one hand, abdicating social responsibility in favor of the seemingly divinely favored security of excessive piety; on the other hand, the all-too-familiar conflation of feeling certain with actual certainty, the overconfident and uncritical identification of what we are unable to imagine being otherwise, and absolute truth. The former takes the *hevel* premise seriously to the point of helplessness, and the latter foolishly ignores it. Qohelet, for one angry moment, binds the two positions together in the harshest of words: "Be not righteous overmuch; nor make thyself overwise: why shouldst thou destroy thyself? Be not wicked overmuch, nor be foolish: why shouldst thou die before thy time?" (16–17).

The meaning of the two verses is straightforward enough, but the Hebrew is better nuanced than its English renditions allow. First, the second clause of the first verse *lama tishomem?* is a rhetorical question, but it is not about being self-destructive so much as about rendering oneself barren. *Sh'mama* does not mean "ruin," but "wasteland." Adopting either position, Qohelet submits, is to lay waste to one's life. The same goes for the second clause of the second verse, *lama tamut b'lo itekha?*—which could mean "why die before your time?" But that makes no sense. Qohelet never claims that the wise live longer, or manage to delay their death longer than the foolish or the wicked. On the contrary: conducting oneself wisely is, for Qohelet, not a way of increasing the number of one's days on earth but of making the most of them. *Lama tamut b'lo itekha?* (literally, "why die without thy time?") is better read as asking rhetorically, "Why die without making anything of your time on earth?" The second clauses of both verses would thus be posing similar rhetorical questions: to allow yourself to be crippled by the *hevel* premise or to ignore it is to lay waste to your life by failing to make proper use of the numbered days granted you under the sun.

Having dealt first with wisely enhancing the scope of our normative self-critique by exposing ourselves to failures and calamities and to the "rebuke" of people who think differently, with added attentiveness to the two opposing positions, Qohelet turns in the last section of the chapter to boldly address the elephant in the room: the deeply rooted, heartfelt, and universally accepted normative convictions that we consider so undeniable that no amount of external critique could possibly destabilize them. These are the normative principles that we claim to have "found out,"[3] or hold true, because we deem them to be self-evident. The example that he chooses is the general directive to always avoid associating with such detestable women "whose heart is snares and nets, and hands are fetters; he who pleases God should escape from her; but the sinner shall be caught by her" (26). Here, as Immanuel Kant would have it, is a maxim, or principle of action that, by virtue of the categorical imperative (namely, finding it to remain valid when formulated as general law binding on all humankind), is endorsed as a universal moral principle that no one could deny or challenge. However, Qohelet wryly notes, even such principles inevitably fall prey to the *hevel* premise, if indirectly. For, certain as we are of the general principle, it is never possible to apply it with certainty. Being a man myself, perhaps, he declares, I can confidently claim to know (to "find out") one in a thousand men but never a woman (27–28). Despite being certain that women belonging to the above-mentioned category should be avoided univocally and at all cost, I can never be certain which of the particular women I actually encounter belong to it and should be avoided.

More generally, claims Qohelet in this remarkably perceptive passage, there are general truths and moral principles that genuinely strike us as being absolute and immune to criticism because they are universally endorsed. Nonetheless, their certainty (real or imagined) can never carry over to the realm of practical reasoning. They relate absolute well-defined directives to well-defined absolutely general categories of people, things, or states of affairs (forever steer clear of women of category *X*) in a way that would seem to defy the *hevel* premise. Yet deeming any actual person, thing, or state of affairs as belonging to the category in question remains thoroughly within the purview of the *hevel* premise: inherently uncertain, time-bound, questionable, context-dependent, and transient.

Prudent attention to our failures and to those of others, to their normative critique, and to the uncertainty of ever validly applying even our most valid principles, Qohelet forcefully argues, combine with our own self-wariness to enable the normative self-distancing required for holding our commitments in self-critical review. This is the best of which we are humanly capable, and it is only thus that we can genuinely claim to act meaningfully while fully endorsing the *hevel* premise.

With this, Qohelet has completed the philosophical portion of his study of the prospects of human wisdom—or perhaps we should say rationality—in conditions of thoroughgoing *hevel*. He embarked on it declaring in the closing verses of chapter 1: "And I gave my heart to know wisdom, and to know madness and folly: I perceived that this also was a striving after the wind. For in much wisdom is much grief" (1:17–18). He has now completed the philosophical part of his journey, and returns to that opening statement almost verbatim, yet stripped clean of any trace of anger, grief, sorrow, or frustration: "I cast about in my mind to know, and to search, and to seek our wisdom, and the reason of things, and to know the wickedness of folly and foolishness which is madness" (25). Again, the Hebrew is better nuanced. *Saboti* connotes "encompassing," coming full circle, thus lending a knowing finality to his quest that "I cast about" does not begin to describe.

NOTES

[1] See Thomas S. Kuhn, *The Structure of Scientific Revolutions*, 2d ed. (Chicago: University of Chicago Press, 1970), 94, 111–14, 150, 151. As I noted in my general introduction (n. 20, the view is forcefully restated in Postscript-1969, which Kuhn appended to the 1970 edition, where he states: "The conversion experience that I likened to a gestalt switch remains therefore at the heart of the revolutionary process" (204).

[2] And not "sorrow," as the KJV and the Jerusalem Bible both have it. The biblical Hebrew term *ka'as* invariably denotes anger, vexation, and frustration.

[3] The verb's root, *m.tz.a.*, "to find," appears in Qohelet eighteen times, in which all but three clearly denote "finding out," rather than merely "finding." The three exceptions are 9:10; 9:15; 11:1.

א טוֹב שֵׁם מִשֶּׁמֶן טוֹב וְיוֹם הַמָּוֶת מִיּוֹם הִוָּלְדוֹ: ב טוֹב לָלֶכֶת אֶל־בֵּית־אֵבֶל מִלֶּכֶת אֶל־בֵּית מִשְׁתֶּה בַּאֲשֶׁר הוּא סוֹף כָּל־הָאָדָם וְהַחַי יִתֵּן אֶל־לִבּוֹ: ג טוֹב כַּעַס מִשְּׂחֹק כִּי־בְרֹעַ פָּנִים יִיטַב לֵב: ד לֵב חֲכָמִים בְּבֵית אֵבֶל וְלֵב כְּסִילִים בְּבֵית שִׂמְחָה: ה טוֹב לִשְׁמֹעַ גַּעֲרַת חָכָם מֵאִישׁ שֹׁמֵעַ שִׁיר כְּסִילִים: ו כִּי כְקוֹל הַסִּירִים תַּחַת הַסִּיר כֵּן שְׂחֹק הַכְּסִיל וְגַם־זֶה הָבֶל: ז כִּי הָעֹשֶׁק יְהוֹלֵל חָכָם וִיאַבֵּד אֶת־לֵב מַתָּנָה: ח טוֹב אַחֲרִית דָּבָר מֵרֵאשִׁיתוֹ טוֹב אֶרֶךְ־רוּחַ מִגְּבַהּ־רוּחַ: ט אַל־תְּבַהֵל בְּרוּחֲךָ לִכְעוֹס כִּי כַעַס בְּחֵיק כְּסִילִים יָנוּחַ:

[1]A good name is better than precious ointment; and the day of death than the day of one's birth. [2]It is better to go to the house of mourning, than to go to the house of feasting: for that is the end of all men; and the living will lay it to his heart. [3]Sorrow is better than laughter: for by the sadness of the countenance the heart is made glad, [4]The heart of the wise is in the house of mourning; but the heart of fools is in the house of mirth, [5]It is better to hear the rebuke of the wise, than for a man to hear the song of fools. [6]For as the crackling of thorns under a pot, so is the laughter of the fool; this also is vapour. [7]Surely oppression makes a wise man mad; and a bribe destroys the heart. [8]Better is the end of a thing than the beginning of it; and the patient in spirit is better than the proud in spirit. [9]Be not hasty in thy spirit to be angry for anger rests in the bosom of fools.

Qohelet continues his characterization of a life well-lived, both in ethical behavior and material achievement. These qualities, he asserts, cannot be anticipated reliably in early or midlife but can be fully assessed only at the end of life, when no more missteps may occur. The illuminations contrast the joy and hopes of a noisy *brit milah* (Jewish ritual circumcision) celebration with the quiet seriousness of the study of a recently deceased scholar.

The scenes are set in a palace room above a garden. On the English page, in front of a window overlooking a blossoming fruit sapling, a mohel (circumcision officiant) of our own day lifts a newly circumcised baby boy to show to the loved ones celebrating his birth. Jewish women and men from across history revel in the newborn's entrance into the community. The prophet Elijah, who, according to tradition, attends every *brit milah*, looks on skeptically, knowing that this innocent new life will face not only joy but also challenge during his days on earth.

The Hebrew page depicts the ending of a life well-lived. Late on a winter's day, the fruit tree outside has grown thick and tall but bent by storms, and now stands coated with ice and snow. The now-quiet room has been the beloved study of a medieval scholar, the desk laden with piles of books and papers. The oil lamp near the window has burned out, the quill lies abandoned on an unfinished page, and flowers have wilted and dried in their vase. A potted palm tree symbolizes righteousness and commitment to God in Psalm 92, while miniature portraits of family members rest among the books, testifying to the respect and love enjoyed by the now-vanished scholar.

The micrographic border across the two pages complements Qohelet's advice with passages from the Mishnah and Talmud relating the value of a good name and ethical personal conduct.[1]

NOTE

[1] Passages from H. N. Bialik and Y. H. Ravnitzky, *Sefer ha-Aggadah* (Tel Aviv: Dvir, 1948), 501–2. Trans. in idem, *The Book of Legends: Sefer ha-Aggadah*, trans. William G. Braude (New York: Schocken, 1992), 642–43. The passages are drawn from Avot 2:1, b. Berakhot 17a, Derekh Eretz Zuta 3, Avot 13, Tanhuma, Vayak'hel 1, b. Yoma 38 a–b, Eduyyot 5:7, Exodus Rabbah 48:1, Avot 4:1, Avot 2:10, b. Berakhot 28b, Deuteronomy Rabbah 4:4.

י אַל־תֹּאמַר מֶה הָיָה שֶׁהַיָּמִים הָרִאשֹׁנִים הָיוּ טוֹבִים מֵאֵלֶּה כִּי לֹא מֵחָכְמָה שָׁאַלְתָּ עַל־זֶה: יא טוֹבָה חָכְמָה עִם־נַחֲלָה וְיֹתֵר לְרֹאֵי הַשָּׁמֶשׁ: יב כִּי בְּצֵל הַחָכְמָה בְּצֵל הַכָּסֶף וְיִתְרוֹן דַּעַת הַחָכְמָה תְּחַיֶּה בְעָלֶיהָ: יג רְאֵה אֶת־מַעֲשֵׂה הָאֱלֹהִים כִּי מִי יוּכַל לְתַקֵּן אֵת אֲשֶׁר עִוְּתוֹ: יד בְּיוֹם טוֹבָה הֱיֵה בְטוֹב וּבְיוֹם רָעָה רְאֵה גַּם אֶת־זֶה לְעֻמַּת־זֶה עָשָׂה הָאֱלֹהִים עַל־דִּבְרַת שֶׁלֹּא יִמְצָא הָאָדָם אַחֲרָיו מְאוּמָה:

[10]Do not say, How was it that the former days were better than these? For thou dost not inquire wisely concerning this. [11]Wisdom is good with an inheritance: and by it, there is profit to them who see the sun. [12]For wisdom is a defense, and money is a defense: but the excellency of knowledge is, that wisdom gives life to those who have it. [13]Consider the work of God: for who can make that straight, which he has made crooked? [14]In the day of prosperity be joyful, but in the day of adversity consider: God has made the one as well as the other, to the end that man should find nothing after him.

ohelet stresses the futility of nostalgia for happier times and the impossibility of predicting what the future holds—humankind sees only a sliver of the total reality that only God knows. Gazing from his palace window at his estates, even privileged Qohelet understands that he sees only part of the reality. Gazing into a garden pool, unpredictable wavelets and spray obscure even the view of his and his companion's faces.

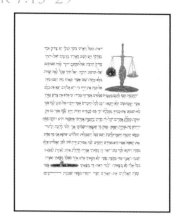

טו אֶת־הַכֹּל רָאִיתִי בִּימֵי הֶבְלִי יֵשׁ צַדִּיק אֹבֵד בְּצִדְקֹו וְיֵשׁ רָשָׁע מַאֲרִיךְ בְּרָעָתֹו: טז אַל־תְּהִי צַדִּיק הַרְבֵּה וְאַל־תִּתְחַכַּם יֹותֵר לָמָּה תִּשֹּׁומֵם: יז אַל־תִּרְשַׁע הַרְבֵּה וְאַל־תְּהִי סָכָל לָמָּה תָמוּת בְּלֹא עִתֶּךָ: יח טֹוב אֲשֶׁר תֶּאֱחֹז בָּזֶה וְגַם־מִזֶּה אַל־תַּנַּח אֶת־יָדֶךָ כִּי־יְרֵא אֱלֹהִים יֵצֵא אֶת־כֻּלָּם: יט הַחָכְמָה תָּעֹז לֶחָכָם מֵעֲשָׂרָה שַׁלִּיטִים אֲשֶׁר הָיוּ בָּעִיר: כ כִּי אָדָם אֵין צַדִּיק בָּאָרֶץ אֲשֶׁר יַעֲשֶׂה־טֹּוב וְלֹא יֶחֱטָא: כא גַּם לְכָל־הַדְּבָרִים אֲשֶׁר יְדַבֵּרוּ אַל־תִּתֵּן לִבֶּךָ אֲשֶׁר לֹא־תִשְׁמַע אֶת־עַבְדְּךָ מְקַלְלֶךָ: כב כִּי גַּם־פְּעָמִים רַבֹּות יָדַע לִבֶּךָ אֲשֶׁר גַּם־[אַתְּ] אַתָּה קִלַּלְתָּ אֲחֵרִים: כג כָּל־זֹה נִסִּיתִי בַחָכְמָה אָמַרְתִּי אֶחְכָּמָה וְהִיא רְחֹוקָה מִמֶּנִּי: כד רָחֹוק מַה־שֶּׁהָיָה וְעָמֹק ׀ עָמֹק מִי יִמְצָאֶנּוּ: כה סַבֹּותִי אֲנִי וְלִבִּי לָדַעַת וְלָתוּר וּבַקֵּשׁ חָכְמָה וְחֶשְׁבֹּון וְלָדַעַת רֶשַׁע כֶּסֶל וְהַסִּכְלוּת הֹולֵלֹות: כו וּמֹוצֶא אֲנִי מַר מִמָּוֶת אֶת־הָאִשָּׁה אֲשֶׁר־הִיא מְצֹודִים וַחֲרָמִים לִבָּהּ אֲסוּרִים יָדֶיהָ טֹוב לִפְנֵי הָאֱלֹהִים יִמָּלֵט מִמֶּנָּה וְחֹוטֵא יִלָּכֶד בָּהּ: כז רְאֵה זֶה מָצָאתִי אָמְרָה קֹהֶלֶת אַחַת לְאַחַת לִמְצֹא חֶשְׁבֹּון: כח אֲשֶׁר עֹוד־בִּקְשָׁה נַפְשִׁי וְלֹא מָצָאתִי אָדָם אֶחָד מֵאֶלֶף מָצָאתִי וְאִשָּׁה בְכָל־אֵלֶּה לֹא מָצָאתִי: כט לְבַד רְאֵה־זֶה מָצָאתִי אֲשֶׁר עָשָׂה הָאֱלֹהִים אֶת־הָאָדָם יָשָׁר וְהֵמָּה בִקְשׁוּ חִשְּׁבֹנֹות רַבִּים:

15 All things have I seen in the days of my vapour: there is a just man who perishes in his righteousness, and there is a wicked man who prolongs his life in his wickedness. 16 Be not righteous overmuch; nor make thyself overwise: why shouldst thou destroy thyself? 17 Be not wicked overmuch, nor be foolish: why shouldst thou die before thy time? 18 It is good that thou shouldst take hold of this; but do not withdraw thy hand from that either: for he that fears God performs them all. 19 Wisdom strengthens the wise more than ten rulers who are in a city. 20 For there is not a just man upon earth, who does good, and sins not. 21 Also take no heed to all words that are spoken; lest thou hear thy servant curse thee: 22 for oftentimes also thy own heart knows that thou thyself hast likewise cursed others. 23 All this have I proved by wisdom; I said, I will be wise; but it was far from me. 24 That which is far off, and exceeding deep, who can find it out? 25 I cast about in my mind to know, and to search, and to seek out wisdom, and the reason of things, and to know the wickedness of folly and foolishness which is madness: 26 and I find more bitter than death the woman, whose heart is snares and nets, and her hands are fetters: he who pleases God shall escape from her; but the sinner shall be caught by her. 27 Behold, this have I found, says Qohelet, counting one thing to another, to find out the sum, 28 which yet my soul seeks, but I have not found it: One man among a thousand I have found; but a woman among all those I have not found. 29 Lo, this only have I found, that God has made man upright; but they have sought out many inventions.

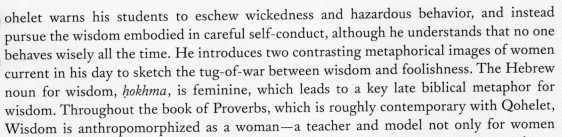

ohelet warns his students to eschew wickedness and hazardous behavior, and instead pursue the wisdom embodied in careful self-conduct, although he understands that no one behaves wisely all the time. He introduces two contrasting metaphorical images of women current in his day to sketch the tug-of-war between wisdom and foolishness. The Hebrew noun for wisdom, *ḥokhma*, is feminine, which leads to a key late biblical metaphor for wisdom. Throughout the book of Proverbs, which is roughly contemporary with Qohelet, Wisdom is anthropomorphized as a woman—a teacher and model not only for women but for all humankind. For instance, Proverbs 8 describes wisdom as God's earliest companion and as a bridge between the divine and human spheres; similarly, Proverbs ends with a paean of praise to the wise and capable mother, homemaker, and businesswoman; this passage is traditionally chanted as the Sabbath table hymn, the "Woman of Power" "Aishet hayil" (Prov 31:10–31) extolling the mystical Sabbath Bride (and many people extend the metaphor to the individual homemaker). Conversely, Qohelet warns of the dangers of temptation by reckless illicit women, characterized in Prov 9:13 by the feminine gender (*k'silut*) of the same word, *k'sil*, "fool," that Qohelet continually applies to his negative role model.[1]

The Hebrew illumination presents the individual's decision-making as a scale, balancing the pursuit of daily needs represented by the pile of coins, with the demands of eternity, symbolized by the cloud of the deep sky. The English illumination uses micrographic texts to contrast the two symbolic women to whom Qohelet alludes in his warning against careless bad behavior. At right, the wise woman, *aishet hayil* of Proverbs, gathers the fruit that she has grown, household keys dangling from her waist. She is composed of Prov 31:10–31 and passages from Proverbs 9, all praising Lady Wisdom. At left, a dancer, such as one might have seen at parties in the Alhambra prior to Christian conquest, rattles a tambourine. Passages from Act I of Verdi's *La Traviata*, the interchange between the courtesan Violetta and Alfredo, form her body. *Libiamo, ne' lieti calici che la bellezza infiora, e la fuggevol ora s'inebrii a voluttà* ("Drink from the joyful glass, resplendent with beauty, drink to the spirit of pleasure that enchants the fleeting moment"), he cries, and Violetta answers: *Tra voi saprò dividere il tempo mio giocondo; tutto è follia nel mondo ciò che non è piacer* ("I shall divide my gaiety among you all; everything in life is folly, except for pleasure").

NOTE
[1] A metaphorical interpretation of these women has precedent in Seow's interpretation of the two women as models of folly and wisdom, albeit using different textual references. See Seow, *The Anchor Bible*, 275.

INTRODUCTION TO CHAPTER EIGHT
KNOWING THE LIMITS OF ONE'S STRENGTH

As Qohelet's idea of a meaningful human life in conditions of utter impermanence and uncertainty gains full philosophical clarity, so does his portrayal of its wise pursuers: critical of themselves and others, deliberative, expecting the worse, and doubtful of anything taken for granted. From this point on, Qohelet devotes much of his text to exploring the social consequences of adopting such an attitude and way of life. He will devote chapter 9 to a piercing examination of such a person's inferior social standing in the context of an honest and decent society that takes a very different view of life from his.

In chapter 8, his focus is different. It is about knowing how far one should go (to paraphrase the title of David Lodge's well-known novel).[1] Assuming that we follow Qohelet's advice, to proceed self-critically, we learn the lesson of past failures and prudently expose ourselves to external criticism and, in time, arrive at an admittedly tentative decision that the time is now ripe for planting, for example, rather than for uprooting the planted. Acting wisely, however, does not end with formulating a tentative diagnosis and action plan. One needs to see it through. The question is, how should one best proceed in the face of a seemingly opposing authority? Two questions present themselves. First, what are the limits of effective action, and how can we be sure that our efforts have become counterproductive and that it is time to rest our case? The second, and more significant, question concerns the limits of our accountability in such circumstances: is it the wise person's duty to stand for what he holds true, come what may? The latter question is also of religious significance. God expects us to make and act upon good time-bound assessments, but at what cost? Does he expect us to remain true to ourselves, no matter what? For Qohelet, doing one's best to do good is God's will, for which he will judge us. But what level of personal risk are we expected to maintain?

Proceeding wisely in God's shadow, to use Michael Walzer's phrase,[2] after an action plan has been wisely made invites such second-order questions, to which Qohelet devotes chapter 8: with reference to the employment of a powerful ruler who thinks differently and to God's ever-presence (8:1–2). As always, it is about steering a justifiably rational course between the Scylla of foolish flaccid piety and the Charybdis of foolish arrogant overconfidence—always a tricky course of significant epistemic and theological import.

As in all occupations under heaven, the duty of councils to powerful monarchs is to do their best to put right what they deem to be wrong. Here, doing one's best is about more than settling on goals and courses of action. It is also about knowing one's strength and assessing one's effectiveness. Monarchs seek advice but can be most averse to criticism. It is one thing to draw the king's attention to a trouble spot, but it can be quite another to question his judgment. For a powerful monarch, the difference between being caught unawares and being proved wrong may well prove fatal.

At first glance, Qohelet's answer might seem bland and trivial. One should not be intimidated by the king and should speak one's mind, he says; yet one must know when to back down, even in cases of wickedness (3)—

which, of course, begs the question of exactly when one is supposed to shift gears and back down. But there is nothing trivial or obvious about Qohelet's answer, especially from the religious perspective from which it is written.

First, Qohelet's indeterminate answer conveys the cruel truth that the *hevel* principle applies here, too. We can never be sure how far to effectively go, and when it is best to persist in protest and when to rest our case (leaving it to God to punish the wicked ruler [5–6])—another example of the type of informed, imaginative, prospective reasoning that Qohelet identifies with acting wisely. We are expected (by God) to do our tentative best in deciding both questions: What is the right thing to do, in principle? Should we continue doing it, given the circumstances?

Second, as noted, the question of whether to "stand on [even] an evil thing" (3) is not merely one of self-preservation. Some things clearly merit taking serious risks. Rather, it is a question of accountability. Qohelet is clear that one cannot be held accountable by God for wrongs that one is powerless to prevent. This is a point worth dwelling on. Qohelet is not merely an epistemologist. He is first and foremost a religious philosopher anxiously concerned about doing the right thing in the eyes of God. As is the case regarding employment in the service of a human monarch, our obligation to God is not only to act appropriately but for our actions to express our commitment and loyalty to God. In religious contexts, these are commonly associated with fanatic zeal, blind to all considerations of reasonable effectiveness. On the contrary, at the time that the book of Qohelet was being written, martyrdom was swiftly emerging as a religious value of great magnitude in the writings of both its contemporaries: the authors of the book of Daniel and those of Maccabees. Qohelet's position is emphatic: zealotry for zealotry's sake is not a religious virtue. The limits of our strength mark the boundaries of our religious responsibilities (4). Where those limits lie is a question about ourselves and our world, about which, like any other such question, we can only hypothesize (7).

But with respect to God, the situation would appear to be radically different. For concerning the divine, we apparently do know something with absolute certainty: that God is the perfectly moral judge. "Yet surely I know," declares Qohelet—which, if there is any truth in my proposed reading of the book, is a very rare statement on his part—"... that it shall be well[3] with those who fear God, who fear before him: But [that] it shall not be well with the wicked [who,] like the shadow, will not prolong his days; because he does not fear before God" (12–13). Qohelet knows that God's judgment is undoubtedly perfect and that therefore those who fear him will ultimately see good, while those who do not will ultimately suffer.

The problem is that "there is *hevel* which is done on the earth," temporary periods[4] during which "there are just men, to whom it happens according to the deeds of the wicked, [and] there are wicked men, to whom it happens according to the deeds of the righteous" (14). This creates two problems for Qohelet, neither of which is the so-called problem of evil—because for Qohelet, no real evil exists in the world but only perfectly just divine retribution. The problems arise "because sentence against an evil work is not executed speedily" and "a sinner [can] do evil a hundred times" before being justly dealt with. Therefore, the true causal relation between human deed and divine reward is forever obscured from human eyes.

The two problems correspond to the two above-mentioned, by now familiar, forms of folly. The first is the overwise, who mistakenly take what they now believe for timeless universal truths. Just like the wise councillor to the evil king, whose obligation is to do all in his power to right the king's wrongs, the overwise, who see wicked kings buried with dignity and pomp and righteous kings banished and forgotten (10), mistake temporary suspension of divine justice for permanent divine *in*justice.

The second kind of fools make the same mistake of identifying the temporary with the absolute, but their confidence in God's perfect judgment causes them to suspend their own judgment. Rather than criticize God, they mistakenly conclude that the temporary good fate of the wicked proves them to be righteous and the ill-fated righteous to be wicked—as if one could infer God's absolute moral code from the momentary fate of his subjects.

Both gravely and dangerously mistaken positions are due to opposite violations of the *hevel* premise. The former delusionally ignore it and criticize God for failing to measure up to what *they* hold right; the latter believe, equally delusionally, that they can validly infer absolute truths from their impressions of the meaning of God's deed and Word.

For Qohelet, the unpredictable and indecipherable timeline of divine justice is no more than the theological equivalent of his original problem, which he forcefully reiterates: "When I applied my heart to know wisdom and to see the business[5] that is done on the earth … then I beheld all the work of God, that a man cannot find out: because a man labour to seek it out, yet he shall not find[6] it; furthermore, though a wise man think to know it, yet he shall not be able to find it" (16–17).

Just as we are to assume responsibility for the world forever lacking certain knowledge of nature's laws, we are to make our moral and ethical decisions forever lacking certain knowledge of those of divine morality or revelation. The idea that we can hold God accountable, as we do a mortal king, like the "Calvinist" idea that divine grace can be inferred from a person's temporary good fortune, is a dangerous and disruptive delusion. Qohelet's conclusion might sound heretical to some ears because we can never determine God's Word or justice with certainty; we can only rely on our own forever temporary and fallible assessments in making our way in the world and, by implication, in making sense of God's Word. In other words, our *hevel* existence cannot be diminished, nor can the prospects of humanly achievable *yitaron* be enhanced by our belief in an all-perfect providential deity who reveals his will to his human creatures. To conduct oneself wisely is to do so as if such a God did not exist, while firmly believing that he does. Because all is *hevel*, states Qohelet, I commend gauging the worth of one's labor on one's own sense of joyous satisfaction (*simha*)—which is all in accord with my ongoing efforts to know wisdom (14–16).

NOTES

[1] David Lodge, *How Far Can You Go?* (London: Penguin, 1987), describes the dilemmas of four young adult Catholics growing up in England under the confusing shadow of the Second Vatican Council's reforms.

[2] Michael Walzer, *In God's Shadow: Politics in the Hebrew Bible* (New Haven, Conn.: Yale University Press, 2012).

[3] The Hebrew word *tov*, "good," connotes a pleasing excellence in biblical Hebrew, which better characterizes God's judgment (as in his assessments of the stages of Creation in Genesis 1) than does "well."

[4] All English translations of 8:14 translate *hevel* here, as elsewhere, as "vanity" (KJV, ESV, JPS, and the Jerusalem Bible), "meaningless" (NIV), or "nonsense" (GNB). Read thus, God is to be unthinkably described by Qohelet as acting nonsensically or meaninglessly, rather than as merely suspending his judgment temporarily.

[5] The Hebrew term is *inyan*, "matter," rather than "business," which clearly and knowingly echoes the *inyan* that God gave us to contend with of 1:13 and 3:10, thus lending it marked theological significance.

[6] As noted with respect to the previous chapter, "to find" for Qohelet is "to find out"—i.e., "to determine."

מִי כְּהֶחָכָם וּמִי יוֹדֵעַ פֵּשֶׁר דָּבָר חָכְמַת אָדָם תָּאִיר פָּנָיו וְעֹז פָּנָיו יְשֻׁנֶּא: ² אֲנִי פִּי מֶלֶךְ שְׁמוֹר וְעַל דִּבְרַת שְׁבוּעַת אֱלֹהִים: ³ אַל תִּבָּהֵל מִפָּנָיו תֵּלֵךְ אַל תַּעֲמֹד בְּדָבָר רָע כִּי כָּל אֲשֶׁר יַחְפֹּץ יַעֲשֶׂה: ⁴ בַּאֲשֶׁר דְּבַר מֶלֶךְ שִׁלְטוֹן וּמִי יֹאמַר לוֹ מַה תַּעֲשֶׂה: ⁵ שׁוֹמֵר מִצְוָה לֹא יֵדַע דָּבָר רָע וְעֵת וּמִשְׁפָּט יֵדַע לֵב חָכָם: ⁶ כִּי לְכָל חֵפֶץ יֵשׁ עֵת וּמִשְׁפָּט כִּי רָעַת הָאָדָם רַבָּה עָלָיו: ⁷ כִּי אֵינֶנּוּ יֹדֵעַ מַה שֶּׁיִּהְיֶה כִּי כַּאֲשֶׁר יִהְיֶה מִי יַגִּיד לוֹ: ⁸ אֵין אָדָם שַׁלִּיט בָּרוּחַ לִכְלוֹא אֶת הָרוּחַ וְאֵין שִׁלְטוֹן בְּיוֹם הַמָּוֶת וְאֵין מִשְׁלַחַת בַּמִּלְחָמָה וְלֹא יְמַלֵּט רֶשַׁע אֶת בְּעָלָיו: ⁹ אֶת כָּל זֶה רָאִיתִי וְנָתוֹן אֶת לִבִּי לְכָל מַעֲשֶׂה אֲשֶׁר נַעֲשָׂה תַּחַת הַשֶּׁמֶשׁ עֵת אֲשֶׁר שָׁלַט הָאָדָם בְּאָדָם לְרַע לוֹ: ¹⁰ וּבְכֵן רָאִיתִי רְשָׁעִים קְבֻרִים וָבָאוּ וּמִמְּקוֹם קָדוֹשׁ יְהַלֵּכוּ וְיִשְׁתַּכְּחוּ בָעִיר אֲשֶׁר כֵּן עָשׂוּ גַּם זֶה הָבֶל:

¹Who is like the wise man? And who knows the interpretation of a thing? A man's wisdom makes his face to shine, and the boldness of his face is changed, ²I counsel thee to keep the king's commandment, and that in the manner of an oath of God. ³Be not hasty to go out of his presence; stand not in an evil thing; for he does whatever pleases him. ⁴For the word of a king has authority: and who may say to him, What doest thou? ⁵He who keeps the commandment shall feel no evil thing: and a wise man's heart discerns both time and method. ⁶For every matter has its time and method, though the misery of man is great upon him. ⁷For he knows not that which shall be: for who can tell him when it shall be? ⁸There is no man who has power over the wind to retain the wind; nor has he power over the day of death: and there is no discharge in that war; nor shall wickedness deliver those who are given up to it. ⁹All this have I seen, and have appointed my heart to every work that is done under the sun: there is a time when one man rules over another to his own hurt. ¹⁰And so I saw the wicked buried, and come to their rest; but those who had done right were gone from the holy place, and were forgotten in the city: this also is vapour.

Qohelet shifts his advice to deal with what might have been the particular situation of many of his students: that of the wise courtier serving a corrupt ruler. Despite their best efforts at mitigating the surrounding corruption, they must behave shrewdly to survive and must choose words—and battles—strategically. For all his supposed power, the king forgets that he, too, enjoys only the limited life span and view of reality of "lesser" humans. His arrogance outstrips his humility. The illuminations offer cautionary images for both the arrogant ruler and the honest courtier. The Hebrew text begins with a painting of a marble statue of Justice, pulling down her blindfold and winking. In contrast, the bordering calligraphy offers the very passage from Deuteronomy (16:18–20) that famously requires the ruler to pursue honest and evenhanded justice for all people:

> Judges and officers shalt thou make thee in all thy gates, which the Lord thy God gives thee, throughout thy tribes: and they shall judge the people with righteous judgment. Thou shalt not wrest judgment; though shalt not respect persons, neither take a bribe: for a bribe blinds the eyes of the wise, and perverts the words of the righteous. Justice, justice shalt thou pursue, that thou mayst live, and inherit the land which the Lord thy God gives thee.

At right, the English text begins with a painting and shows a crown lying in a gutter, jewels scattered among the weeds coming through the stones. This image offers a cautionary tale inspired by Napoleon's remark about the crown of France lying in the gutter, and General George Patton's observation that in Roman generals' triumph parades, "A slave stood behind the conqueror holding a golden crown and whispering in his ear a warning: that all glory is fleeting."

The decorative text bordering the English page illustrates the dangers attendant upon the honest courtier, even when that courtier is the monarch's beloved child. King Lear casts his sole honest daughter, Cordelia, from his court when she refuses to compete with her malignant sisters at flattering him. Cordelia's honesty, of course, demonstrates her virtue; yet her father's and sisters' hateful reactions, and subsequent abuse of one another, result in the once-mighty king's humiliation—and ultimately, death for all four of them.

> Good my lord,
> You have begot me, bred me, loved me:
> I return those duties back as are right fit:
> Obey you, love you, and most honor you.
> Why have my sisters husbands, if they say
> They love you all? Haply, when I shall wed,
> That lord whose hand must take my plight shall carry
> Half my love with him, half my care and duty:
> Sure, I shall never marry like my sisters,
> To love my father all.
> (*King Lear*, 1.1)

יא אֲשֶׁר אֵין־נַעֲשָׂה פִתְגָם מַעֲשֵׂה הָרָעָה מְהֵרָה
עַל־כֵּן מָלֵא לֵב בְּנֵי־הָאָדָם בָּהֶם לַעֲשׂוֹת רָע:
יב אֲשֶׁר חֹטֶא עֹשֶׂה רָע מְאַת וּמַאֲרִיךְ לוֹ כִּי
גַּם־יוֹדֵעַ אָנִי אֲשֶׁר יִהְיֶה־טּוֹב לְיִרְאֵי הָאֱלֹהִים
אֲשֶׁר יִירְאוּ מִלְּפָנָיו: יג וְטוֹב לֹא־יִהְיֶה לָרָשָׁע
וְלֹא־יַאֲרִיךְ יָמִים כַּצֵּל אֲשֶׁר אֵינֶנּוּ יָרֵא מִלִּפְנֵי
אֱלֹהִים: יד יֶשׁ־הֶבֶל אֲשֶׁר נַעֲשָׂה עַל־הָאָרֶץ
אֲשֶׁר | יֵשׁ צַדִּיקִים אֲשֶׁר מַגִּיעַ אֲלֵהֶם כְּמַעֲשֵׂה
הָרְשָׁעִים וְיֵשׁ רְשָׁעִים שֶׁמַּגִּיעַ אֲלֵהֶם כְּמַעֲשֵׂה
הַצַּדִּיקִים אָמַרְתִּי שֶׁגַּם־זֶה הָבֶל:

[11]Because sentence against an evil work is not executed speedily, therefore the heart of the sons of men is fully set in them to do evil. [12]A sinner does evil a hundred times, and his days are prolonged, yet surely I know that it shall be well with those who fear God, who fear before him: [13]but it shall not be well with the wicked, and, like the shadow, he will not prolong his days; because he does not fear before God. [14]There is a vapour which is done upon the earth; that there are just men, to whom it happens according: to the deeds of the wicked: again, there are wicked men, to whom it happens according to the deeds of the righteous: I said that this also is vapor.

Like its companion in the adjacent painting, this illumination continues Qohelet's meditation about the consequences for appearances of divine justice, arising from God's timelessness and the evanescence of all material existence. In these two paintings, he observes two trees. He reflects upon the ultimate doom of the soul of the arrogant and the eternal favor that the soul of the wise and just person will enjoy. In this painting, a once-tall and mighty cedar proudly planted within a tiled surround has died. Its stump reveals the rot at its core, and its decaying branches and leaves rest on the surrounding tile. The clear sky gives way to a view of the deep sky filled with stars, symbolizing God's distant eternity.

The border presents verses from Psalm 49, promising—as Qohelet understands—ultimate divine justice for both the arrogant and powerful:

Why should I fear in the days of evil,
when the iniquity of my persecutors compass me about?

They that trust in their wealth,
    and boast themselves in the multitude of their riches;
None of them can by any means redeem his brother,
    nor give to God a ransom for him:
For the redemption of their soul is too dear, and he leaves it forever:
That he might still live forever, and not see the pit.
When he sees that wise men die, that the fool and the brutish person perish together,
            And leave their wealth to others:
    Their inward thought is, that their houses shall continue forever,
    And their dwelling places to all generations;
    They call their lands after their own names.

וְשִׁבַּחְתִּי אֲנִי אֶת־הַשִּׂמְחָה אֲשֶׁר אֵין־טוֹב לָאָדָם טו
תַּחַת הַשֶּׁמֶשׁ כִּי אִם־לֶאֱכֹל וְלִשְׁתּוֹת וְלִשְׂמוֹחַ וְהוּא
יִלְוֶנּוּ בַעֲמָלוֹ יְמֵי חַיָּיו אֲשֶׁר־נָתַן־לוֹ הָאֱלֹהִים תַּחַת
הַשָּׁמֶשׁ: טז כַּאֲשֶׁר נָתַתִּי אֶת־לִבִּי לָדַעַת חָכְמָה
וְלִרְאוֹת אֶת־הָעִנְיָן אֲשֶׁר נַעֲשָׂה עַל־הָאָרֶץ כִּי גַם
בַּיּוֹם וּבַלַּיְלָה שֵׁנָה בְּעֵינָיו אֵינֶנּוּ רֹאֶה: יז וְרָאִיתִי
אֶת־כָּל־מַעֲשֵׂה הָאֱלֹהִים כִּי לֹא יוּכַל הָאָדָם לִמְצוֹא
אֶת־הַמַּעֲשֶׂה אֲשֶׁר נַעֲשָׂה תַחַת־הַשֶּׁמֶשׁ בְּשֶׁל
אֲשֶׁר יַעֲמֹל הָאָדָם לְבַקֵּשׁ וְלֹא יִמְצָא וְגַם אִם־
יֹאמַר הֶחָכָם לָדַעַת לֹא יוּכַל לִמְצֹא:

[15] So I commend mirth, because a man has no better thing under the sun, than to eat, and to drink, and to be merry: for that shall accompany him in his labour during the days of his life, which God gives him under the sun. [16] When I applied my heart to know wisdom, and to see the business that is done upon the earth: (how one sees no sleep with one's eyes either by day or by night); [17] then I beheld all the work of God, that a man cannot find out the work that is done under the sun: because though a man labour to seek it out, yet he shall not find it: furthermore, though a wise man think to know it, yet he shall not be able to find it.

In this painting, Qohelet muses on the happier attitude of the humbler, more realistic, person who eschews greed and pretension and instead finds contentment in whatever pleasures surround him. In contrast to the once-prized, now-dead cedar tree, on the other side of the hedge a small apricot tree has asserted itself, growing unnoticed among the hedge bushes. A wild rosebush springs near its roots, among this hidden corner's rocks and grass. The plant's diminutive size, thorns, and blossoms caused the authors of Exodus Rabbah to identify the Burning Bush as a rose, embodying Israel's humility, as well as Israel's inclusion of both the righteous and the wicked.[1] Hidden from view, enjoying privacy away from the celebrity and attention within the palace and its manicured garden, a couple has taken pleasure in the hidden spot; traces of a picnic—a bottle of wine and spilled glasses and fruit rest on a rumpled blanket in the fragrant shade.

In the poetry inscribed around the border, the eleventh-century Sephardic poet and grand vizier of Granada, Samuel the Nagid, who trod its palace courtyards daily, passed along Qohelet's advice:

My friend, we pass our lives as if in sleep;
Our pleasures and our pains are merely dreams.
But stop your ears to all such things, and shut
       Your eyes—may Heaven grant you strength!—
Don't speculate on hidden things; leave that
       To God, the Hidden One, whose eye sees all.

But send the lass who plays the lute
       To fill the cup with coral drink,

Put up in kegs in Adam's time,
       Or else just after Noah's flood,
A pungent wine, like frankincense,
       A glittering wine, like gold and gems,
Such wine as concubines and queens
       Would bring King David long ago.

The day they poured that wine into the drum,
       King David's singer Jerimoth would strum
And sing: "May such a wine as this be kept
       Preserved and stored in sealed-up kegs and saved
For all who crave the water of the grape,
       For every man who holds the cup with skill,
Who keeps the rule Ecclesiastes gave,
       Revels, and fears the tortures of the grave."[2]

NOTES

[1] H. Freedman and Maurice Simon, eds., *Midrash Rabbah*, vol. 3: *Exodus*, trans. S. M. Lehrman (London: Soncino, 1939), 54.

[2] Trans. Scheindlin, *Wine, Women, and Death*, 54–55.

INTRODUCTION TO CHAPTER NINE
THE CASE AGAINST HEDONISM

There are good reasons for hedonism: the harrowing thought, articulated in morbid detail in verses 1–6, that "all things come alike to all"; that all are in the unknowable hands of God, never knowing what life might hold in store for them, whether love or hate; that the same fate awaits all—the righteous and the wicked, the good (and the bad), the pure and the impure, those who worship, and those who do not; that after death, the great leveler, all is forgotten, renders wholly meaningless every consideration other than to enjoy our brief respite on earth to the hilt. Such is Qohelet's dark version of Louis the XV's infamous "Après moi, le déluge" (replacing *déluge* by *décès* in 9:3). If there is a decisive argument against the perpetually anxious, precarious, self-doubting, and uncertain life of worth prescribed by Qohelet, it has to be this.

To make it even stronger, Qohelet paints the hedonistic alternative in the most appealing pastoral colors:

> Go thy way, eat thy bread with joy, and drink thy wine with a merry heart; for God has already accepted thy works. Let thy garments be always white; and let thy head lack no oil. Live joyfully with the wife whom thou lovest all the days of the life of thy *hevel*, which he has given thee under the sun, all the days of thy *hevel*. (7–9)

Suburban paradise! Qohelet's rhetoric contains no trace of the usual accusation of anarchic, carefree, degenerate, and often violent self-indulgence so typical of religious diatribes against hedonism. Indeed, Qohelet plays the devil's advocate to hedonism so effectively that almost all his readers take him to be advocating his own position. But they are wrong.

The problem with even the most benign form of hedonism, Qohelet goes on to argue, resides not in the quality of its argument (we can know nothing for certain, and death is indeed the great leveler) or in its questionable morality (certainly not in the version he describes) but in it being an extremely bad strategy from the hedonist's own point of view. Hedonists do not deny the *hevel* premise. They do not overestimate it, as do passive, pious fools, nor do they underestimate it, as do *uber*-wise fools. Qohelet has convinced them of what a life of *yitaron* consists of, in the face of thoroughgoing *hevel*. But they are not willing to pay the price of such a life for reasons that Qohelet cannot but accept.[1] The only thing we can be sure of, they argue cynically, is that our days are numbered; that nothing we can achieve can be of lasting value; that the only advantage we have over the dead is that they know nothing, while we know that we are sure to die (4–5); that with respect to life's cruel trials, talent and learning offer no advantage; and that the race is not won by the swift, or the battle by the strong, or bread by the wise, or riches by men of understanding, "or yet favor" by "men of skill; but time and chance happens to them all" (11). Under such bleak conditions, hedonists see no *yitaron* in Qohelet's recommended life of wisdom and make a calculated choice to take their chances and invest their strength and talent in enjoying the little time they are granted on earth as best they can.

Interestingly, unlike the two forms of foolishness that Qohelet contends with throughout the book, the hedonist option is not described by him as foolish. Qohelet is well aware that what he has to offer is not much and that the advantages of what he terms *yitaron* cannot be tested or confirmed. On Qohelet's showing, the wise can perhaps feel satisfied that, in their efforts to improve their world and their picture of it, they have done their best. But our best does not guarantee success, and even his firm conviction that this is what God expects of us may perhaps be argued for; but that, too, can never be tested or confirmed.

Candidly realizing that in the lucid and reasoned hedonist option that he describes, he finds his keenest external normative challenge, Qohelet, true to his own philosophy, treats it with enormous respect and takes it with utmost seriousness. More important, unlike as with any other position he confronts, he makes for it the best case possible. Perhaps most significant is that he levels his argument against it from squarely within the premises on which it builds.

Hedonists, argues Qohelet, live their life in order to best enjoy it precisely because it is short and inherently unpredictable. However, constructing one's very existence around enjoying life's pleasures renders the hedonist, by his own admittance, vulnerable to the catastrophes that are bound to occur from time to time (11). Wholly unprepared when disaster befalls, they will resemble frantically squirming fish or aimlessly squawking birds that are caught unawares in an unnoticed fateful trap—"so are the sons of men snared in an evil time, when it falls suddenly upon them" (12). But if future disasters are unpredictable, the hedonist presumably answers, how could we have prepared? We enjoy life while it lasts, and if and when disaster hits, so be it! Here, at the point where hedonism morphs into fatalism, claims Qohelet, is where hedonism gets it gravely wrong. The source of their mistake is to identify being prepared with predictability. "This wisdom," he declares, which I have "seen also under the sun, ... [is]² great to me!" (13).

A community can prepare for such contingencies despite the fact that they can seldom predict them. Preparing for them requires seriously imagining and planning in advance for worst-case scenarios. Forever wary of life's cruel surprises, and always expecting the worse, those best positioned to deal with such emergencies, as when a great king suddenly attacks and lays siege on a small city (14), are those whom Qohelet deems to be wise. They will have considered the possibility on the basis of close studies of past calamities, planned for it as best they can, exchanged notes with their equally critical colleagues, and, although never able to say when such an emergency will present itself, will still be in a position to save the city when it does.

The problem with hedonism is hence twofold. Such pleasure-bound societies as Qohelet describes not only are unprepared for such scenarios but will have had little patience and no room for the perpetually misanthropic, always critical, party poopers who are capable of saving them in times of need. Wretched and rejected, they will go unheeded when most needed (15–16). Pleasure-seeking societies, especially of the benign "suburban" variety described by Qohelet, not only disagree with the advocates of Qohelet's philosophy as to what the true meaning of life should be, but they view their pessimistic way of thinking and ever-critical disposition as affronts to their very value system, and as socially disruptive and threatening, not unlike the Athenians' persecution of Socrates.

Hedonism cannot count as a viable alternative to Qohelet's life philosophy because it is forced to affirm it. People are free not to follow Qohelet's advice and to spend their lives pursuing the pleasures of food, drink, and loving spouses. But if they refuse to revere and properly accommodate dedicated devotees of Qohelet's philosophy as bona fide members of society, they will be their own undoing. The tragedy of purporting to meet the *hevel* premise by means of a serious and reasoned philosophy of pleasure- and comfort-seeking is that it lacks the social and psychological resources necessary for truly revering and granting social standing and voice to the required number of Qohelet devotees. Viewed thus, as Qohelet brilliantly argues, hedonism is its own undoing, almost of necessity.

NOTES

¹ In general, when Qohelet opens a statement with the word *yada'ati*, he signals awareness of a widely held opinion that is not his own (see, e.g., 3:12, 14). But when he says *shavti ve-er'eh*, "I returned and saw [understood]," he is stating his own opinion (e.g., 4:1, 7).

² Both the KJV and Jerusalem Bible render the last clause "and it *seemed* great to [or unto] me." The Hebrew phrase is *u-g'dolah he a'lai* and does not state that this piece of wisdom *seems* great to me, but *is* great to me. There is nothing hesitant or qualified in Qohelet's argument against his most powerful adversary.

א כִּי אֶת־כָּל־זֶה נָתַתִּי אֶל־לִבִּי וְלָבוּר אֶת־כָּל־זֶה אֲשֶׁר הַצַּדִּיקִים וְהַחֲכָמִים וַעֲבָדֵיהֶם בְּיַד הָאֱלֹהִים גַּם־אַהֲבָה גַּם־שִׂנְאָה אֵין יוֹדֵעַ הָאָדָם הַכֹּל לִפְנֵיהֶם:

ב הַכֹּל כַּאֲשֶׁר לַכֹּל מִקְרֶה אֶחָד לַצַּדִּיק וְלָרָשָׁע לַטּוֹב וְלַטָּהוֹר וְלַטָּמֵא וְלַזֹּבֵחַ וְלַאֲשֶׁר אֵינֶנּוּ זֹבֵחַ כַּטּוֹב כַּחֹטֶא הַנִּשְׁבָּע כַּאֲשֶׁר שְׁבוּעָה יָרֵא:

ג זֶה ׀ רָע בְּכֹל אֲשֶׁר־נַעֲשָׂה תַּחַת הַשֶּׁמֶשׁ כִּי־מִקְרֶה אֶחָד לַכֹּל וְגַם לֵב בְּנֵי־הָאָדָם מָלֵא־רָע וְהוֹלֵלוֹת בִּלְבָבָם בְּחַיֵּיהֶם וְאַחֲרָיו אֶל־הַמֵּתִים:

ד כִּי־מִי אֲשֶׁר יְבֻחַר [יְחֻבַּר] אֶל כָּל־הַחַיִּים יֵשׁ בִּטָּחוֹן כִּי־לְכֶלֶב חַי הוּא טוֹב מִן־הָאַרְיֵה הַמֵּת:

ה כִּי הַחַיִּים יוֹדְעִים שֶׁיָּמֻתוּ וְהַמֵּתִים אֵינָם יוֹדְעִים מְאוּמָה וְאֵין־עוֹד לָהֶם שָׂכָר כִּי נִשְׁכַּח זִכְרָם:

ו גַּם אַהֲבָתָם גַּם־שִׂנְאָתָם גַּם־קִנְאָתָם כְּבָר אָבָדָה וְחֵלֶק אֵין־לָהֶם עוֹד לְעוֹלָם בְּכֹל אֲשֶׁר־נַעֲשָׂה תַּחַת הַשֶּׁמֶשׁ:

¹For all this I laid to my heart, and sought to clarify all this, that the righteous, and the wise, and their deeds, are in the hand of God: no man knows whether love or hatred is in store: all is before them. ²All things come alike to all: there is one event to the righteous, and to the wicked: to the good and to the clean, and to the unclean: to him who sacrifices, and to him who does not sacrifice: as is the good, so is the sinner: and he who swears, as he who fears an oath. ³This is an evil in all things that are done under the sun, that there is one event to all: yea,⁴ also the heart of the sons of men is full of evil, and madness is in their heart while they live, and after that they go to the dead. ⁵For to him that is joined to all the living there is hope: for a living dog is better than a dead lion. For the living know that they shall die: but the dead know nothing, nor do they have any more a reward; for the memory of them is forgotten. ⁶Also their love, and their hatred, and their envy, is now long perished; nor have they any more a portion forever in any thing that is done under the sun.

ohelet resigns himself to the evident arbitrariness of fate, at least as it is perceptible to humankind down "under the sun." The individual's condition or fate may bear no relationship to his or her goodness or evil, obedience, or disregard of religious practice. Yet "while there is life, there is hope," as the aphorism says. Death, however, is like a closed book, an ended story, with no potential for further action or self-improvement in the world.

The illuminations depict the painful uncertainty of fate in the context of the life of a single innocent family and in the lives of blameless individuals caught up in national turmoil.

In the Hebrew illumination, Qohelet, safe in his palace, imagines a young husband and wife clinging together amid Jerusalem's destruction by Babylonian forces—perhaps only a few centuries before his own lifetime. However innocent of misdeed they might be, the young people cannot escape the maelstrom of national destruction. Sights of Jerusalem's disaster—a woman and her daughter grieving beside an infant's corpse, burning timbers and buildings, and cracked and spilling storage jars—flash across couple's view.

The border presents Lam 2:15–19, mocking once-beautiful Jerusalem for her humiliation:

> All that pass by clap their hands at thee; they hiss and wag their head at the daughter of Jerusalem, saying, Is this the city that men call the perfection of beauty, the joy of the whole earth? All thy enemies have opened their mouth against thee; they hiss and gnash the teeth; they say, We have swallowed her up: certainly this is the day that we have looked for; we have found it, we have seen it.

The Hebrew illumination focuses on the individual's vulnerability to national fortunes; but in the English illumination, Qohelet imagines the sudden death of an aristocrat from illness or accident, a very personal tragedy. A physician draws the stained bedsheet over the man's head; the bloodied rags, medicines, and the pomander with which he tried to rouse the dying man lie abandoned on a bedside table. The prince's grieving wife, horrified courtiers, and palace staff gather round the bed—a nurse entering the sickroom drops a basin of water as she covers her face in shock, and one man falls to the ground in grief. In the window, the narrow waning moon among the eternal stars signals the draining away of this life. A closed book, alluding to the end of the dying man's story, lies on the floor of his palace bedroom; this metaphor came to my mind in the days after my beloved first husband's death from cancer. The black-and-white tiled floor resembles the board on which we play so many games of chance. Modern pills rolling out of the scene relate the medieval physician's labors to the medical efforts of our own day.

The painting is surrounded by verses from Psalm 42, in which the Psalmist cries out in hope for deliverance—not only from pain but from uncertainty about God's care:

> [2]As the deer pants after the water brooks, so my soul pants after thee, O God. [3]My soul thirsts for God, for the living God: when shall I come and appear before God? [4]My tears have been my bread day and night, while they say to me all the day, Where is thy God?... [12]Why art thou cast down, O my soul? And why dost thou moan within me? Hope thou in God: for I shall yet praise him, who is the health of my countenance and my God.

׳ לֵךְ אֱכֹל בְּשִׂמְחָה לַחְמֶךָ וּשֲׁתֵה בְלֶב־טוֹב יֵינֶךָ
כִּי כְבָר רָצָה הָאֱלֹהִים אֶת־מַעֲשֶׂיךָ: ׳׳ בְּכָל־עֵת
יִהְיוּ בְגָדֶיךָ לְבָנִים וְשֶׁמֶן עַל־רֹאשְׁךָ אַל־יֶחְסָר:
׳ רְאֵה חַיִּים עִם־אִשָּׁה אֲשֶׁר־אָהַבְתָּ כָּל־יְמֵי חַיֵּי
הֶבְלֶךָ אֲשֶׁר נָתַן־לְךָ תַּחַת הַשֶּׁמֶשׁ כֹּל יְמֵי הֶבְלֶךָ כִּי
הוּא חֶלְקְךָ בַּחַיִּים וּבַעֲמָלְךָ אֲשֶׁר־אַתָּה עָמֵל תַּחַת
הַשָּׁמֶשׁ: ׳ כֹּל אֲשֶׁר תִּמְצָא יָדְךָ לַעֲשׂוֹת בְּכֹחֲךָ
עֲשֵׂה כִּי אֵין מַעֲשֶׂה וְחֶשְׁבּוֹן וְדַעַת וְחָכְמָה
בִּשְׁאוֹל אֲשֶׁר אַתָּה הֹלֵךְ שָׁמָּה:

[7]Go thy way, eat thy bread with joy, and drink thy wine with a merry heart; for God has already accepted thy works. [8]Let thy garments be always white; and let thy head lack no oil. [9]Live joyfully with the wife whom thou lovest all the days of the life of thy vapour, which he has given thee under the sun, all the days of thy vapour: for that is thy portion in life, and in thy labour in which thou dost labour under the sun. [10]Whatever thy hand finds to do, do it with thy strength, for there is no work, nor device, nor knowledge, nor wisdom, in She'ol, whither thou goest.

Qohelet considers that the best humankind can do in this uncertain world is to seize each fleeting moment, each opportunity for pleasure and useful work before it floats away like vapor.

In the Hebrew painting, a fine, if somewhat battered, wine cup[1] lists slightly against a disk golden as the sun. Despite its wear, the cup still brims with rich red wine of celebration, alluding to David's joyful declaration, "My cup runs over" (Psalm 23). The droplets fall in a pattern observed in pioneering strobe photography made by Harold Edgerton at MIT during the 1940s,[2] suggesting the need to notice even the imperceptibly brief moment. The English painting offers a cluster of fruits, sweet and ripe at the moment, but which will only wizen and sour if not enjoyed in their prime.

NOTES

[1] This cup is modeled on sacramental wine cups by the Shevach family of Yemenite Jewish silversmiths, presently working in Jerusalem.
[2] Harold "Doc" Edgerton, *One Milk Drop* (Putney, Vt.: Optical Toys, 1996).

יא שַׁבְתִּי וְרָאֹה תַחַת־הַשֶּׁמֶשׁ כִּי לֹא לַקַּלִּים הַמֵּרוֹץ וְלֹא לַגִּבּוֹרִים הַמִּלְחָמָה וְגַם לֹא לַחֲכָמִים לֶחֶם וְגַם לֹא לַנְּבֹנִים עֹשֶׁר וְגַם לֹא לַיֹּדְעִים חֵן כִּי־עֵת וָפֶגַע יִקְרֶה אֶת־כֻּלָּם: יב כִּי גַּם לֹא־יֵדַע הָאָדָם אֶת־עִתּוֹ כַּדָּגִים שֶׁנֶּאֱחָזִים בִּמְצוֹדָה רָעָה וְכַצִּפֳּרִים הָאֲחֻזוֹת בַּפָּח כָּהֵם יוּקָשִׁים בְּנֵי הָאָדָם לְעֵת רָעָה כְּשֶׁתִּפּוֹל עֲלֵיהֶם פִּתְאֹם: יג גַּם־זֹה רָאִיתִי חָכְמָה תַּחַת הַשָּׁמֶשׁ וּגְדוֹלָה הִיא אֵלָי: יד עִיר קְטַנָּה וַאֲנָשִׁים בָּהּ מְעָט וּבָא־אֵלֶיהָ מֶלֶךְ גָּדוֹל וְסָבַב אֹתָהּ וּבָנָה עָלֶיהָ מְצוֹדִים גְּדֹלִים: טו וּמָצָא בָהּ אִישׁ מִסְכֵּן חָכָם וּמִלַּט־הוּא אֶת־הָעִיר בְּחָכְמָתוֹ וְאָדָם לֹא זָכַר אֶת־הָאִישׁ הַמִּסְכֵּן הַהוּא: טז וְאָמַרְתִּי אָנִי טוֹבָה חָכְמָה מִגְּבוּרָה וְחָכְמַת הַמִּסְכֵּן בְּזוּיָה וּדְבָרָיו אֵינָם נִשְׁמָעִים: יז דִּבְרֵי חֲכָמִים בְּנַחַת נִשְׁמָעִים מִזַּעֲקַת מוֹשֵׁל בַּכְּסִילִים: יח טוֹבָה חָכְמָה מִכְּלֵי קְרָב וְחוֹטֶא אֶחָד יְאַבֵּד טוֹבָה הַרְבֵּה:

¹¹I returned, and saw under the sun, that the race is not to the swift, nor the battle to the strong, nor yet bread to the wise, nor yet riches to men of understanding, nor yet favour to men of skill; but time and chance happens to them all. ¹²For man also knows not his time: like the fishes that are taken in an evil net, and like the birds that are caught in the snare; so are the sons of men snared in an evil time, when it falls suddenly upon them. ¹³This wisdom have I seen also under the sun, and it seemed great to me: ¹⁴there was a little city, and few men within it; and there came a great king against it, and besieged it, and built great siegeworks against it: ¹⁵now there was found in it a poor wise man, and he by his wisdom saved the city; yet no man remembered that same poor man. ¹⁶Then said I, wisdom is better than strength; nevertheless the poor man's wisdom is despised, and his words are not heard. ¹⁷The words of wise men heard in quiet are better than the cry of him who rules among fools. ¹⁸Wisdom is better than weapons of war: but one sinner destroys much good.

ohelet's thoughts turn back to the arrogance and foolishness of the person—whether powerful or seemingly insignificant—who believes that his or her deeds will necessarily triumph, bring glory to his or her name, or stand forever in the human world. Only God, who assigns each person his or her life span, is timeless. While the pleasure (or pain) of the immediate moment may be all that we can be sure of, as he argued in the last section, time and chance happen to all; even our best efforts and actions may never be recognized or remembered. Above all, wise living requires careful judgment—while we have the time. And as Qohelet reiterates throughout his book, the wise person *must* persevere, even struggle, in his or her work in this world under the sun.

On the English illumination, the hourglass with which he measures minutes and hours holds, he imagines, not sand but floating, fleeting vapor. Dice tossed on the surface before him suggest the gamble of every moment. At his side, the intricately carved frieze, the fruit of many hours of a nameless craftsman's days, shows careless damage, yet still fills the room with beauty.

The Hebrew painting offers a view of a lion fountain in the Alhambra, originally built by its fourteenth-century craftsmen as a water clock that sprayed water from a different lion's mouth for each hour of the day. Three centuries earlier, Sephardic poet and philosopher Solomon ibn Gabirol described a similar fountain in a wondrous Andalusian palace that reflected its master's vast power:

> It had a basin brimming, like Solomon's basin,
>   but not on the backs of bulls like his—
> lions stood around its edge
>   like whelps that roar for prey;
> for they had wells in them, wells that emitted
>   water in streams through their mouths like rivers.[1]

The Andalusian craftsmen's ingenious design, too, vanished like mist. Following the 1492 conquest of Granada by the Christian forces of Isabella of Castile, workmen from her court who were assigned to refurbish the fountain instead destroyed its water-clock function.

The poem that Ibn Gabirol—not only poet but also philosopher—composed about the palace reveals his own struggle against Qohelet's assertion of the limits of human deeds. In this painting, the entire panegyric poem, which extols both the palace and its lord's power, is inscribed in micrography, in a pattern that still decorates the Alhambra's Generalife Gardens.[2] Raymond P. Scheindlin has described how the poet likens the unnamed patron's powers to God's own creative powers; Ibn Gabirol characterizes his patron's palace as a microcosm of Creation: the shifting light within the palace dome rivals the creation of day and night, and the animal statuary throughout its rooms and gardens comes to life and speaks. "The patron shows his power over nature by creating with his wealth, spirit, and good taste, an artificial world to rival the real one."[3] Ibn Gabirol compares the palace to King Solomon's legendary re-creation of nature; yet he ultimately infers that, since the poet's imagination will control the *memory* of the impermanent stone, his immortal verses will outlive the stone that will one day crumble. Indeed, his creative skills led this poet to "measure himself against God"[4]—all the more poignant, in the light of Ibn Gabirol's lifelong ill health and early death.

The caper sprig in the foreground symbolizes Israel's quality of perseverance in the Babylonian Talmud (Beitsa 25b).[5] Able to sprout among dry rocks, with no water or nourishment, and produce a fresh bud, blossom, and fruit every day, the caper reminded the rabbis of Israel's ability to persevere through adversity with only God's unseen—Qohelet might say inscrutable—support.

NOTES

[1] From "Come with Me," in Raymond P. Scheindlin, *Vulture in a Cage: Poems by Solomon ibn Gabirol* (New York: Archipelago, 2016), 221.

[2] Y. Demiriz, *Islam Sanatinda: Geometrik Süsleme* (Istanbul: Hayalperest, 2017), 377.

[3] Raymond P. Scheindlin, "Poet and Patron: Ibn Gabirol's Poem of the Palace and Its Gardens," *Prooftexts* 16, no. 1 (January 1996): 35.

[4] Scheindlin, "Poet and Patron," 42.

[5] Nogah Hareuveni, *Tree and Shrub in Our Biblical Heritage*, trans. Helen Frenkly (Kiryat Ono, Israel: Neuot Kedumim, 1984), 42.

INTRODUCTION TO CHAPTER TEN
A FOOL'S DYSTOPIA

hough bitterly worded, chapter 10 is as close as Qohelet will get to a moment of comic relief. As if to counter the impression left by the end of chapter 9, that despite psychological and sociological problems, a small group of properly situated and appreciated wise people of voice and standing will suffice in order to prepare for the worst (amid a pleasure-bent majority hoping for the best), Qohelet turns to consider the disturbingly disruptive potential of energetic fools of voice and standing: how a single death-fly can rot a precious ointment (10:1). As before, both varieties of foolishness make their appearance.

Unlike hedonists who have somehow overcome their antagonism to pessimistic faultfinders and have come to their senses, both types of fool stand in vociferous and active opposition to those whom Qohelet deems to be wise. Both remain familiar to the modern reader. Fools belonging to the first category deny Qohelet's *hevel* principle. They object to the claim that all human knowledge is time-bound and hypothetical. Qohelet's *uber*-wise are still very much with us today. The triumphs of science, our widely accepted moral principles, and the marvels of technology, many people argue, are living proof of our ability to recognize certitude. But they confuse broad, momentary agreement with actual truth,[1] and *feeling* certain with *proving* certitude. If history teaches us anything, it is that radical paradigm shifts puncture and dissect the long march of human accomplishment into a discontinued patchwork of undeniable, yet later abandoned, certitudes. Take Euclidean geometry, the five axioms of which were considered, until recently, the paradigm of humanly achievable absolute certitude. The first shock came with the discovery of equally viable non-Euclidean geometries during the first half of the nineteenth century, which rendered the truth of the Euclidean variety no longer necessary. But with the advent of general relativity during the 1910s, physical space ceased to be Euclidean, rendering Euclidean geometry not even empirically true.

Even when much is at stake theoretically, and even theologically, as our picture of the world is radically transformed—as in the hard-won Copernican shift from a geocentric to a heliocentric world picture—little harm can be done by obstinate reactionaries incapable of thinking "out of the box." But when it comes to running a city, the blinkered dogmatism of *uber*-wise fools can be a real danger. Although "no man can tell what shall be, and what shall be after that"[2] (14), such fools, who don't even "know to get to the city" (15), multiply their words as if they know everything (14). Their brazen, cocksure self-confidence, for which the hesitant, self-doubting, deliberating, and humbly thoughtful wise are seldom a match, is capable of winning over the heart of a city.

Fools of the second type fully accept Qohelet's *hevel* premise but answer his big question negatively: because our knowledge of the good and the true can never be ascertained, our worldly undertakings can never be properly deemed worthy. As a result, they face the world with paralyzed apathetic indifference (relying, if religious, on divine intervention).

As in previous chapters, Qohelet refrains here from reasoning with them. From his perspective, they do not merit serious response. Unlike the real challenge of reasoned hedonism, dealt with brilliantly in the previous chapter, neither category of fools, Qohelet believes, offers an alternative solution to the problem with which he is grappling. Rather, they both deny that there is a problem—by rejecting the *hevel* premise, as do fools of the first category, or by rejecting the very idea of humanly achievable *yitaron*, as do those of the second.[3] Rather than take them seriously, Qohelet engages them by means of an Aristophanic, no-holds-barred, tragicomic ridicule of two fool-run cities going to rot, far more effectively than any reasoned argument could achieve.[4]

> Folly is set in great dignity, and the rich sit in low places. I have seen servants upon horse and princes walking as servants on the earth. He who digs a pit, will fall into it, and whoever breaks through a hedge, a snake shall bite him. He who transports[5] stones shall be hurt by them; and he who chops wood will be endangered by that. If the iron is blunt, and one does not whet the edge, then he must put to more strength. (6–10)

> By much slothfulness the beams collapse; and through idleness of the hands the house leaks. A feast is made for laughter, and wine makes life joyful. (18–20)

To properly appreciate the force of Qohelet's slapstick satire, it should really be read side by side with his portrayal in the next chapter of the paradigmatically wise farmer. Nonetheless, his animated depiction of the topsy-turvy disruption of the city's social fabric and the slapdash projects of cocky, reckless fools, which unwittingly bring greater harm than they were meant to prevent, together with the pathetically neglectful disrepair caused by the idle fools of the second category, is more effective than any philosophical argument to bar such strategies from entering the discussion.

NOTES

[1] See the insightful exchange between Jürgen Habermas and Richard Rorty around the latter's claim that the very concept of truth should be dropped in favor of levels of agreement, in *Rorty and His Critics*, ed. Robert B. Brandom (Oxford: Blackwell, 2000), chaps. 1–2.

[2] Virtually all English versions translate *aḥarav* as "after him," namely, as referring to the foolish predictor. But that renders the second part of the verse wholly redundant.

[3] As opposed to the hedonist, who accepts both premises—but, for seemingly good reasons, refuses to pay the price.

[4] On the rationality and effectiveness of degrading and ridicule, see Simon Goldhill, "The Insider's Joke," and reply by Fisch and Benbaji in *Trusted Critics: Critical Engagements with Menachem Fisch and Yitzhak Benbaji, the View from Within*, ed. Noah J. Efron and Ariel Furstenberg (Tübingen: Mohr-Siebeck, 2023 [forthcoming]).

[5] "Transports" fares better with the Hebrew *mesi'a*, than "removes," as the KJV and Jerusalem Bible have it.

א זְבוּבֵי מָוֶת יַבְאִישׁ יַבִּיעַ שֶׁמֶן רוֹקֵחַ יָקָר מֵחָכְמָה מִכָּבוֹד סִכְלוּת מְעָט: ב לֵב חָכָם לִימִינוֹ וְלֵב כְּסִיל לִשְׂמֹאלוֹ: ג וְגַם־בַּדֶּרֶךְ כְּשֶׁהַסָּכָל [כְּשֶׁסָּכָל] הֹלֵךְ לִבּוֹ חָסֵר וְאָמַר לַכֹּל סָכָל הוּא: ד אִם־רוּחַ הַמּוֹשֵׁל תַּעֲלֶה עָלֶיךָ מְקוֹמְךָ אַל־תַּנַּח כִּי מַרְפֵּא יַנִּיחַ חֲטָאִים גְּדוֹלִים: ה יֵשׁ רָעָה רָאִיתִי תַּחַת הַשֶּׁמֶשׁ כִּשְׁגָגָה שֶׁיֹּצָא מִלִּפְנֵי הַשַּׁלִּיט: ו נִתַּן הַסֶּכֶל בַּמְּרוֹמִים רַבִּים וַעֲשִׁירִים בַּשֵּׁפֶל יֵשֵׁבוּ: ז רָאִיתִי עֲבָדִים עַל־סוּסִים וְשָׂרִים הֹלְכִים כַּעֲבָדִים עַל־הָאָרֶץ: ח חֹפֵר גּוּמָץ בּוֹ יִפּוֹל וּפֹרֵץ גָּדֵר יִשְּׁכֶנּוּ נָחָשׁ: ט מַסִּיעַ אֲבָנִים יֵעָצֵב בָּהֶם בּוֹקֵעַ עֵצִים יִסָּכֶן בָּם: י אִם־קֵהָה הַבַּרְזֶל וְהוּא לֹא־פָנִים קִלְקַל וַחֲיָלִים יְגַבֵּר וְיִתְרוֹן הַכְשֵׁיר חָכְמָה: יא אִם־יִשֹּׁךְ הַנָּחָשׁ בְּלוֹא־לָחַשׁ וְאֵין יִתְרוֹן לְבַעַל הַלָּשׁוֹן: יב דִּבְרֵי פִי־חָכָם חֵן וְשִׂפְתוֹת כְּסִיל תְּבַלְּעֶנּוּ: יג תְּחִלַּת דִּבְרֵי־פִיהוּ סִכְלוּת וְאַחֲרִית פִּיהוּ הוֹלֵלוּת רָעָה: יד וְהַסָּכָל יַרְבֶּה דְבָרִים לֹא־יֵדַע הָאָדָם מַה־שֶׁיִּהְיֶה וַאֲשֶׁר יִהְיֶה מֵאַחֲרָיו מִי יַגִּיד לוֹ: טו עֲמַל הַכְּסִילִים תְּיַגְּעֶנּוּ אֲשֶׁר לֹא־יָדַע לָלֶכֶת אֶל־עִיר:

[1]Dead flies cause the perfumer's ointment to give off a foul odour; so does a little folly outweigh wisdom and honour. [2]A wise man's heart inclines him to his right hand: but a fool's heart to his left. [3]Yea also, when a fool walks by the way, his understanding fails him, and he reveals to everyone that he is a fool. [4]If the spirit of the ruler rise up against thee, do not leave thy place; for deference appeases great offenses. [5]There is an evil which I have seen under the sun, when an error proceeds from the ruler: [6]folly is set in great dignity, and the rich sit in low place. [7]I have seen servants upon horses, and princes walking as servants upon the earth. [8]He who digs a pit shall fall into it; and whoever breaks through a hedge, a snake shall bite him. [9]He who removes stones shall be hurt by them; and he who chops wood shall be endangered by that. [10]If the iron is blunt, and one does not whet the edge, then he must put to more strength: but wisdom increases skill. [11]If the serpent bites and cannot be charmed, then there is no advantage in a charmer. [12]The words of a wise man's mouth are gracious; but the lips of a fool will swallow up himself. [13]The beginning of the words of his mouth is foolishness: and the end of his talk is grievous madness. [14]A fool also multiplies words: yet no man can tell what shall be; and what shall be after him, who can tell him? [15]The labour of fools wearies himself; for he does not know to get to the city.

*T*he wise person must negotiate a path through incompetence and vainglory in even the highest places, Qohelet warns his listeners. The loveliest golden perfume vessel, left carelessly ajar, can be ruined by flies—harbingers of decay and death throughout the Hebrew Bible. Misfortune can follow foolish actions as surely as a cobra might strike if inadequately hypnotized by an unskilled snake charmer. Without careful judgment and wise management, individual and public welfare can crumble like the rock wall behind the initial word of the painting. And, as we shall see, when the merest unthinking movement overturns a wine glass, more may be wasted than a few ounces of wine.

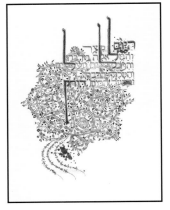
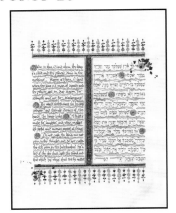

טז אַשְׁרֵיךְ אֶרֶץ שֶׁמַּלְכֵּךְ בֶּן־חוֹרִים וְשָׂרַיִךְ בָּעֵת יֹאכֵלוּ בִּגְבוּרָה וְלֹא בַשְּׁתִי: יז בַּעֲצַלְתַּיִם יִמַּךְ הַמְּקָרֶה וּבְשִׁפְלוּת יָדַיִם יִדְלֹף הַבָּיִת: יט לִשְׂחוֹק עֹשִׂים לֶחֶם וְיַיִן יְשַׂמַּח חַיִּים וְהַכֶּסֶף יַעֲנֶה אֶת־הַכֹּל: כ גַּם בְּמַדָּעֲךָ מֶלֶךְ אַל־תְּקַלֵּל וּבְחַדְרֵי מִשְׁכָּבְךָ אַל־תְּקַלֵּל עָשִׁיר כִּי עוֹף הַשָּׁמַיִם יוֹלִיךְ אֶת־הַקּוֹל וּבַעַל הַכְּנָפַיִם [כְּנָפַיִם] יַגֵּיד דָּבָר:

[16]Woe to thee, O land, when thy king is a child, and thy princes dine in the morning! [17]Happy art thou, O land, when thy king is a man of dignity, and thy princes eat in due season, for strength, and not for drunkenness! [18]By much slothfulness the beams collapse; and through idleness of the hands the house leaks. [19]A feast is made for laughter, and wine makes life joyful: and money answers all things. [20]Do not curse the king, no, not even in thy thought; and do not curse the rich even in thy bedchamber: for a bird of the sky shall carry the sound, and that which has wings shall tell the matter.

Spilled wine has spattered onto a pair of illuminated court documents, the pride of the childish ruler. That careless act has undermined the very grandeur and authority of his decrees—in which policies, we might understand, Qohelet assumes that his audience has been involved. In late biblical texts such as Esther, the importance of the preparation of royal documents was carefully marked. Illuminated books and documents gleaming with precious gold and paints were the pride and envy of medieval Muslim court culture. These paintings were inspired by illuminated manuscripts made in the Ottoman palaces of the sixteenth and seventeenth centuries.

The painting at right presents the text of these verses. The page at left illuminates a passage from the small ethical tract of the Mishnah, *Pirke Avot*, attributed to Rabbi Tarfon:

> The day is short and the work much;
> the workers are lazy and the wages high;
> and the Master of the house presses. (2:20)[1]

Rabbi Tarfon might indeed have had Qohelet's words in mind, for just as his next words warn that "you are not obliged to complete the work, but you are not free to neglect it," Qohelet admonishes his listeners and readers that they cannot neglect their responsibilities despite the foolishness and danger surrounding them.

NOTE

[1] Berkson, trans., *Pirke Avot*, 101.

By chapter 11, Qohelet has completed to his satisfaction his penetrating inquiry into the prospects of a worthy human life, one of real *yitaron*, in the *hevel* conditions of thoroughgoing human impermanence. Chapter 11, the first of the book's two concluding chapters, offers a powerful example of wisdom at its best: a Qohelet-wise farmer tilling his field in the face of uncertainty. We can assume that he belongs to a community resembling the one described in chapter 4, has closely studied past failings and calamities, has formulated his plans and discussed them with others, and has taken their criticisms to heart, as he sets about his work, taking no heed of the advice of pleasure seekers, overconfident know-it-alls, and piously passive fools. What Qohelet presents us with here is not a reiteration of how a wise person forms a worthy plan of action but what a wisely deliberated and decided worthy plan of action looks like—not what goes into making a wise decision but how a wise decision should look.

"Cast thy bread upon the waters, for thou shalt find it after many days" (11:1) is the motto that captures the precariousness of prospective action, hoping that, yet never knowing if, our investments might eventually yield a reward. But the mention of bread and water lends a pungent urgency to the cliché piece of friendly advice. Our very existence depends on bread, and our bread on water—the great unpredictable necessity on which Qohelet's agrarian world depended for its very life. Yet clever farmers do eventually "find it." Uncertain as to which crops will survive, or when the rain will come, they wisely hedge their bets by subdividing their plots (2). They have to sow in advance of rain, but not too early. If they wait for clouds to gather, they will have missed their chance and will never sow in time. Nor can they predict the rainfall by gauging the ever-changing wind (3–4). It is as impossible to chart nature's course as it is to chart the formation of a fetus in its mother's womb (5). Acutely aware of the *hevel* premise, as of the vital *yitaron* of bringing forth bread from the earth, good farmers wisely hedge their bets again by subdividing their time, as they did their fields: sowing both morning and evening, instead of vainly forming futile forecasts or gambling recklessly. Science has since improved such predictions, of course, but only by knowingly using the same methods in the face of the same predicament.

And so, from being the critical obstacle to life's *yitaron*, Qohelet's cruel *hevel*-premise as to our inherent and unsurmountable mist-like temporality and fallibility has morphed into the key to achieving life's *yitaron*. We are able to live worthy lives devoted to the great tasks with which God has given us to contend. To do so, we are not required to overcome and transcend the time-bound uncertainties of our *hevel* existence—the idea that we can do so is a dangerous delusion—but, on the contrary, to properly endorse and internalize the idea. Being forever on the lookout from what we deem to be failings and problems, shortcomings and wrongs, we form tentative plans to solve and right them, forever humbly aware, that others, past and present, may well have seen and done things differently, and still do. Availing ourselves to the mutual challenge of such a constructively critical environment, we can rest assured by the end of the day that we have done our humanly best.

Qohelet has solved the problem from which he anxiously set forth and can boldly declare to his readers, in stark and deliberate contrast to the dark despair of chapter 2, that raising our eyes from our human vantage point under the sun, "Truly the light is sweet, and a pleasant thing it is for the eyes to behold the sun" (7). Against the dismal backdrop of the end of chapter 2, this is a powerful image. Looking up not merely at the sun but to face "the high one who watches over" us (5:7), we are no longer crushed by the insurmountable chasm between "God … in heaven" and we "upon the earth" (5:1). We have come to better understand our position under the sun, and to behold it[1] as holding, despite the *hevel* premise, real promise for a divinely approved life wisely led and worth living. The light, as we now gaze upward toward the sun and beyond it, has been finally transformed into a sweet and pleasant thing from our own perspective under it.

But to fully endorse the *hevel* premise is to fully internalize the obvious: to realize that, in addition to the knowledge we possess, the norms by which we abide and whatever we achieve by means of them, we, as living subjects and agents of reasoned change, are also inherently and unavoidably impermanent. We can never know when our time is finally up (9:12), but we do know with all certainty, and should never forget, that our days under the sun are few and numbered. But on no account should we live our lives in the morbid shadow of death.[2] Now that we have come to understand how it is possible to lead a meaningful life worth living, the fact that it will eventually come to an end should lend an exuberant urgency to making the most of it while we are still young and able.

"Rejoice, O young man in thy youth; and let thy heart cheer thee in the days of thy youth, and walk in the ways of thy heart and in the sight of thy eyes" knowing "that for all these things God will bring thee into judgment" (9). The wholly positive combination of this verse's three elements, "joyous cheer" at the prospect of "walking in the ways of one's heart and sight of one's eyes"—a clear echo of 6:8–9 that marks the first major step in Qohelet's positive solution—fully aware, yet no longer dreading that in doing so, we are accountable to God, says it all. Qohelet's undertaking is as religiously motivated as it is profoundly philosophical. Despite his losing all hope close to the outset, the sweetly lit joy and cheer that mark its final chapter bear clear witness to its deeply gratifying successful culmination.

NOTES

[1] The choice of the major English translations to translate the Hebrew *lir'ot* as "to behold," rather than "to see" captures how "seeing" in biblical Hebrew most often connotes "comprehending," in addition to mere viewing.
[2] Ingmar Bergman's *The Seventh Seal* (1957) brings this point home forcefully in how, acting under the morbid shadow of the Black Death, none of the story's characters, from the knight and his squire to the last of the churchmen, is capable of realizing his identity and acts wholly out of character, except for the traveling troupe of players who remain wholly dedicated to their art.

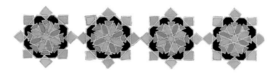

^א שַׁלַּח לַחְמְךָ עַל־פְּנֵי הַמָּיִם כִּי־בְרֹב הַיָּמִים תִּמְצָאֶנּוּ: ^ב תֶּן־חֵלֶק לְשִׁבְעָה וְגַם לִשְׁמוֹנָה כִּי לֹא תֵדַע מַה־יִּהְיֶה רָעָה עַל־הָאָרֶץ: ^ג אִם־יִמָּלְאוּ הֶעָבִים גֶּשֶׁם עַל־הָאָרֶץ יָרִיקוּ וְאִם־יִפּוֹל עֵץ בַּדָּרוֹם וְאִם בַּצָּפוֹן מְקוֹם שֶׁיִּפּוֹל הָעֵץ שָׁם יְהוּא: ^ד שֹׁמֵר רוּחַ לֹא יִזְרָע וְרֹאֶה בֶעָבִים לֹא יִקְצוֹר: ^ה כַּאֲשֶׁר אֵינְךָ יוֹדֵעַ מַה־דֶּרֶךְ הָרוּחַ כַּעֲצָמִים בְּבֶטֶן הַמְּלֵאָה כָּכָה לֹא תֵדַע אֶת־מַעֲשֵׂה הָאֱלֹהִים אֲשֶׁר יַעֲשֶׂה אֶת־הַכֹּל: ^ו בַּבֹּקֶר זְרַע אֶת־זַרְעֶךָ וְלָעֶרֶב אַל־תַּנַּח יָדֶךָ כִּי אֵינְךָ יוֹדֵעַ אֵי זֶה יִכְשָׁר הֲזֶה אוֹ־זֶה וְאִם־שְׁנֵיהֶם כְּאֶחָד טוֹבִים: ^ז וּמָתוֹק הָאוֹר וְטוֹב לַעֵינַיִם לִרְאוֹת אֶת־הַשָּׁמֶשׁ: ^ח כִּי אִם־שָׁנִים הַרְבֵּה יִחְיֶה הָאָדָם בְּכֻלָּם יִשְׂמָח וְיִזְכֹּר אֶת־יְמֵי הַחֹשֶׁךְ כִּי־הַרְבֵּה יִהְיוּ כָּל־שֶׁבָּא הָבֶל: ^ט שְׂמַח בָּחוּר בְּיַלְדוּתֶיךָ וִיטִיבְךָ לִבְּךָ בִּימֵי בְחוּרוֹתֶךָ וְהַלֵּךְ בְּדַרְכֵי לִבְּךָ וּבְמַרְאֵי עֵינֶיךָ וְדַע כִּי עַל־כָּל־אֵלֶּה יְבִיאֲךָ הָאֱלֹהִים בַּמִּשְׁפָּט: ^י וְהָסֵר כַּעַס מִלִּבֶּךָ וְהַעֲבֵר רָעָה מִבְּשָׂרֶךָ כִּי־הַיַּלְדוּת וְהַשַּׁחֲרוּת הָבֶל:

¹Cast thy bread upon the waters: for thou shalt find it after many days. ²Give a portion to seven, and even to eight; for thou knowst not what evil shall be upon the earth. ³If the clouds are full of rain, they empty themselves upon the earth: and if the tree falls toward the south, or toward the north, in the place where the tree falls, there it shall lie. ⁴He who observes the wind shall not sow; and he who regards the clouds shall not reap. ⁵As thou knowst not what is the way of the wind, nor how the bones grow in the womb of her that is with child: even so thou knowst not the works of God who makes all. ⁶In the morning sow thy seed, and in the evening do not withhold thy hand: for thou knowst not which shall prosper, whether this or that, or whether they both shall be alike good. ⁷Truly the light is sweet, and a pleasant thing it is for the eyes to behold the sun; ⁸for if a man live many years, let him rejoice in them all; yet let him remember the days of darkness; for they shall be many. All that comes is vapour. ⁹Rejoice, O young man in thy youth; and let thy heart cheer thee in the days of thy youth, and walk in the ways of thy heart, and in the sight of thy eyes: but know thou, that for all these things. God will bring thee into judgment. ¹⁰Therefore remove vexation from thy heart, and put away evil from thy flesh *on account of* childhood and youth being vapour.

esilience offers humankind our best chance to survive life's arbitrary fortunes in the face of our inability to predict divine intent. As he considers farmers caring for their crops and land, Qohelet fulfills his search for wisdom under the sun. The wise farmer, he realizes, may seem tiny from the king's height, yet his lands, carefully divided into multiple plots as orderly as the mosaics on the palace walls, offer him the best chance of reward for his labors. While some plots' crops languish from little rainfall and beating sun, other plots receive a balance of sun and rain, and the crops burgeon. Careful planning for diverse contingencies, embedded in a life of clear vision and righteous conduct—together with one's beloved—offers the clearest path to resilience and consequent serenity not only for the farmer but for all humankind. Observing the wise farmer, Qohelet attains the elusive secret to a meaningful life beneath the unknowable heavens.

Introduction to Chapter Twelve
When All Is Said and Done

Qohelet's passionate plea to rejoice in the prospects of a divinely approved life, by emulating the wise farmer in prudently following our hearts and what we see fit (11:9), stands in sharp and calculated contrast to the bitter loathing of life expressed in 2:17–20. Still seeking to somehow overcome, rather than to meaningfully live with, our *hevel* existence, Qohelet was devastated by death, the radical termination point that he believed rendered life pointless by erasing all difference between wise and foolish, good and bad. In chapter 12, having worked out how a time-bound, finite life can be of real value, he comes full circle and returns to death with profoundly new eyes—death no longer as the rude disruptive leveler but as natural an occurrence as birth.

Death, Qohelet has come to realize, is powerless to deny life's worth because the full awareness of our transience is the only thing that can guarantee it. After we live a life of *yitaron* while still young and able, as did the wise farmer of chapter 11, death inevitably approaches as our limbs gradually weaken and our faculties slowly wane. "Remember now thy Creator" (12:1), cautions Qohelet, before the end of life draws near, before the sun, and[1] the light, the moon, and the stars are darkened, and the clouds return after the rain; (before) the day when the keepers of the house tremble, and the strong men stoop, and the grinders cease because they are few, and the eyes dim, and one starts from the sound of a bird; before "the man goes to his eternal home, and the mourners go about the streets" (2–5).

Qohelet tenderly describes us departing the world, symbolically accompanied by the equally transient, soon to be outmoded, fruits of our accomplishments, our silver cord that will inevitably loosen, our golden bowl eventually shattered, our pitcher broken at the fountain, and our wheel at the cistern (6).

"Never was there a gentler poem on the approach of death," keenly observes Harold Fisch. "[D]eath becomes … the beauty of a golden sunset"[2] as "the dust returns to the earth and the spirit" to meet its maker (7).

Read in the light of Qohelet's conclusions, the book's last four verses read far less like a later apologetic appendage, as so many people have interpreted. As indicated in my notes to chapter 1, there is much to suggest that Qohelet viewed the problem of meaningful accomplishment, in the face of human time-boundedness, as applying equally to the two tasks that "God has *given* the sons of man to be exercised with" (1:13; 3:10): to make sense of both his divinely authored books: the Book of Nature, and of humankind within it; and the Book of His Revealed Word. As we have seen, the added anxiety and urgency of articulating a viable notion of achievable *yitaron* in the face of our *hevel* existence (with which he set forth), by adding the God axiom into the mix, transforms the entire text, from 1:13 onward, into a profoundly penetrating religious meditation.

What the God axiom actually adds to the mix has nothing to do with worship or prayer, religious law, ritual or rite, or with any other aspect of institutionalized religion. God's ever-presence in Qohelet's discourse is limited to our being judged by him for the quality of our time-bound normative decisions. In Qohelet's discourse, we are held accountable to him for the quality of our decision-making, lacking reliable knowledge of "the works of God who makes all" (11:5), not as obligated to him as religious practitioners. As I have noted, the concept of a transcendental, intervening, and providential God who ultimately "brings [us] into judgment" (11:9) more than implies the monotheism of revealed religion, of which, at the time Qohelet was writing, only one such religion existed. The idiom of his discourse is universal, but the religious setting, despite being stripped of specific ritual laws, rites, or liturgy, is undeniably Jewish.

But why would an undeniably Jewish deliberation, written with no monotheistic alternative in sight, strip itself of all decisively Jewish content? Doing so does not render its argument more general or lend it a more universalist appeal. If what it says about God is enough to narrow its envisaged readership exclusively to Jews, why does their Jewish religiosity make no appearance in the text (except to taunt the over-pious for their excessive investment of effort in Temple rituals [4:17; 5:1–5])?

The only answer that comes to mind, which I have insinuated from the start, is that Qohelet believed that articulating a viable notion of humanly achievable *yitaron* in the face of Qohelet's uncompromising *hevel* premise is general and applies equally, therefore, to both undertakings with which God gave us to contend. Insofar as our capacity to comprehend, assess, and react is time-bound and fallible, it matters little to what end we apply it. Working out philosophically how best to weigh a situation and react to it, aware of our inherent close-mindedness and alert to how different people do so differently, is an undertaking that necessarily precedes all forms of human endeavor—including that of making sense of God's revealed Word and its practical implications. Qohelet never says any of this in so many words; nonetheless, the last four verses of his book render the point almost explicit.

The first of these verses suggestively deems "the words of the wise" and those of "the masters of collections" to be "given by the one shepherd" (11). Until now, Qohelet was concerned with conducting oneself wisely in one's work or labor under the sun. The words of the wise are referred to previously by Qohelet as being soft-spoken, as opposed to the cries of fools (9:17). Verse 12:11 is unique in referring not only to their content but to the fact that they originate in God and are spoken in "collections"—addressed to audiences, or deliberated in study sessions. The Talmud uses this verse as the basis for a homily advocating the radical diversity of rabbinic opinion in matters of halakha as the God-sanctioned master norm of Torah study,[3] much in line with my proposed reading of Qohelet.

The next verse warns against vainly attempting to render one's inevitably tentative findings permanent by committing them to writing. "And further, by these, my son, be admonished: of making many books there is no end" (12). This, too, suggests an echo of the rabbis' later insistence that the Oral Torah (the ways in which God's revealed written Word is understood) should remain forever oral and not be committed to writing. Apparently, Qohelet believed that the only book worth committing to writing is the one that makes the case for the inherently tentative nature of all human understanding.

Only then, after Qohelet's discourse has been all "said and done," can we be in a position to "fear God and keep his commandments" (13), not because we can now know them for certain but because we are now in a position to confidently claim to have done our best to understand them for the time being—"for that is the whole duty of man" (13). After making clear that everything he has said and done applies equally to making sense of God's Word as it does to making one's way in God's world, Qohelet can summarize the religious message of his book in full generality: "God shall bring every work into judgment, with every secret thing, whether it be good, or whether it be evil" (14). The Hebrew term *ma'ase* connotes "act" rather than "work." When all is said and done, declares Qohelet, we can live divinely approvable time-bound lives that are nonetheless worth living, and knowing, as he put it at the end of chapter 11, yet no longer dreading, that God will bring into judgment our every action—manifest or hidden, performed, spoken or thought—for better or for worse.

NOTES

[1] For some reason, the KJV, Jerusalem Bible, and several other English translations render the list disjunctive by inserting "or" between the sun, the light, the moon, and the stars, instead of conjunctive by using "and," as is clearly implied by the Hebrew.

[2] H. Fisch, "Qohelet: A Hebrew Ironist," 177–78.

[3] B. Ḥagiga 3b. Elsewhere, I have referred to this particular homily as a "Hillelite or antitraditionalist manifesto." See M. Fisch, *Rational Rabbis*, 88–95.

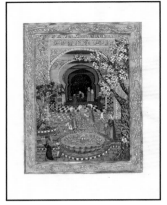

א וּזְכֹר֙ אֶת־בּֽוֹרְאֶ֔יךָ בִּימֵ֖י בְּחוּרֹתֶ֑יךָ עַ֣ד אֲשֶׁ֤ר
לֹא־יָבֹ֙אוּ֙ יְמֵ֣י הָֽרָעָ֔ה וְהִגִּ֣יעוּ שָׁנִ֔ים אֲשֶׁ֣ר תֹּאמַ֔ר
אֵֽין־לִ֥י בָהֶ֖ם חֵֽפֶץ: ב עַ֠ד אֲשֶׁ֨ר לֹֽא־תֶחְשַׁ֤ךְ הַשֶּׁ֙מֶשׁ֙
וְהָא֔וֹר וְהַיָּרֵ֖חַ וְהַכּֽוֹכָבִ֑ים וְשָׁ֥בוּ הֶעָבִ֖ים אַחַ֥ר הַגָּֽשֶׁם:
ג וְסֻגְּר֤וּ דְלָתַ֙יִם֙ בַּשּׁ֔וּק בִּשְׁפַ֖ל ק֣וֹל הַֽטַּחֲנָ֑ה וְיָקוּם֙
לְק֣וֹל הַצִּפּ֔וֹר וְיִשַּׁ֖חוּ כָּל־בְּנ֥וֹת הַשִּֽׁיר: ד גַּ֣ם מִגָּבֹ֤הַּ
יִרָ֙אוּ֙ וְחַתְחַתִּ֣ים בַּדֶּ֔רֶךְ וְיָנֵ֤אץ הַשָּׁקֵד֙ וְיִסְתַּבֵּ֣ל
הֶֽחָגָ֔ב וְתָפֵ֖ר הָֽאֲבִיּוֹנָ֑ה כִּֽי־הֹלֵ֤ךְ הָֽאָדָם֙ אֶל־בֵּ֣ית
עֽוֹלָמ֔וֹ וְסָבְב֥וּ בַשּׁ֖וּק הַסּֽוֹפְדִֽים: ה עַ֣ד אֲשֶׁ֤ר לֹֽא־
יֵרָתֵ֣ק [יֵרָחֵק] חֶ֣בֶל הַכֶּ֔סֶף וְתָרֻ֖ץ גֻּלַּ֣ת הַזָּהָ֑ב
וְתִשָּׁ֤בֶר כַּד֙ עַל־הַמַּבּ֔וּעַ וְנָרֹ֥ץ הַגַּלְגַּ֖ל אֶל־הַבּֽוֹר:
ו וְיָשֹׁ֧ב הֶֽעָפָ֛ר עַל־הָאָ֖רֶץ כְּשֶׁהָיָ֑ה וְהָר֙וּחַ֙ תָּשׁ֔וּב
אֶל־הָֽאֱלֹהִ֖ים אֲשֶׁ֥ר נְתָנָֽהּ: ז הֲבֵ֤ל הֲבָלִים֙ אָמַ֣ר
הַקּוֹהֶ֔לֶת הַכֹּ֖ל הָֽבֶל:

[1]Remember now thy Creator in the days of thy youth, before the evil days come, and the years draw near, which thou shalt say, I have no pleasure in them; [2]before the sun, or the light, or the moon, or the stars, are darkened, and the clouds return after the rain: [3]in the day when the keepers of the house tremble, and the strong men bow themselves, and the grinders cease because they are few, and those that look out of the windows are dimmed, [4]and the doors are shut in the street, when the sound of the grinding is low, and one starts up at the voice of the bird, and all the daughters of music are brought low, [5]and when they are also afraid of that which is high, and terrors are in the way, and the almond tree blossoms, and the grasshopper drags itself along, and the caper-berry fails; because the man goes to his eternal home and the mourners go about the streets; [6]before the silver cord is loosed, or the golden bowl is shattered, or the pitcher is broken at the fountain, or the wheel broken at the cistern; and the dust returns to the earth as it was; [7]and the spirit returns to God who gave it. [8]Vapour of vapours, says Qohelet; all is vapour.

K now before whom you stand, Qohelet might have said at this moment, anticipating the talmudic motto that crowns the grand portal to this palace, just as it has crowned the holy ark in synagogues across the centuries. In all the diverse and busy lives lived in the palace, whether child or adult, laborer or scholar or aristocrat, all paths ultimately lead away from the sunlit courtyard toward shadow, oblivion—and certain divine judgment.

A fragile, elderly laborer lugs a basket of grapes destined for a rich table, pregnant women celebrate one another's joy, a child bounces a ball across the pavement, aristocrats chat, and an old man hobbles into the inescapable misty darkness at the end of the grand halls. Even the solid stone palace itself is ephemeral. The golden bowl of the courtyard fountain not only sprays but also leaks the water that is essential to human life. Weeds have invaded the meticulously laid courtyard tiles, and the intricate mosaics have begun to crumble. The almond tree is heavy with fragrant white blossoms, yet even that may be a contemporary metaphor for the white hair of old age.[1] Nothing in the palace of human existence—even in this grandest of palaces—lasts forever.

Then what does last forever, if not human accomplishment? Only God, and Qohelet begins his paean to the end of human life "under the sun" by warning us to live constantly aware of the inevitability of divine judgment of our personal actions. The courtyard of his palace is filled with exhortations to live mindful of divine law. The pomegranate tree reminds the courtiers of fertility—we see pregnant women and the fruits of all humankind's labors—but its many seeds also symbolize the 613 Commandments. Midrashic associations with the pink lily[2] at its root reminds them of the value of the Ten Commandments in the corrupt human world, and the thorny rose climbing its trunk recalls the humility of the Burning Bush.[3] The grass that springs up between the courtyard tiles suggests the warning that occurs throughout biblical texts that sinners will vanish like dry grass (e.g., Ps 90:5–6). As throughout Jewish lore, the water that sprays from the fountain also symbolizes the necessity of Torah to humankind throughout our lives under the sun.

NOTES

[1] See Seow, *The Anchor Bible*, 361.

[2] The comparison of the fragrant lily to the value of the Ten Commandments is found in Simon, *The Song of Songs*, 95. It is also found in Leviticus Rabbah 23:3.

[3] The association of the Burning Bush with the rose is drawn from William G. Braude, *The Midrash on Psalms* (New Haven, Conn.: Yale University Press, 1959), 1:381.

ט וְיֹתֵר שֶׁהָיָה קֹהֶלֶת חָכָם עוֹד לִמַּד־דַּעַת אֶת־הָעָם וְאִזֵּן וְחִקֵּר תִּקֵּן מְשָׁלִים הַרְבֵּה: י בִּקֵּשׁ קֹהֶלֶת לִמְצֹא דִּבְרֵי־חֵפֶץ וְכָתוּב יֹשֶׁר דִּבְרֵי אֱמֶת: יא דִּבְרֵי חֲכָמִים כַּדָּרְבֹנוֹת וּכְמַשְׂמְרוֹת נְטוּעִים בַּעֲלֵי אֲסֻפּוֹת נִתְּנוּ מֵרֹעֶה אֶחָד: יב וְיֹתֵר מֵהֵמָּה בְּנִי הִזָּהֵר עֲשׂוֹת סְפָרִים הַרְבֵּה אֵין קֵץ וְלַהַג הַרְבֵּה יְגִעַת בָּשָׂר: יג סוֹף דָּבָר הַכֹּל נִשְׁמָע אֶת־הָאֱלֹהִים יְרָא וְאֶת־מִצְוֹתָיו שְׁמוֹר כִּי־זֶה כָּל־הָאָדָם: יד כִּי אֶת־כָּל־מַעֲשֶׂה הָאֱלֹהִים יָבֵא בְמִשְׁפָּט עַל כָּל־נֶעְלָם אִם־טוֹב וְאִם־רָע:

[9]And besides being wise, Qohelet also taught the people knowledge; for he weighed, and sought out, and set in order many proverbs. [10]Qohelet sought to find out acceptable words: and words of truth written in proper form. [11]The words of the wise are like spurs and like nails well driven in are the sayings of the masters of collections; they are given by one shepherd. [12]And furthermore, my son, be admonished: of making many books there is no end; and much study is a weariness of the flesh. [13]The end of the matter, when all is said and done: Fear God, and keep his commandments: for that is the whole duty of man. [14]For God shall bring every work into judgment, with every secret thing, whether it be good, or whether it be evil.

Far beneath the heavens, night falls over the palace of the philosopher-king. The golden bowl framing the scene has cracked, perhaps rendered even more precious by knowledge of its fragile impermanence. Luckily, while planning the paintings for this final chapter, I happened upon *Ben Qohelet* (Son of Qohelet), the book of poetry reflecting on Qohelet, composed by the first of the two Jewish grand viziers who ruled in Granada, Samuel the Nagid.[1] It was the Nagid's son, Joseph ibn Naghrella, who constructed the great Solomonic-scale palace that lies under the present-day Alhambra. That palace might be the model for the Ibn Gabirol poem presented in the illuminations of 9:18 above. The micrographic border offered in this painting bears the first forty-four poems of *Ben Qohelet*. The pattern of the micrography is adapted from a tiling pattern found in the palace complex in Granada.

One brief poem from *Ben Qohelet* surrounds the text page, expressing the poet's insistence on pursuing life despite its transience:

> Soul opens inside you on beauty—
> then tells you to seek in the world
> and ignore its flaws.
>
> Heart says: you'll live forever—
> and death as it speaks
> grasps you with claws.[2]

Qohelet's last words rest within imagery of fig branches across the four seasons—spring buds; ripening summer fruits cloaked in lush foliage; ripening, even bursting, autumn fruit and yellowing leaves; and the bare branches of winter. Here, fig branches hint at the birth and passing of generations, as well as the value of divine law. Throughout Jewish lore, figs embody many qualities of Israel, humankind, and the world. In the Song of Songs, young figs budding from their branches symbolize spring rebirth, while the author of the medieval midrash *Yalkut Shimoni* compares the fig to the divine law that Qohelet advises us to heed:

> Why is the Torah likened to a fig tree? Because all other fruits contain useless [inedible] matter. Dates have pits, grapes have seeds, pomegranates have rinds. But the fig, all of it is edible. So words of Torah have no worthless matter in them.[3]

The oak branch embedded in the micrography of the final illumination bears the acorns that carry forward its heritage despite that tree's yellowing leaves. The image alludes to Israel's strength to endure, despite the passing of every individual—of even the Davidic kingdom itself. Isaiah prophesied that Israel would be reborn after conquest, "like the terebinth and the oak, of which stumps are left even when they are felled: its stump shall be a holy seed."[4] Like the oak's seed and regenerating stump, long after his own death Qohelet's words continue to offer humankind guidance toward a realistic, yet meaningful, life.

NOTES

[1] S. Abramson, trans. and ed., *Samuel haNagid: Ben Qohelet* (Tel Aviv: Mossad haRav Kook, 1952), 5–19.

[2] Peter Cole, trans. and ed., *Selected Poems of Shmuel haNagid* (Princeton, N.J.: Princeton University Press, 1996), 123. In Abramson, cited above, this is poem 66, p. 28.

[3] Quoted from *Yalkut Shimoni*, Joshua, in Bialik and Ravnitzky, eds., *The Book of Legends*, 405.

[4] Isa 6:13, in *JPS Hebrew-English Tanakh*, 859.

MYSTERIES DISPELLED: QOHELET IN BIBLICAL AND LITURGICAL CONTEXT

Menachem Fisch

All readings, we have come to realize, are readings *in*. Such conceits as the early Protestant contention that Scripture concedes its one true, divinely intended, message to prudently unbiased literalist reading *out*, and that of empiricism's contention that external reality somehow excites our sensual nerve-endings in conceptually pre-informed bundles, are no longer considered viable positions. Human beings actively conceptualize the texts that they read and the reality that they experience by means of the internalized vocabularies at their disposal—whether thoughtlessly as second nature[1] or, more thoughtfully, as when one ponders what ones reads or perceives. Different people will hence read the same text, or perceive the same state of affairs as differently as their different vocabularies dictate.

Language, on such a showing, is not a medium capable of representing an independently experienced external reality or of expressing an independently experienced self.[2] Language transforms our "raw feels" into experience, lending them the form, meaning, and value that they have for us. Our knowledge of the world and of ourselves is not mediated, but thoroughly constituted by the words that we have and use. Needless to say, the languages by which we perceive, think, and judge are the contingent and historical products of our particular upbringing.

This being the philosophy of human comprehension to which I adhere, it is not surprising that the view that I attribute to the book of Qohelet resembles it so closely. I admit that had this not been a position with which I was intimately acquainted, it would never have occurred to me to read Qohelet the way I do—or, for that matter, to attribute a similar view to the rabbinic literature. However, there is a world of difference between the kind of bias that accounts for spotting a fruitful interpretive opportunity while attempting prudently to make sense of a text and the kind of bias responsible for tendentiously appropriating it to one's own position. In philosophy, argues Robert Brandom, one's own position acquires normative authority by reading past philosophers as having anticipated that authority.[3] This form of appropriative reading, Yael Gazit states, is unique to philosophy. It explains how philosophical traditions are retroactively formed and provides the key to accounting for the history of philosophy.[4]

That it is the position by which I philosophically abide does not prevent me from identifying very different positions in others, especially in those whose thinking long predates the philosophical developments that gave rise to the position I hold—in my case, the specifically post-Kantian developments in Anglophone analytical philosophy. Martin Shuster, whose reading of Qohelet steers closest to my own, describes his interpretive undertaking as "using Martin Heidegger to re-read the book of Ecclesiastes." Shuster is clearly a follower of at least the early Heidegger, but he uses Heidegger's thinking to insightfully tease out unnoticed elements of Qohelet's discourse; but on no account can he be described as using Qohelet to appropriate Heidegger. My motivations are similar: to employ my latter-day position to make maximal philosophical, religious, and, as we shall see, liturgical sense of this remarkable text.

As I explained at the outset of this work, I purport to read Qohelet not merely as how a latter-day philosopher of language, mind, science, and self might see it but as Judaism's formative rabbinic canon of late antiquity would

the View from Within. Ed. Noah J. Efron and Ariel Furstenberg. Tübingen: Mohr-Siebeck, 2023 (forthcoming).

Gordis, Robert. *Koheleth: The Man and His World*. New York: Schocken, 1968.

Grabar, Oleg. *The Alhambra*. Cambridge, Mass.: Harvard University Press, 1978.

Halbertal, Moshe. *People of the Book: Canon, Meaning, and Authority*. Cambridge, Mass.: Harvard University Press, 1997.

———, and Stephen Holmes. *The Beginning of Politics: Power in the Biblical Book of Samuel*. Princeton, N.J.: Princeton University Press, 2017.

Hareuveni, Nogah. *Tree and Shrub in Our Biblical Heritage*. Trans. Helen Frenkley. Kiryat Ono, Israel: Neot Kedumim, 1984.

Harrison, Peter. *The Bible, Protestantism and the Rise of Natural Science*. Cambridge: Cambridge University Press, 2006.

Hengel, Martin. *Judaism and Hellenism*. 2d ed. Trans. John Bowden. Minneapolis: Fortress, 1991.

Hobbes, Thomas. *Leviathan or the Matter, Forme and Power of a Commonwealth Ecclesiasticall and Civil*. London: Andrew Crooke, 1651.

Howell, Kenneth J. *God's Two Books: Copernican Cosmology and Biblical Interpretation in Early Modern Science*. South Bend, Ind.: University of Notre Dame Press, 2004.

Hume, David. *A Treatise of Human Nature*, 1739.

Irwin, Robert. *The Alhambra*. Cambridge, Mass.: Harvard University Press, 2004.

Israeli, Yael. *Made by Ennion: Ancient Glass Treasures from the Shlomo Moussaieff Collection*. Jerusalem: Israel Museum, 2011.

———, et al. *Treasures of the Holy Land: Ancient Art from the Israel Museum*. New York: Metropolitan Museum of Art, 1986.

Japhet, Sara, and Robert B. Salters, eds. and trans. *The Commentary of R. Samuel Ben Meir RASHBAM on Qoheleth*. Leiden: Brill, 1985.

Jewish Publication Society. *JPS Hebrew-English Tanakh*. Philadelphia: Jewish Publication Society, 1999.

King, Philip J., and Lawrence E. Stager. *Life in Biblical Israel*. Louisville, Ky.: Westminster John Knox, 2001.

Knobel, Peter S. "The Targum of Qohelet." In *The Aramaic Bible*. Vol. 15: *The Targum of Job, the Targum of Proverbs, the Targum of Qohelet*. Collegeville, Minn.: Liturgical Press, 1991.

Kuhn, Thomas S. *The Structure of Scientific Revolutions*. 2d ed. Chicago: University of Chicago Press, 1970.

Levine, Lee I. *The Ancient Synagogue: The First Thousand Years*. 2d ed. New Haven, Conn.: Yale University Press, 2005.

———. *Jerusalem: Portrait of the City in the Second Temple Period (538 B.C.E.–70 C.E.)*. Philadelphia: Jewish Publication Society, 2002.

Loewe, Raphael. *Ibn Gabirol*. New York: Grove Weidenfeld, 1989.

McDowell, John. *Mind and World*. Cambridge, Mass.: Harvard University Press, 1996.

Meek, Russell L. "Twentieth- and Twenty-First-Century Readings of *Hebel* (הֶבֶל) in Ecclesiastes." *Currents in Biblical Research* 14, no. 3 (2016): 279–97.

Meyerson, Emile. *Identity & Reality*. Trans. Katie Loewenberg. Mineola, N.Y.: Dover, 1965.

Mitchell, Stephen. *Gilgamesh: A New English Version*. New York: Free Press, 2004.

Otto, Rudolf. *The Idea of the Holy: An Inquiry into the Non-Rational Factor in the Idea of the Divine and Its Relation to the Rational*. Trans. J. W. Harvey. Oxford: Oxford University Press, 1958.

Panofsky, Erwin. *Early Netherlandish Painting: Its Origins and Character*. New York: Harper and Row, 1971.

Popper, Karl R. *The Poverty of Historicism*. New York: Harper & Row, 1957.

———. *Conjectures and Refutations: The Growth of Scientific Knowledge*. New York: Harper & Row, 1963.

Rankin, O. S. *Israel's Wisdom Literature: Its Bearing on Theology and the History of Religion*. New York: Schocken, 1969.

Rawls, John. *Political Liberalism*. Expanded ed. New York: Columbia University Press, 2005.

Rorty, Richard. *Contingency, Irony, Solidarity*. Cambridge: Cambridge University Press, 1989.

Rowse, A. L. *The Annotated Shakespeare*. 3 vols. New York: Clarkson N. Potter, 1978.

Samet, Nili. "Qoheleth's Idiolect and Its Cultural Context." *Harvard Theological Review* 114, no. 4 (2021): 451–68.

Sandberg, Ruth. *Rabbinic Views of Qohelet*. Lewiston, N.Y.: Edwin Mellen, 1999.

Scheindlin, Raymond P. "Poet and Patron: Ibn Gabirol's Poem of the Palace and Its Gardens." *Prooftexts* 16, no. 1 (January 1996): 31–47.

———. *Vulture in a Cage: Poems by Solomon ibn Gabirol*. New York: Archipelago, 2016.

———. *Wine, Women, and Death: Medieval Hebrew Poems on the Good Life*. Philadelphia: Jewish Publication Society, 1986.

Scherman, Nosson. *The Complete Artscroll Machzor: Yom Kippur*. Brooklyn, N.Y.: Mesorah, 1986.

Schiffman, Lawrence H. et al., *From Text to Tradition: A History of Second Temple & Rabbinic Judaism*. Hoboken, N.J.: Ktav, 1991.

Scott, R. B. Y. *The Anchor Bible*. Vol. 18: *Proverbs, Ecclesiastes*. Garden City, N.Y.: Doubleday, 1965.

Sellars, Wilfrid. "Empiricism and the Philosophy of Mind." Repr. with introduction by Richard Rorty, study guide by Robert Brandom. Cambridge, Mass.: Harvard University Press, 1997.

Seow, Choon-Leong. *The Anchor Bible*. Vol. 18C: *Proverbs, Ecclesiastes*. New York: Doubleday, 1997.

Sharf, Andrew. *Byzantine Jewry: From Justinian to the Fourth Crusade*. London: Routledge & Kegan Paul, 1971.

Smith, Howard A. *Let There Be Light: Modern Cosmology and Kabbalah—A New Conversation Between Science and Religion*. Novato, Calif.: New World Library, 2006.

Shuster, Martin. "Being as Breath, Vapor as Joy: Using Martin Heidegger to Re-Read the Book of Ecclesiastes." *Journal for the Study of the Old Testament* 33, no. 2 (2008): 219–44.

Steinsaltz, Adin. *The Thirteen Petalled Rose: A Discourse on the Essence of Jewish Existence and Belief*. Trans. Yehudah Hanegbi. New York: Basic Books, 2006.

Stone, Michael E., and David Satran, eds. *Emerging Judaism: Studies on the Fourth & Third Centuries B.C.E.* Minneapolis: Fortress, 1989.

Teplitz, H., et al. "Hubble Ultra Deep Field 2014." NASA photograph found at *Astronomy Picture of the Day*, June 5, 2014. https://apod.nasa.gov/apod/ap140605.html.

Walzer, Michael. *In God's Shadow: Politics in the Hebrew Bible*. New Haven, Conn.: Yale University Press, 2012.

———. *Interpretation and Social Criticism*. Cambridge, Mass.: Harvard University Press, 1987.

Williams, James G. "Proverbs and Ecclesiastes." In *The Literary Guide to the Bible*. Ed. Robert Alter and Frank Kermode, 263–82. Cambridge, Mass.: Belknap Press of Harvard University Press, 1987.

Key to Bible Translation Abbreviations

ESV   English Standard Version

GNB Good News Bible

JB   Jerusalem Bible (Fisch translation, 2008)

KJB   King James Bible, sometimes referred to as the King James Version (KJV)

NASB   New American Standard Bible

NIV   New International Version

NKJB   New King James Bible sometimes referred to as the New King James Version (NKJV)

INDEX

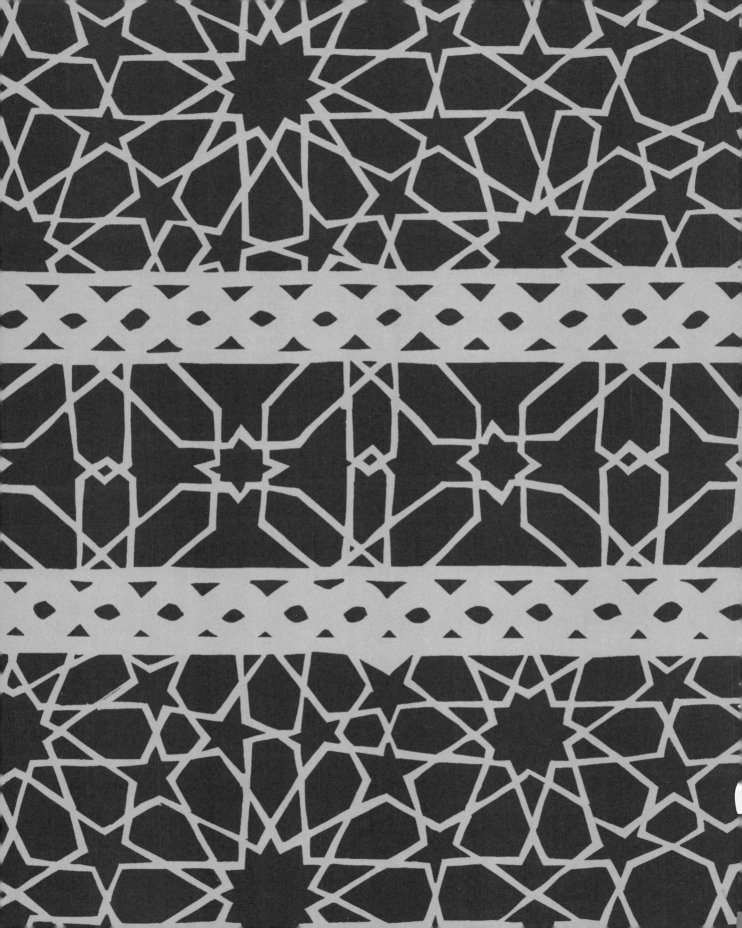